# Ferrari

## *The Machines And The Man*

### BY PETE LYONS

A Foulis Motoring Book

Copyright © 1989 Publications International, Ltd.
All rights reserved. No part of this book may be
reproduced or transmitted in any form or by any
means, electronic or mechanical, including photo-
copying, recording or by any information storage
or retrieval system, without permission of the
Haynes Publishing Group.

Printed and bound in Yugoslavia

ISBN 0 85429 758 8

This edition first published 1989 by
Haynes Publishing Group,
Sparkford, Nr. Yeovil, Somerset BA22 7JJ,
England

Printed and bound in Yugoslavia

# CREDITS

Technical sidebars covering Ferrari engine and chassis by Dean Batchelor.

## Photography

The editors gratefully acknowledge the photographers who helped make this book possible. They are listed below, along with the page number(s) of their photos:

Franco Zagari—7, 10, 11, 12, 13, 15, 16, 18, 19, 20, 21, 23, 24, 25, 26, 27, 28, 29, 30, 31, 32, 33, 34, 35, 36, 37, 38, 40, 41, 42, 43, 48, 49, 50, 51, 52, 54, 55, 56, 60, 61, 62, 64, 65, 70, 73, 75, 76, 77, 80, 81, 82, 83, 84, 85, 86, 88, 89, 92, 93, 94, 96, 97, 98, 99, 100, 102, 107, 110, 113, 114, 121, 122, 124, 125, 129, 134, 135, 156-57, 158-59, 174, 176, 177, 178-79, 197, 202, 203, 204, 205, 206, 207, 208, 209, 213, 214, 217, 223, 224, 234, 235, 236, 237, 246-47, 249, 250-51, 257, 258, 259, 280, 304, 307, 308, 312, 315. Nicky Wright —6, 9, 58, 59, 89, 98, 103, 109, 111, 112, 114, 115, 116, 117, 118, 126, 130-31, 132, 133, 136, 137, 139, 140, 141, 143, 146, 152, 153, 154, 172-73, 174, 175, 182, 183, 190-91, 192, 196, 197, 198, 199, 200, 201, 202, 203, 204, 205, 208, 209, 210, 211, 254, 262, 263, 268, 306, 308, 311, 314. Mirco Decet—57, 69, 87, 90, 144-45, 160-61, 163, 164, 166-67, 168-69, 178, 181, 194, 195, 209, 216, 228, 229, 256, 264, 265, 268, 269, 278, 286, 291, 292, 293, 309, 310. David Gooley—44, 45, 46, 47, 228, 229, 249, 252. Doug Mitchel—95, 96, 97,
101, 305, 307. Sam Griffith—104, 105, 184, 185, 186, 187, 188, 189, 204, 205, 208, 211, 226, 227, 230, 231, 232, 233, 238, 239, 242, 282, 284, 302, 312, 316. Roland Flessner—71. Dean Batchelor—57, 215, 305, 310. Indianapolis Motor Speedway Museum—63, 108. Mitch Frumkin—68, 69, 70, 73, 275, 277, 302, 315. A. Van De Putte-138, 170, 171. Bill Bailey—148-49, 150-51. Autocar & Motor Magazines —8, 72, 292, 293, 294, 295, 296, 297, 298, 299, 301, 302. Chuck Giametta—162, 265. Vince Manocchi—218, 219, 220, 221. Hank Forssberg Inc., Nancy Talarico, Pietro DeFranchi Ferrari/Maranello (MO)—4-5, 238, 240-41, 243, 244, 245, 248, 253, 270-71, 272, 276, 278, 279, 281-82, 283, 284, 314, 315. Pete Lyons—129, 266-67. Pinin Farina—224, 225, 257, 260, 261. Quadrant Picture Library—273, 274, 275, 287-88, 316. L.A.T. Photographic —289-90.

## Owners

Special thanks to the owners of the Ferraris featured in this book for their enthusiastic cooperation. They are listed below, along with their automobiles and the page number(s) on which the cars appear:

Bernd. Schneider—'79 Boxer: 18. John Weinberger, Continental Motors, Hinsdale, Illinois —302, 315, 316; Testarossa: 19, 275; 3.2 Mondial: 238, 239; 328 GTS: 242; GTO: 282, 284. Auburn-Cord-Duesenberg Museum—'52 340 Mexico: 58, 59. David Carte—'52 340 Mexico: 111, 112. Thomas Mittler—342 Ferrari: 111, 112. Bob Des Marais—'53 375 MM: 9, 114, 115. Wayne Golomb—375+ America: 116, 127. Wayne Nelson—11; 410 SA: 117;
'57 250 CA: 6, 140, 141, 143; 250TR: 89, 308; '64 500 SuperFast: 9; '64 Lusso 250 GTL: 172, 173; '65 275 GTB 6C: 182, 183; 365 GTS: 198, 199; '66 365 2+2: 200, 201; 365 GTC: 208, 209; 365 Spyder: 203, 210, 311. Hilary Raab Jr.—'59 410 SA: 118, 126; '69 365 GTB/4: 202, 203; '78 308 GT4 2+2: 254; '75 365 GT/4BB 2+2: 262; 512 BB: 268; 400i: 314. Edsel Pfabe—'50 195/S: 95. Ben Caskey Estate—400SA: 120. Dave Cummins —410SA: 9, 126; '67 275 GTB/4: 190, 191, 192. J. Harrison—250 GTO: 90. George Shelly —121 LM: 96, 97, 306. Terry Buy—212 Export: 101, 305. Brooks Stevens Museum—'53 250 Eu.: 98. Ken Hutchison—'52 212 Export: 104, 105. Carlyle Fraser—'52 212 MM: 103. David B. Smith—'53 250 MM: 130-33, 306; '60 250 GT: 138. Charles Glapinski—'57 250 TDF: 136-37, 146. Roger Meiners—250 SWB: 148-49, 150-51. Michael A. Leventhal—'61 250 SWB GT: 152, 153, 154. Martin Hilton —250 GTO: 160-61, 163. Jack Sears—250 GTO: 164, 166-67, 309. Monte C. Shalett—'62 250 GT Speciale: 174, 175. Michael Feldman —'66 275 GTB: 184, 185, 186, 187. Glenn & Lynn Hanke—'70 365 GT 2+2: 204, 205. Dennis Machul—275 GTB: 188, 189. Ed McCoughlin—'71 Daytona: 204, 205, 208, 211. Henry Haga—250 LM: 215, 310. Richard Giacobetti—'72 246 GT: 226, 227. Secondo J. Colombero—'72 246 GTS: 228, 229, 249, 252. Bob Cortese—'75 308 GT4: 230, 231, 232, 233. Terry Gordon—Dino 240 GTS: 227; '74 246 GTS: 312. Dr. Ronald Mulacek-400 SA: 309.

Special thanks to: Ken McKay of Ferrari North America Tech Center.

# CONTENTS

# Introduction

# Catching the Fever

I became a believer one afternoon on the Angeles Forest Highway in the mountains of California. The car was a 308 GTB Quattrovalvole, glossy black. I'd been invited to participate in a multi-car evaluation with the staff of *Car and Driver* magazine, and had been assigned to pick up the Ferrari a couple of days before. It was the first one I'd driven. My first impression was lukewarm.

The seating position seemed a little awkward, with the steering wheel tilted so the top of the rim was too far away. The pedal cluster was canted toward the middle of the car, and I'm always sensitive to that feeling of driving down the road crooked. On

concrete freeway surfaces the car tended to wander on the rain grooves, and the steering had an on-center stickiness that made correcting an annoyingly conscious act. The gear change was stiff and a bit notchy in its big machined gate. And the engine seemed unnecessarily noisy—whiny, whistley, fussy. The whole car seemed flashy. I felt conspicuous. I thought, with distaste, "This car is a bauble. It's for people who wear gold chains and expose their chest hair."

Then I left the freeway. I headed into the hills for home. The road began curling on itself as it climbed.

The traffic died away. The Ferrari awakened.

Its steering came to life. Its chassis grew lithe. Its transmission became lighter. Its engine started to sing. "I was born to live in the high country," it seemed to carol in gratitude, "You're taking me home, too." Toward the end we were taking the timber-lined curves in long, smooth sweeps at a speed that may have looked fast on the outside, but which was relaxed, effortless, and satisfying inside.

Yet, I didn't understand, not fully, until the day of the comparison test. Each journalist climbed into car after

Ferrari as a force of nature: a black stallion on a field of gold, the *cavallino rampante*, Ferrari's regal insignia (*opposite page*); the 250 GTE (*above*), like all classic designs, is at home anywhere. No other marque so embodies passion, speed, beauty, and timelessness.

car and launched them into the empty, echoing mountains over a set course of many twisting miles. They were all fine cars, great cars, even, famous for their speed and handling. Each car had its good points, and each its less good. Some I really enjoyed driving, but one I turned around before the halfway point and brought back early, disgusted.

I couldn't turn the Ferrari around. It seemed possessed. It flashed past the nominal end of the evaluation route at a very high speed. It kept going, over the hills, arcing through the bends, making quick work of the Forest Highway, singing at its work, in love with the road, the mountains, the day. I felt my blood running hot.

After a long time, I returned my beautiful glossy black Ferrari to the staging point. With deep reluctance, I climbed out so someone else could drive. I noticed I was still breathing deeply, and that my body tingled. I thought, "I understand. I believe."

If the marque Ferrari had not come into being naturally, those for whom sporting automobiles are a passion would have found it necessary to invent it. Trouble is, no one but Enzo Ferrari could have invented something as rich and glorious as the fabulous machines from Maranello.

Many men have given their names to their cars, but only the names of strong men survive—and perhaps Enzo Ferrari was the strongest of them. In 41 years of automaking he created nothing less than a legend. To many, the Ferrari is the epitome of personal automotive expression. To say "Ferrari" is to invoke a dream at once desirable and fearful. Let it roll off your tongue. How redolent it is: iron, hot blood, sleek steel, speed, sex appeal.

If you were sealing one vehicle into a time capsule to present the highest meaning of the automobile in this century to future eras, would you not choose a Ferrari?

Ah, but which Ferrari? There are so very many, and many are racing cars. Ferrari's factory was founded to race, with the road cars second in the man's heart. Yet the old line about racing improving the breed was true at Ferrari. The most ordinary of Ferraris was extraordinary because of Enzo's love of racing. His race cars gave all Ferraris their flavor and their cachet. Competition-derived engines gave them

8

A pride of Ferraris: 1988 F40 (*opposite page*);
'59 410 Superamerica (*top*); '64 500 Superfast
(*left*). The initials "SF" on the Ferrari shield
(*above*) stand for Scuderia Ferrari, Enzo's old
racing team. This one is on a '53 375 MM.

their excitement. Yet, it's by his road cars that most enthusiasts contact the passion of Ferrari. That's why this book concentrates on the sports and GT models. They're the road cars most akin to racing Ferraris.

What a complex and broad subject it is. That's partly because of Enzo Ferrari's sheer enthusiasm for building cars. It's also because he began building at a time when automobiles were really handmade, when they were individual artifacts having importance in themselves as *objets d'art et du sport*.

For many years, each Ferrari was virtually unique, and always of the highest possible quality. They were sold literally to kings.

Yet, even when produced in small series, Ferraris of the classic period often showed many variations, both in style and, frequently, in dimension. During the era of hand-hammered bodies, a given car might exhibit amazing asymmetry. The left fender wouldn't be a mirror image of the right. Wheel arches and door openings would differ, sometimes by

inches. Owners who had their cars stripped of paint said the sight of the bare metal, with dozens of little welded pieces and lots of Italian bondo filling the seams, would make them weep.

This visibly human touch is at the opposite pole of automotive appreciation from the clinical replication of perfection found at, say, Porsche.

In just that way, this is a personal book. It reflects the interests and prejudices of a car nut set on his path by a father who talked a lot about all cars,

but who seemed to say the most memorable things about Ferraris. In his work as a photographer, Ozzie Lyons would often go shoot a new Ferrari. He'd come home, his eyes dancing with it. "You don't slip a Ferrari clutch," he instructed me once, "you slip the wheels." I've endeavored to practice that teaching at every opportunity since. Another time he reported enlivening his daily commute by keeping the family Volvo in second gear all the way. "Just like driving a Ferrari!"

No wonder the very first Ferrari I encountered on the highway made me gasp. I was driving along a narrow country road, and reached a hillbrow just as a Ferrari coupe popped over the top at speed from the other direction, all glistening red and with its jaws open, snarling. I heard my breath suck in with fear, yes, but also with admiration and desire.

So the same thing that made professional race drivers sacrifice to join Ferrari's racing team works in the blood of the rest of us. Yet this book isn't blind to shortcomings natural in a creation more of spirit than of science. Ferraris are not mechanically seamless. Driving one has always called for knowledge and dedication and a certain mind-set. Ownership would be awkward and strange, and ultimately entirely unsatisfactory, for someone who approached a car as an appliance.

The correct approach, I think, is from the other direction: How fortunate and privileged one is to possess an automobile of a racing breed that might be driven on the highway. If its needs are finicky it's because they descend from extraordinary high performance that required tuning and careful warm-ups by professional racing mechanics. If you were willing to bring that kind of care and attention to your own Ferrari, you might be worthy. If you just wanted to have something flashy for stopping in at the country club, shop another manufacturer.

In the automotive world at large today this is a lost thought, old-fashioned, even otherworldly. It is still part of operating and enjoying a motorcycle, an airplane, a sailboat. These vehicles also require knowledge, skill and commitment. Most cars do not.

That's why this is also a romantic book. There's a human thread running through the tale of these cars. You won't find here an exhaustive record of chassis numbers, or a recital of every race victory, or engineering developments point by minute point. I would not presume to trespass in the province of lifelong specialists. Dean Batchelor, one of the foremost of Ferrari authorities, a man who has owned

several and driven most, was asked to collaborate by supplying his insight into the most technical matters and to describe the important engine and chassis milestones.

Sadly, most of us have missed our chance to own one of the classic Ferraris. This grand marque has finally become as widely cherished as its partisans have always known it deserved to be. Aesthetic appreciation has resulted in monetary appreciation, often to stunning heights. Our approach is not that of players in the investment game, however. We're out to fashion some idea of what it would be like to *drive* these fabulous cars, to live with them as Enzo intended.

One thing we know without further investigation: Ferraris were always on the cutting edge of performance in their times. As Dean Batchelor points out, Enzo Ferrari set the pace. He was always the moving target for his rivals, both on track and on the road. He was not always at the forefront of technology—his cars in fact were often the most conservative in design—but he was always the prime opposition.

Enzo Ferrari should be thanked by enthusiasts for every other automobile. "He put the zip in it," Dean says. I'll stand by that. I'm a believer.

Pete Lyons
Big Bear, California
1989

Racing was Enzo Ferrari's automotive passion. The Dino 246 S (*opposite page*) was a V-6 sports-racer of the late 1950s and early '60s. A Ferrari Formula 2 V-12 of 1950 (*top*) is a work of art with or without its aluminum skin.

## Pronunciation Guide to Selected Italian Names and Words

*Antonio* and *Alberto Ascari* (Ah-**SKAH**-ree); Ferrari drivers

*barchetta* (bar-**KETTA**); "little boat," a body style

*Luigi Bazzi* (**BAHT**-see); Ferrari technician

*berlinetta* (bair-lee-**NET**-a); closed-coupe body style

*Bertone* (Bair-**TONE**-ay); coachbuilding company

*Bologna* (Boh-**LOAN**-yah); city in Italy

*Carrozzeria* (Kah-**RAWT**-sah-**REE**-ah); coachbuilder

*Cavallino* (Kah-vah-**LEE**-no); little horse

*Luigi Chinetti* (Ki-**NETTY**); Ferrari driver

*Gioacchino Colombo* (**GEE**-oh-ah-**KEE**-no Ko-**LUM**-bo); Ferrari engine designer

*Granturismo* (Gran-tyoo-**REES**-mo); grand touring

*Ingegnere* (**EEN**-jen-**YAIR**-ay); engineer

*Vittorio Jano* (Vee-**TOR**-ee-oh **YAH**-no); Ferrari engine designer

*Aurelio Lampredi* (Aw-**RAY**-lee-o Lam-**PRAY**-dee); Ferrari engine designer

*lusso* (**Loo**-so); luxury

*Mille Miglia* (**MEE**-lay **MEEL**-yah); "thousand miles," a race

*Tazio Nuvolari* (**TAHTS**-ee-oh Noo-voh-**LAH**-ree); a race driver

*Pininfarina* (**PEE**-neen-fah-**REE**-nah); coachbuilding company

*quattrovalvole* (kwatro-val-**VOL**-ay); having four valves

*Scaglietti* (Skahl-**YETTY**); coachbuilding company

*Testa Rossa* (**TES**-tah **RAW**-sah); "red head"

*Tipo* (**TEE**-poh); type (of car or engine)

*Vignale* (Vee-**NYA**-lay); coachbuilding company

The F40 during a test at the factory proving grounds in 1987 (*left*). Enzo Ferrari, 1898-1988 (*right*). His achievements afforded him many opportunities to smile, but Enzo could also be far less revealing about his true emotions.

# Chapter 1:

# Enzo Ferrari:
# The Caesar of Speed

There was always a haunting feeling that the Old Man might be listening, watching perhaps, through the red-shuttered windows of the stately old farmhouse inside the factory test track.

The feeling was that he might be studying you as you made your first acquaintance with his latest supercar, the newest Ferrari, the automobile that would carry into the world his name, his spirit, his very honor. Would he be watching to gauge your reaction to his work, anxiously hoping for your approval?

No more than the lion fears you will judge him maladroit at his kill.

Enzo Ferrari, a born king of men who made himself a titan in a giant's world, knew well and surely what he was: a genius. Such men do not trouble their lives with the opinions of others.

His was a long life, 90 years, and he lived every day of it on his own terms. For most of us, an average way of life presents adversity and challenge and turmoil enough; Enzo Ferrari sought these things as if they nourished him. His was the farthest thing imaginable from an average life. Starting with nothing but his ambition and his wit, he built a personal empire that has stood for generations, and will stand for generations to come, as one of the most remarkable feats of individual enterprise in automotive history. He called this work of his life "La Ferrari," as though it lived on its own.

His cars express the man, and they are wondrous. But the man was even more interesting than all of his machines together. Seen almost universally as a forbidding figure, he knew everyone, but he himself was really known to none. One of the few even remotely close to him, coachbuilder Pinin Farina, said Ferrari's character was "closed like a walnut." Others, even those speaking with affection— and there were many who spoke without it—used words such as difficult, petulant, rigid, harsh, distant, manipulative, stubborn, hostile, cruel. He was "a prideful egomaniac" to some, a "lord in his feudal holdings." He had a screaming temper that could make grown men whisper. He could hold a grudge for decades.

Yet Ferrari could also hold you in the palm of his hand. There was a reverential mood in any gathering around him. "The Pope of the North," they often called him, acknowledging his genuine charisma. If reluctantly, they also recognized the power of his mind. He was astute and logical, intuitive, even visionary—though he could also display an infuriating dogmatism. Not well educated in a formal sense, nor widely traveled, but well and very widely read, Enzo Ferrari was in many ways a better man of the world than most he met. He was employed for a time as a journalist and later, displaying considerable literary skill, he wrote his own autobiography, *Le Mie Gioie Terribili (My Terrible Joys)*, published in 1962. Some 20 years later, he expanded on some of this material for a second book about the drivers he had known, *Piloti, che gente... (Drivers, What People!)*. Both are works of considerable elegance, strength, and depth. They're also a considerable frustration to the historian, riddled as they are with selective memory, veiled reference, and dubious interpretation. All of that was entirely in keeping with the man.

Automotive journalist Denise McCluggage writing in *AutoWeek* observed that Ferrari was adroit with spoken language, and his conversation was often witty, even mischievous. He could be courtly and charming, as well as abrupt and rude. "A man easier to love than to like," she decided. Others were impressed most by the ruthlessness that showed in both his commercial and personal life. "I'm not sure he was a nice man," racing journalist Nigel Roebuck remarked in Britain's *Supercar Classics*, "but I know he was a great one."

Certainly, he had an imperial presence. Enzo Ferrari in his prime was

*(continued on page 17)*

Enzo Ferrari ruled an empire and nurtured a legend from this office at his Maranello headquarters. "[A] spider central in his web, sensing its vibrations, manipulating, planning, attacking when need be," said writer Doug Nye. Six decades earlier *(inset)* Enzo sits behind the wheel of an Alfa Romeo Grand Prix car. A moderately successful race driver, his competition experiences influenced the flavor of later Ferrari road cars.

described by a friend, Griff Borgeson, in the Automobile Quarterly book *Ferrari The Man The Machine*. Borgeson portrayed a "splendid figure of a man—tall, powerfully built, dynamic, vital. His handsomeness is classical; given a toga and laurel wreath he would make a convincing member of the Roman Senate . . . or a Caesar. He speaks rich and eloquent Italian, good French, and even says cheese for English-speaking photographers. He has a good sense of humor, an engaging smile, a rollicking laugh, flashing eyes. At the same time, his dignity and authority are absolute. . . . He is a *very* hard man and I can't say that I have ever heard any kind words spoken of him."

This hard man, whose family name derived from the Latin word for iron, was a true man of steel. Yet surely a softer character would not have made as much of the life allotted Enzo Anselmo Ferrari.

He came squalling into the world two years before the close of the nineteenth century. It was February, a bitter month in northern Italy, and the birth actually occurred on the 18th. However, snow prevented word reaching the local registry office until two days later, so official records fix it on the 20th.

He was the second of two sons of Alfredo Ferrari, who himself fulfilled the apparent destiny of his surname—

a common one in Italy—by starting a metalworking company. Although Alfredo came originally from the town of Carpi, where he was a butcher's son, he set up premises on the eastern outskirts of Modena, that venerable capital of artisans on the southern edge of the broad Po river valley. It was in the adjoining modest home that his sons were born and reared.

Enzo awoke each morning to the heavy ring of tools below his window. The Ferrari business specialized in what Enzo described as gangways and sheds for the railroad. It employed some 15 to 30 depending on workload, and conferred a measure of prosperity and stature uncommon in a chronically poor, primarily agrarian nation. It also gave little Enzo a first-hand grounding in essentially the very industry that would absorb his adult energies.

The father hoped that for both sons the grounding would be formalized with higher education. His first-born, also named Alfredo, two years older than Enzo, dutifully earned good grades in engineering subjects. But his

Formula 1 dominated Ferrari's racing efforts from the 1970s on. Enzo inspects the '76 312 T 2 (*left*). Its No. 1 denotes Niki Lauda's 1975 world driving championship. Ferrari considered master coachbuilder, Battista "Pinin" Farina (*above*) among his friends and few equals. Enzo called him, "That singular man."

headstrong younger son proved to be no scholar. "I had a most deep-rooted aversion to study," Enzo confessed in his memoirs. "I wanted to start working." After but four years of elementary schooling, plus three at a trade school, Enzo dropped out to pursue his vocation his own way.

That this vocation would involve the automobile was established early. Some historians credit the Ferrari family with ownership of a car, which he easily learned to drive well before the conventional age. They also speak of a garage workshop on the factory premises, where the boy found his first formal employment. But Enzo did not mention either in *Le Mie Gioie Terribili*. For him, the grand passion of his life was ignited on a hot summer's day in 1908, when he was 10. Alfredo Ferrari, Sr., took his two boys down to Bologna, the large town of the region, to watch an open-road automobile competition. "This race made a great impression on me," Enzo wrote of that bright event. So much so that, more than 50 years later, Enzo clearly recalled that Vincenzo Lancia set fastest lap and that Felice Nazarro won at about 74 mph.

His memory was accurate. The race would have been the Coppa Florio, contested over ten laps of a 32.8-mile loop of roads to the west and north of Bologna. Nazarro's Fiat, a great roaring locomotive of a thing, was undoubtedly painted a bright, fire-engine red, the national racing color of Italy. Pounding along the unpaved highway in a comet of dust, taking the curves in lurid, dirt-showering slides, wood-spoke wheels flashing in the sun, Nazarro beat the second-place car, a Lorraine Dietrich, by almost 10 minutes. Lancia wound up fifth.

Ten-year-old Ferrari also noted a clever safety idea at a certain curve along Bologna's Via Emilia: "The ground alongside the road had been flooded to a distance of forty yards with a foot of water ... [this] kept the spectators at a safe distance and, at the same time, provided harmless thrills with the clouds of spray and the unexpected shower baths...."

The next summer, auto racing came almost into Enzo's backyard. He had only to walk a couple of miles over farm fields and across a railroad track to watch as a driver named Da Zara thundered to a record speed of 87.148 mph along a measured, watered-down stretch of the Modena-Ferrara provincial highway. "I still remember ... as clearly as if it had happened yesterday," he wrote. And, "I found these events immensely exciting."

They were indeed exciting enough to signpost a career. Some wait decades for a true calling to emerge, but Enzo Ferrari knew his very early. What he knew was that he would never be a trained engineer, as his father had hoped. Neither would he

18

be an opera singer, his own first ambition—because "I had neither voice nor ear." Sports reporting attracted him, too, and later he would actually pursue that; at 14 he was contributing to a local newspaper. But by the age of 12,

he said later, his life's true purpose was apparent. He would be a racing driver.

He would have to wait. The golden age of his youth and adolescence ended in his 18th year. It was early in

A dapper Ferrari in 1929 (*left*), shortly after he was made a *commendatore*—"commended" for his automotive accomplishments. Eight years earlier (*this page, top*), Enzo and his bride, Laura, pose aboard an Alfa Romeo in a Modena courtyard. (*Above*) Mechanics tune the Alfa that Ferrari would drive in the 1924 Targa Florio.

1916, and Italy was enmeshed in the horrors of World War, when his father died of pneumonia. A few months later Alfredo Jr. succumbed to an unspecified ailment contracted in military service. Although it is believed his mother was still alive, Enzo says he abruptly "found myself quite alone and at a turning point in my life."

Of course, a teenager's feelings were a matter of indifference to the army. In 1917, young Enzo Ferrari was drafted into a detachment of the Mountain Artillery. An assignment was found for him in apparent keeping with his background in the metalworking industry: they had him shoe mules (the Italian for blacksmith is *ferraro*). The comic aspect of this episode was probably more apparent in later years than at the time, and it too nearly ended in tragedy. Like his father and brother, Enzo fell seriously ill. His book does not explain the nature of the ailment, except to say that it required an operation, and that afterward he was put into "a group of dilapidated wooden huts reputedly intended for incurables." How close the Ferrari story came to ending there we can only guess, but Enzo was in fact to have periodic bouts of poor health all during the rest of his long life.

Finally discharged from the army at war's end, he took a letter of introduction from his colonel to the offices of mighty Fiat in Turin. Fiat said it had no job for him. It was wintertime, and his clothes were thin. Enzo Ferrari never forgot trudging to a bench in the city's Valentino Park, where he wiped off the snow and sat down. "I was alone, my father and my brother were no more. Overcome by loneliness and despair, I wept."

Ferrari behind the wheel of a CMN in his very first race, the 1919 Parma-Berceto run (*opposite page, top*). The 21-year-old rookie finished 4th in the 3-liter class. In 1935, as chief of Alfa's racing arm, Scuderia Ferrari (*opposite page, bottom*), Enzo surveys the pits at Monza, the site of the Italian Grand Prix. At age 74 (*below*), Enzo oversees the 1972 opening of Fiorano, the private Ferrari test track across the road from his Maranello factory.

# Chapter 2:

# Scuderia Ferrari: Enzo Establishes Himself

Enzo Ferrari did bring his dark hour to an end by finding work, and portentous work it was. He was hired as a test and delivery driver for an entrepreneur in Turin. The entrepreneur stripped the bodies off surplus military trucks and sold the bare chassis to a firm in Milan, which built sporty civilian coachwork on them. If not a racing driver, Enzo was at least a professional driver, and he began hanging out in the bars at both ends of his delivery route where the leading lights of local motorsport gathered. Stalwart, intelligent, and gregarious, young Ferrari soon made many friends. And one of them, a racing driver named Ugo Sivocci, opened the next door.

A former bicycle racer, Sivocci had been racing small cars since at least 1906, when he won a hillclimb in a single-cylinder Otav. He was now working for a Milanese automaker called CMN, or Costruzioni Meccaniche Nazionali. This company, which had been making four-wheel-drive artillery tractors, was now installing surplus Isotta Fraschini engines into new chassis for sale to a car-starved public. There were ambitious plans for an all-new model. Sivocci was chief test driver and in that capacity he apparently got his new friend Ferrari hired as his assistant.

It was 1919, and the opinion was widely held that an automaker's best method of proving the quality of its cars was by winning races with them. In those informal days the concept of

racing as a special profession had not yet developed. Running an employer's latest model in speed competitions was just part of a test driver's job. And so it was that at the age of 21, Enzo Ferrari had almost literally fallen into a situation fulfilling his decade-old dream. Presto! He was a racing driver.

His first competition for CMN was in October of 1919. Probably the first major Italian automotive event after the war, it was a hillclimb conducted one-way along 32.9 miles of a dirt-surfaced road south out of the foothill city of Parma to the mountain town of Berceto. Overall winner was Antonio Ascari, in a 4.5-liter Fiat. The rookie Enzo Ferrari placed fourth in the three-liter class.

Just a month later, he and Sivocci embarked on a real adventure: the Targa Florio in Sicily. To get there, they and their riding mechanics simply climbed aboard the cars they would race and drove them all the way from Milan to the ferry at Naples.

Photos of this expedition show Enzo's CMN to have been a considerably more advanced machine than the rather buckboardish Parma car. A gracefully simple sports runabout of conventional layout, the new racer had a bold, roundish nose, a stout leather hold-down strap over the hood, and wood-spoke wheels shod with white rubber tires. Its two-seat cockpit perched high behind a huge steering wheel, which, in Italian racing fashion, was mounted on the right. In racing trim there was nothing re-

sembling a windshield. The rear wheels were fenderless, the fronts were barely protected by what may have been a canvas arrangement. There were brakes only on the rear. Enzo and crew drove bundled to the ears with heavy clothing, the November wind rippling their rakishly baggy caps, their eyes protected by oval racing goggles.

En route to Naples, the intrepid young men ran through a blizzard, and at one point in the wild, hilly Abruzzi they attracted the attention of a pack of famished wolves. Enzo drove them off with a pistol "which I always kept under the seat cushion."

After that, and a dismally uncomfortable sea crossing to Palermo, the race itself must have seemed a bit of an anti-climax. It had been created in 1906 by a powerful Sicilian named Don Vincenzo Florio—the same who had given the Coppa, or cup, as a trophy to the winner of the first race

Alfa Romeo's sturdy RLTF (for Targa Florio) (*opposite page*) was developed specifically for Alfa's participation in the 1923 running of the grueling Sicilian endurance race. Its 6-cylinder engine of roughly 3-liters displacement gave it a top speed of about 110 mph. RLTFs finished 1st, 2nd, and 4th in the '23 Targa. Alfa was the de facto national racing team of Italy at this time and Enzo Ferrari was one of its drivers.

that Enzo Ferrari ever attended. The Targa ("plate" or "plaque") Florio was held in the rugged Madonie region, east along the coast from Palermo. The course of November 23, 1919, was a 67.1-mile loop of narrow, twisting, precipitous mountain roads that had to be covered four times.

Racing began with the clay surface slick from rain, and there were numerous crashes. Ascari's was one; he skidded off into a ravine and had to wait many hours for rescue. Even the eventual race winner crashed—seven times. Andre Boillot's last crash came in the last yards of the last lap, when he spun his 2.5-liter Peugeot off the road a few yards from the finish. The exhausted, filthy driver was plucked from a mud puddle, his car was manhandled back to the road and, since it happened to be facing the wrong way, the Peugeot was simply driven backwards across the line.

The Frenchman was "greeted as a hero until cries went up that he should be disqualified for finishing in reverse," writes historian Chris Jones in his book, *Road Race*. "There were no regulations to support this view, but in the heat of the moment nobody thought of that." A rival demanded that the still-dazed Boillot climb aboard one more time, turn around, and cross the line properly. "Which he did, saying before he fainted from exhaustion, "'C'est pour la France.'"

Jones' book doesn't record a death in connection with the incident, but Ferrari's own account says it cost the life of a hapless spectator, and that this was his own first brush with death in motor racing. Someone running across the road could well explain Boillot's spinning out.

In any event, Ferrari was many miles from the scene. His race had been twice delayed, first by a loose fuel tank and then by a speech. Yes, a speech. Pelting into the village of Campofelice on the last lap, already very late, he found the road blocked by a trio of policemen, who politely but firmly told him to shut off the motor until the president of Italy had finished addressing the crowd. "You never ignore the *carabinieri*," Enzo noted dryly. This hold up, a wonderfully original excuse, meant he didn't arrive at the checkered flag until the flagman and everybody else had gone home. The only soul left at the finish line was a policeman, who was methodically recording times—to the nearest minute—with an alarm clock. But young Ferrari was awarded ninth place anyway. Sivocci placed seventh.

By the time of the 1920 Targa, Enzo Ferrari had taken another significant career step. He had followed Sivocci to Alfa Romeo, the manufacturer now on its way to supplanting Fiat as Italy's

From Enzo's days with Alfa Romeo (*clockwise, from above, left*): Ferrari, sans helmet, wrestling a 20/30 ES Sport in a hillclimb; teammates Antonio Ascari (open coveralls), Ferrari (goggles) and Giuseppe Campari (stripe on sleeve); Enzo at the wheel of a RLS with mechanic Giulio Ramponi in 1923; and the start of a typical European road race, circa 1924.

de facto national auto racing team. Still only 22 years old, he was suddenly a fellow driver to such as the great Ascari and Giuseppe Campari. On October 20, Enzo's second assault on the wild Sicilian mountains earned him second place behind Campari. It also earned him 10,000 lire, which at the time was a lot of money.

Perhaps more important than any victory, however, was the idea that Ferrari's concept of automobiles and automobile racing was formed in those golden days. The color and fire of that pioneering era emerged decades later in the cars he built.

As a racing driver, Ferrari certainly was no international Grand Prix star. Indeed, on the one occasion he was entered in a top-level GP, to drive one of four team Alfa P2s at Lyon, France, in 1924, he backed out. The official excuse was poor health, but there have always been observers who said that

Ferrari had simply realized that the car was too much for him. Driving tamer machinery, he did have moderate success in various local events, in both road races and hillclimbs, for a dozen years or so. And by his own account, there was a time when he was faster than Tazio Nuvolari. The fiery little man from Mantua would come to be held as one of the greatest drivers of all time, and one day would be the central member of Ferrari's own team, but Enzo didn't know that when he held the unknown newcomer at bay to win two successive races at Savio and Polesine in 1924.

It was also in 1924, he wrote, when "I finally made my name as a driver" in an event called the Coppa Acerbo at Pescara. On this occasion he drove an Alfa to an upset victory over a pair of Mercedes cars of the same type that had just beaten Alfa at the Targa Florio.

This win gained him more than a "name." He actually got a title out of it. The race promoter, a government minister named Acerbo, had the power to bestow the honor of *cavaliere*, or knight, on the winner of his Coppa. It was the first of several similar honors Ferrari would gather over the years.

His racing also garnered the dramatic emblem that would come to identify Ferrari worldwide. One story has the famous "prancing horse" insignia bestowed on the dashing young racer in 1923 by the parents of a deceased World War I flying ace, Francesco Baracca. The design has been traced to a 17th-Century Italian cavalry regiment, and young Baracca's first military posting was in fact to the cavalry. When he switched to fighters, he painted the proud little animal on his Spad. An alternative trail leads back to the city of Stuttgart, Germany, once a

noted center of equine enterprise (there's a similar horse on the Porsche crest). This theory holds that the device came to Italy as a trophy of a World War I aerial battle.

The prancing horse is said to have appeared on the other aircraft of Baracca's squadron. And Enzo's brother is thought to have worked for that very unit. At some point, too, an insignia featuring a *cavallino rampante* apparently was taken over by the entire Italian Air Force. So it's not entirely certain whether the badge was in fact the Baracca's to bestow.

Tough Tazio Nuvolari was Ferrari's teammate at Alfa, then his employee at Scuderia Ferrari. Nuvolari relaxes in 1930 on an Alfa P2 with fellow drivers (*opposite page, top*). To his right is Eugenio Siena; to his left is Luigi Arcangeli, who would die in an Alfa at Monza. Tazio with an obviously proud Enzo (*above*). Two years earlier, on the Circuit of Mugello, (*bottom left*) Ferrari himself storms past an enthusiastic onlooker.

27

Nonetheless, Enzo preserved the letter from the Baracca family "in which they entrust the horse to me," and obviously felt no compunction about adopting the cavallino as his own. He did make a number of changes: he reversed the direction it faced, altered some details of its outline and stance, and switched its white background to a warm yellow, or gold—the traditional heraldic color of Modena, his birthplace.

Cavaliere Ferrari's once-dark life had turned rich and good. The early opera buff and racing spectator was moving in some exalted company these days. Stories survive of joyous dinner parties, some featuring the informal singing duo of Campari and Ferrari, with guitar accompaniment by Ascari's young son, Alberto, who would himself one day become a champion driver for Ferrari. Also, Enzo had gotten involved in selling Alfa Romeos, and as a purveyor of some of the finest performance road cars of the day, he was literally mingling with royalty. Portraits of the time show all the juicy self-satisfaction of the successful athlete. Enzo was not precisely a handsome fellow, but he was striking, with strong features dominated by that imperious nose. His eyes affected a certain heavy-lidded wariness that failed to conceal intelligence and sensitivity.

He'd also married. Sometime after moving to Turin to join CMN—his book is vague about the exact date—he met "a pretty and smartly dressed little blond with a vivacious manner. I fell head over heels." This was Laura, who would stand in the wings of the Enzo Ferrari opera for the next six decades.

Ferrari continued his racing through 1931. That season, he won a hillclimb outside of Piacenza in a 2.3-liter Alfa 8. According to Borgeson's research, this was Enzo's ninth career victory. A little later, says historian Doug Nye, he had an epic battle with Nuvolari and finished a close second. The following January his first son was born, and he used this turning point as a reason to retire. But he probably would have quit anyway.

"I don't think I did too badly as a racing driver," he summed up his career. But he knew he hadn't made it really big—and wasn't sure he could have. "I was beset by doubts," he recorded, "....because I knew I had one big fault:

I drove always with consideration for the car, whereas to be successful, one must on occasion be prepared to mistreat it." A ruthless driving style was "against all my instincts. In fact, when I drive, I do so not only because I want to get somewhere, but because I find enjoyment in the sensation of the car's response."

"Enjoyment in the sensation of the car's response"—did Enzo Ferrari not define here the very meaning of the exciting cars he would one day build?

Auto manufacturing was still in Ferrari's distant future, of course, and it's difficult to imagine that such a step had even occurred to him at this point. He was plenty busy with everything else his restless energies had led him to take on. As do so many racers, Ferrari had discovered an off-track aptitude for business and management, and Alfa was happy to let him exercise it. As early as 1923, according to his book, he conducted a talent raid on

Fiat. Among those brought to the upstart Alfa fold was the great designer Vittorio Jano. Ferrari prided himself on acquiring "this extraordinary man and his fertile brain."

Quite soon, Ferrari's hands were in a lot of his employer's business. "During my years with Alfa Romeo my work had been many-sided," he wrote. "I had endeavored above all to learn to know men and things. I was driver, organizer, racing manager, and other

(continued on page 31)

Standing with an Alfa P3, Achille Varzi (*above*), was an arch rival of Nuvolari and was among the first drivers hired by Ferrari. Varzi once won the Targa Florio in a car that was on fire from spilled fuel. The danger and excitement of early road racing was heightened by the proximity of spectators to the racers and by the lack of sophisticated safety measures. Enzo Ferrari at the wheel of an Alfa 6C (*opposite page, top*) trails a cloud of dust in the Circuit of Mugello in 1928. Varzi muscles an Alfa P2 (*opposite page, bottom*) around a corner in 1930.

No Alfa is more valued today than the classic 6C, a fast, strong, beautiful sports car introduced in 1925. This 1928 example has the 1.5-liter six derived from Vittorio Jano's Grand Prix straight-8; others ranged to 1.9 liters. Ferrari raced 6Cs in the '20s and '30s.

things besides, without any clear-cut boundaries to my fields of responsibility. At the same time, I was in charge of Alfa Romeo sales in Emilia, Romagna, and the Marche, living alternately in Milan and Bologna and managing to avoid complete severance of my ties with Modena.... With my natural aggressiveness I began by exercising my innate talent for 'stirring up' men and technical problems. (And I have not changed—I have never considered myself a designer or an inventor, but only one who gets things moving and keeps them running.)"

He was also finding time, somehow, to pursue his journalism ambitions, writing reports of various sports events; indeed, he says he was for a while the managing director of *Corriere dello Sport*, the famous Italian sports newspaper then headquartered in Bologna. And at one point he says he worked in Switzerland, but gives no details.

Small wonder, then, that 1924, the year that "made" him as a racing driver, also made him ill. In *Gioie Terribili* Enzo says he became "seriously rundown...the beginning of trouble with my health that was to afflict me throughout the years to come." In *Piloti* he calls the trouble "a serious nervous breakdown." Automobile competition affords racers unrestrained scope for their talent and enterprise, but it also harbors an insatiable hunger for their energy.

And it was racing that remained the centerpiece of Enzo's life. Even before he stopped driving, he took on the role of a team owner. Late in 1929, after ten racing seasons as an Alfa Romeo employee, he quit to go on his own, returning to Modena and forming Scuderia Ferrari, a private enterprise to race Alfa cars.

The word *scuderia* literally means "stable," but in this context, it is better translated as "team." Scuderia Ferrari was started as little more than a maintenance service for some of Enzo's wealthy sportsman friends, a way to let them buy all the pleasures of racing with none of its drudgery. Not surprisingly, Enzo rapidly made something more of the business. The team began hiring professional drivers, such as the fabulous Nuvolari, the moody Achille Varzi, and future World Champion Giuseppe Farina. So well was the "stable" operated that

31

Ferrari-entered Alfas, running primarily against Maseratis and Bugattis, virtually dominated Grand Prix racing in 1932 and again in '33. That second season was the beginning of a five-year period in which the financially troubled manufacturer—its affairs would soon come under control of the Italian government—actually appointed Ferrari's team its official competition arm. The Scuderia remained independent of Alfa Romeo, but the black-and-yellow prancing horse emblem replaced Alfa's green-and-white cloverleaf on the factory cars.

About this time Enzo inaugurated publication of a magazine and also of an annual book, both about Scuderia Ferrari and its doings. Some of Ferrari's motivation is obvious: to publicize the team and also to scratch his old journalism itch. But Nye adds a deeper thought: "He wielded them as self-promotion, flattering European race organizers with glowing profiles, occasionally chivvying a recalcitrant driver by some pointed (and very public) remark. The great manipulator was learning to pull the strings...."

The latter years of the 1930s saw the great onslaught from Mercedes-Benz and Auto Union, and without the resources to counter the government-backed Germans, the Italian team was usually overpowered. In 1935, Nuvolari did manage a magnificent in-your-face triumph for Enzo's Alfas at the Nürburgring, the German back yard. The following year, the little horse emblem scored its first victory in America, in the Vanderbilt Cup event on Long Island, New York.

In 1934, the frustrated team constructed two examples of a free-formula model with dual engines (one in front, the other in the rear), and although these Bimotori hot rods were not a success on the track, one did set a speed record of just over 200 mph. Three years later Ferrari got Alfa to authorize participation in the comparatively small-engined *voiturette*, or Formula Two, class, which the Germans considered beneath them. His own shop in Modena took part in planning and building the resulting model 158, a design that matured into the 159 Alfetta that would eventually dominate the early post-World War II scene.

Ferrari also ran a motorcycle racing

team for a few seasons. His British-made Rudge and Norton bikes took the Italian national championship in several classes two years straight. One of the things he learned from this episode was that good riders have a lot of the traits he looked for in drivers.

By 1938, the 40-year-old entrepreneur already could very legitimately be called the Grand Old Man of Italian

(continued on page 36)

Cigarette between his lips, racing coveralls as yet unsoiled by competition, Nuvolari (*above*) talks with Scuderia Ferrari teammates before the start of the German Grand Prix at the Nürburgring. As the 1930s drew to a close, Alfa Romeo could seldom steal victory from the mighty Mercedes-Benz team. On this day, however, Nuvolari would best Mercedes and its great driver, Rudy Caracciola. Scuderia Ferrari (*opposite page*) was one of the first European competition teams to use specially modified trucks to transport its racing cars.

Engine maven Vittorio Jano, whom Ferrari would later snap away from Alfa, furthered his growing reputation with the Alfa Romeo 8C 2300, a splendid sports-racer introduced in 1931. Its 138-horsepower 2.3-liter straight-8 was actually two fours ingeniously joined back to back.

auto racing, and therefore one of the significant figures in European motorsports.

Even his government officially recognized his stature. To his first title of *cavaliere* had been added *cavaliere ufficiale*, and then, in 1928, he was made a *commendatore*. This simply meant he was "commended" for his accomplishments, not—as many English-speak-ing Ferraristi seem to want to think—that he was in any way a "commander." The amusing fact is that, as Ferrari explains in his book, this was a Fascist government honor wiped out after the war. He could have applied to renew it, but "I myself made no such application and am thus no longer a *commendatore*." But that never stopped people from calling him one.

Alfa reshouldered its own racing program in 1938 and offered Enzo the job of team manager. He closed down Scuderia Ferrari and moved to Milan. But having been his own man for nine years, he soon chaffed at being someone else's. There were also personality clashes. One dispute, with a manager he otherwise admired, casts more light on the Ferrari character: "(Ugo)

Gobbato...was no believer in improvisation or in snap decisions..." Ferrari wrote. "[He] hated having to adapt himself to sudden changes, whereas for me the art of makeshift was almost a part of my religion."

Another dispute was over the value of the chief engineer, a Spaniard named Wilfredo Ricart, who was later responsible for the Pegaso automobiles. Enzo found Ricart peculiar both in ideas and in person. When he asked the man one day why he wore shoes with such thick rubber soles, he received the straight-faced response that it was to protect his delicate engineer's brain from shocks. Enzo's snort of derision was that of the self-made man for the college boy.

So it was probably no surprise on

The Alfa Romeo 158 of 1939 (*above and opposite page, bottom*) was the first car built by Ferrari's Modena racing shop. Competing in a class below the German-dominated Grand Prix category, its wins gave Italian fans something to cheer about. A racing version of the 8C prepares to leave the pits (*opposite page, top*) in a 1935 Grand Prix race in Budapest.

either side that in November of 1938 Enzo left Alfa again. In two places in his book he admits he was "dismissed," but in another place he speaks of a "crisis of conscience that led me to abandon [Alfa]." In yet another, he says, "I had been for too long a time with Alfa Romeo ... to spend a whole lifetime with one firm was a mistake for someone who wanted to learn; to learn, one must move about.... I left Alfa so that I might show the people in Alfa what I was made of—an ambitious idea that might have ruined me!"

Besides all that, he saw a war coming, and obviously perceived that there were better places to ride it out. The place he went was back to Modena to work for himself. As part of a financial settlement with Alfa, he had agreed not to revive the Scuderia Ferrari or compete in racing for four years. On September 1, 1939, he set up a contract design and manufacturing firm, Auto-Avio Costruzioni di Ferrari Enzo, and tried to busy himself with industrial accounts. But if he ever actually intended to stay out of racing for four years, he was unable, and soon his shop was assembling a pair of little sports racing hot rods out of Fiat parts. These cars were no threat to anything Alfa was doing at

the time, and their genesis could have been no secret to his old teammates, but Enzo went through the subterfuge of keeping his own name off them. The first Ferraris in fact, they were simply called by a type number: 815, for their 8-cylinder engines of 1.5-liters displacement.

They first ran in the last pre-war Mille Miglia ("Thousand Miles") race on April 28, 1940. Alberto Ascari, the guitarist son of Antonio, drove one. Both cars actually led the 1500-cc class early on, but neither lasted to the finish. "Despite a promising start," Enzo summarized, "the car was not a success, mainly on account of the haste with which it had been constructed."

We can only speculate where the 815 project might have led, because Ferrari himself makes no further reference to it. But it must be significant that the first car to bear his name, the model 125 of six years later, differed from the 815 more in degree than in kind. And from the outset, the 125 concept included roadgoing sports cars for the wealthy enthusiast. So, although it may not have been wholly formed in his mind by 1940, it is logical to presume that even this early, Enzo harbored an ambition to found an actual auto factory.

Building his plan around the wealthy enthusiast was only natural to Ferrari. Fewer than one Italian in 100 in the late 1930s could afford to own a car of any sort, and only the central circles of society could aspire to a car built for fun. But of course those were the circles in which this workman's son had long since grown used to moving. It simply would not have occurred to Enzo Ferrari to make a car to please anyone but a prince.

All of that ceased to matter a few weeks after the Mille Miglia, however. On June 10, 1940, the Fascist government of Benito Mussolini took Italy into World War II on the side of the Nazis. For the second time in less than 25 years, Enzo's life was derailed. Of course, this time he had the disaster under some semblance of control. "There followed years of interesting experience," he wrote, "although sad ones, as I could have nothing to do with cars." This time, at least, he need have nothing to do with mules.

Prepared to do battle in the Mille Miglia, a squadron of Scuderia Ferrari Alfa Romeos lines up before the team's headquarters building in Modena. Scuderia was formed in 1929 and lasted until 1939, when Enzo severed his ties with Alfa.

# Chapter 3:

# La Ferrari:
# "A Psychosis for Racing Cars"

Italy's plunge into war was a national disaster and of course wasn't anything Enzo Ferrari would have chosen. However, if he had foreseen the storm, he was truly prescient, for his Modena enterprise was well conceived to ride it out. Placing racing on a back burner, he concentrated on his existing subcontract work for a factory in Rome that produced small engines for flight training. Then he found an even more solid enterprise, making high-quality copies of German ball-bearing grinding machines. Ferrari's company prospered during the war years, and grew from a workforce of about 40 to more than 100.

It also expanded onto a new site. In 1943, when the tide was turning against the Axis, Ferrari was forced by a government decentralization policy to move his operation away from the attractive military target of Modena. Apparently because his wife already owned some orchard land there, he chose a place some ten miles south of the city, on national highway 12 just before a village named Maranello. There on the east side of the road he built a small complex of buildings around a tri-cornered, cobblestoned courtyard.

The move failed to hide him from the Allies. The plant was bombed twice, in October 1944 and again the next February. But the attacks caused little more damage than did the retreating Nazis, who one day late in the conflict made off with truckloads of Ferrari's copied grinders. There's little evidence that Enzo really cared, however. His mind had already turned from machine tools to more passionate ambitions. "The end of the war did not find me altogether unprepared," he confessed in his memoirs. "I had always continued to work on designs for racing cars."

Here was a man in his late forties, one with responsibilities to both a small family and a substantial staff of employees, who had achieved a measure of economic success by manufacturing quality industrial equipment. Surely it was a product of which his ravaged nation had sore need, and his continued supply of it would guarantee his prosperity. But now he was turning his back on that sound, solid business to play with fast, noisy cars.

As irresponsible as the scheme might seem, Ferrari was actually well placed to start up as an automaker. He had 20 years of top-quality experience in every aspect of the high performance motor industry. He also owned a small gem of a plant, one stocked with much of the machinery needed for his new enterprise. It fit a model he had developed back at Alfa Romeo: "I took the view that a racing car should be the compendium of the work of a small auxiliary workshop, well fitted out and with its own specialized staff, so that the ideas and designs of the engineers might rapidly be translated into reality." This notion was at variance with Alfa's established practice, which featured a huge, ponderous op-

eration. The disagreement was one of the reasons Ferrari had left Alfa in 1939. It essentially describes what he'd now built at Maranello.

He'd also taken care to staff his "workshop" with excellent people, some of whom had come with him from the old Scuderia Ferrari/Alfa Romeo days, and others whom he had spent six years selecting in a region respected internationally for its manufacturing talent. As Griff Borgeson notes, Modena is renowned as a center of craftsmanship. "Absurdly gifted artisans abound, so that you can have almost anything made, made surpassingly well, and so cheaply that you never get used to the miracle. It's an incredible place, where master pattern makers are a dime a dozen and skilled metal workers of every kind seem to surge out of the black humus.... Hence the stature, in the automotive world, of this otherwise bucolic and utterly boring backwater of civilization."

Ferrari himself put it this way: "In Modena there is a species of psychosis for racing cars.... The worker in these parts, whether of muscle or of mind, is extremely intelligent and very active. What is more, the people in this part of the country are by nature of a rebellious character—they are not easygoing folk. In short, the union of blood and brain is such that the result is a type of man who is stubborn, capable, and daring—the very qualities that are needed for building racing cars."

Enzo's own "psychosis for racing cars" was even stronger than that of any of his neighbors. The rest of his country was still reeling from war when Ferrari, who Borgeson calls "the great agitator," had his staff at work on his first one.

Decades later, Ferrari recalled that this first automobile to bear his name, "came into being as an orthodox car; it was not the result of any experimentation. All we wanted to do was to build a conventional engine, but one that would be outstanding." Well, the car itself may have been orthodox, but this one man's idea of a "conventional" engine would strike most of the rest of the world as quite awesome.

It certainly was outstanding—particularly as the first automotive product of such a small company in the cli-

mate of desperate poverty that was immediate postwar Italy. For almost anyone else, even some quite large factories in that other hotbed of specialty car manufacture, England, it has often proved difficult enough to produce a new car powered by an existing engine. But Ferrari had the great fortune to be able to draw on Italy's notable facility with metallurgy. Creating an all-new engine to go into a truly all-new automobile was all in a day's work to Enzo's skilled and enthusiastic workmen.

All of them were heir to a wealth of good Italian automotive tradition. For one thing, because of the endless mountain roads running not only through the mighty Alps to the north, but over the Apennines down the whole length of the country, Italian

cars had been naturally selected in the Darwinian sense for excellent handling. Also, fuel had always been costly and taxation savage, so engines needed to be small and efficient. And since the 1920s, Italian drivers had enjoyed a network of high-speed Autostradas, so their engines had to be as durable as they were powerful. All these factors resulted in cars in tune with the native brio. No wonder Italy was widely known as "the nation of enthusiasts."

To arch-enthusiast Ferrari, the most interesting and important element of any car was its engine. He'd demonstrated that with the pre-war 815, where he'd gone to great lengths not to just modify an existing powerplant, but to virtually construct his own. For the new model he'd go to

even greater lengths. Its power was not going to come from anything ordinary and simple, anything rational— certainly not from a hopped-up Fiat. No, he was going to create a brand new, scratch-built, all-aluminum, overhead-camshaft V-type engine with 12 cylinders.

In explaining this seemingly extravagant choice, Ferrari cited aesthetics at least as much as any engineering rationale. "I had always liked the song of twelve cylinders; what is more, I must confess that the fact that there was then only one firm in the world making such engines acted on me as a challenge and a spur."

That other manufacturer was America's Packard, and he claimed to have long admired its twelve. In fact, Enzo was mistaken to call it a con-

temporary of his own. Packard's V-12 had not survived 1939. Nor was it in any way comparable to his own project—the American powerplant had been a huge thing, 7.7 liters (473 cubic inches) in displacement, a slow-revving, side-valve luxury-car engine.

So is the Packard citation a smokescreen? Enzo did mention a Delage V-12 he'd once admired, but he was silent about several similar engines much closer to his own experience, such as those raced against him by Mercedes and Auto Union. Nor did he discuss the twelves of both Vee and flat-opposed configuration built by Alfa Romeo. How could Enzo have forgotten that his team's 1936 victory at the Vanderbilt Cup was gained with an Alfa V-12? Was he sensitive that people might think he was copying his

old employer? As an historical trace, *My Terrible Joys* has its slippery spots.

But its author was on firm ground when he suggested it took courage to specify a tiny V-12 for his first car. "I came in for a good deal of criticism; it was forecast that I was digging my

Ferrari ran a motorcycle racing team for a few seasons in the late 1930s (*opposite page*). His British-made Rudge and Norton bikes took the Italian national championship in several classes two years straight. Enzo is the third figure from the right in the photo. To his left is Tazio Nuvolari. The pageantry of the Targa Florio, the epic long-distance race through the mountains of northern Sicily, is captured in this view (*above*). Enzo competed in the grueling race many times and its lessons were an important influence upon him.

own grave, the experiment being judged too daring and presumptuous." How easy it is to picture his imperial smile as he pens those words years later.

Even the model designation was a bold stroke. Like his pre-war 815 it was going to be a 1.5-liter, but rather than follow the same logic and calling the new car, say, the 12-15, Enzo settled on 125, which was simply the displacement in cubic centimeters of one cylinder (7.6 cubic inches). This rather confusing base-12 arithmetic would be preserved in Ferrari nomenclature for many years. One always had to stop and carry out a sum to figure out the full size of the motor. But how cunning: The calculation always reinforced one's appreciation that a Ferrari was a V-12.

Perhaps the new marque would have earned the same public acclaim had its power come from more pedestrian mechanicals—but don't bet on it. The hustling, rustling, exciting "song of twelve cylinders" is a good part of what made Ferrari's name as a carmaker. Making the first Ferrari engine a V-12 was a masterstroke from the image viewpoint alone.

But there also was an engineering rationale. It centers on the way a piston engine makes horsepower. Every time it revolves, it draws in a certain quantity of air, adds fuel, and burns the mixture to release energy. The more mixture processed, the more energy released and the more horsepower generated. One way to more power is more displacement—a physically bigger engine that takes larger bites of air with every revolution. That's the way American automakers did it for so many years. But taxation policies, which were reflected in racing regulations, almost universally constrained European engines to specific displacement categories. So their designers took another route to performance: They spun their smaller engines faster to take more bites per minute.

An Alfa Romeo 8C driven by Tazio Nuvolari leads another Alfa and a Maserati 8CM through a corner of the Italian Grand Prix in the late 1930s. The courage, skill, and technology bred by motorsports inspired Ferrari's love of cars and became his guiding automotive light. Of his own driving career, Enzo said, "...I had one big fault: I drove always with consideration for the car, whereas to be successful, one must on occasion be prepared to mistreat it."

Of course, there are inherent restrictions on the rotational speed of a piston engine. One is the weight and metallurgical strength of the various reciprocating parts. To reduce this factor, the designers can divide the engine's displacement into a larger number of smaller cylinders. They also may equip them with more elaborate valve-operating mechanisms, specifically overhead camshafts. These eliminate the oscillating weight of pushrods and other intermediate parts, therefore allowing the springs to keep the valves under control at higher rpm.

Given proper engineering of these factors, engines of a certain displacement will produce more power the more cylinders they have. More cylinders usually mean smoother, sweeter operation, too. And in Ferrari's case at least, a fabulous sound.

There are drawbacks. Such a "multi-cylinder" engine is necessarily bulkier, heavier, more complex, and more expensive. But in the rarified heights of the automotive world that Ferrari was planning to address, he believed the traffic would bear such an exotic powerplant. After all, since the early 1920s he'd known no other kind of customer.

He was planning to service racers primarily, but he was operating in a happy period when the traditional family relationship between racer and roadster was still close. A racing sports car could be driven on the highway quite easily, and it often was, and not only en route to the race venue. So it was perfectly feasible, in 1946, to design one basic engine that could fill a broad spectrum of uses and thus satisfy a wide base of customers.

Ferrari's game plan was announced in a 1946 story describing the project published in the Italian magazine *Inter Auto*. The famous Scuderia Ferrari had been revived, and there would be three models: a 125 S, for Sport, would come first, followed by a Com-petizione, meaning a competition version of the sports car, and a Gran Premio—a Grand Prix racer. Although in the hurly-burly of actual events the plan was not followed precisely, and while Enzo's heart always beat for his race cars first and foremost, he would write: "Ever since I built the first 1500, I had ambitious plans for launching out into the manufacture of high quality cars." His initial hope was to reach an output of a car a day; his factory would eventually exceed that goal by several times.

The seminal Ferrari 125 Competi-

*(continued on page 48)*

The 166 Sypder Corsa had great success in a variety of racing classes in the late 1940s. It's 2-liter Colombo V-12 was durable enough to outlast larger-displacement machines in endurance races, and its headlamps and cycle-type fenders could be removed for participation in formula and sports-car events. Maximum speed was about 125 mph and the car had a 0-60-mph time of about 10 seconds.

This beautifully preserved 166 Spyder Corsa freezes in time a bygone era of motorsports. Note the absence of seatbelts and the minimal lateral bolstering for the driver in its two-place cockpit (*opposite page, bottom*). Twin windscreens and the tachometer-dominated dashboard (*above*) are both functional and charming. Roman numerals on the shift knob show the 5-speed transmission's gear pattern.

zione was an open two-seater of rather bluntly utilitarian lines. Designed by Gioacchino Colombo, who started work as early as August 1945, it was developed and built by Aurelio Lampredi and several other engineers and technicians during 1946. The first example actually raced on May 11, 1947, at Piacenza. Franco Cortese started from pole position, and Enzo's account says he was leading two laps from the end when the fuel pump seized. "It was at least a promising failure," he commented.

The historic first-ever Ferrari victory came two weeks later, at Rome at the hands of Cortese. He scored three

more wins out of five starts in June. In July, Tazio Nuvolari rejoined Scuderia Ferrari and was responsible for more success.

That began it, the most remarkable sustained accomplishment ever seen in auto racing. In the coming years and decades the *cavallino rampante* would prance the length and breadth of the motorsports world, building a record of race wins and series championships unequaled now or perhaps ever.

In the course of all this activity, Ferrari produced a bewildering number and variety of models. Even before the end of that impressive first racing sea-

The first car to wear the Ferrari badge was the 125 S (Sport), a two-place roadster introduced in 1947 (*opposite page*). Its 1497-cc V-12 produced about 100 horsepower. The car was first raced on May 11. Franco Cortese started from the pole position at Piacenza in Italy, but fuel-pump failure retired him three laps from the end. Two weeks later, Cortese scored Ferrari's first victory with a win at Rome's Caracalla circuit. That began an unmatched record of international triumphs. Here, Ferrari's race-team transporters await loading on a ship bound for the United States (*above*).

son of 1947, his engine people were enlarging the original Tipo ("type") 125 to make a Tipo 159 at—multiply by 12 to get the displacement—just over 1900 cc. Over that winter the engine was taken out to 1995 cc, creating the Tipo 166. In January 1948, an example of this model was the first Ferrari ever sold. According to historian Stanley Nowak, it probably was just one of the previous year's 1.5 racing chassis with the new two-liter engine installed.

Nineteen forty-eight turned out to be an epochal year for the fledgling Ferrari factory. That summer another version of the 166 won both the Targa Florio and the Mille Miglia. The winning machine was actually the same car wearing two different bodies. These just happened to be the two most prestigious sports car races in Italy. And of course the Sicilian victory was a special triumph, coming at long last on Enzo's old stomping grounds. Then came an important international success; a win at the Paris 12-hour endurance event.

Behind the scenes, work was going forward on a supercharged version of the original 1.5 engine to suit postwar Formula One Grand Prix racing. This was finally ready in the fall, and one car finished third at the Turin GP behind Alfa's aging, but still very potent, type 159 Alfettas. Meanwhile, fenderless versions of the 2-liter, normally-aspirated car had already started winning Formula 2 events.

At the same time, Ferrari had been letting out a few chassis to coachbuilders to have genuine, everyday highway cars constructed. A sales brochure issued that fall described four production models; three were racers, including an F2 single-seater, but one was a roadgoing coupe. All were powered by the same Tipo 166 engine.

On the track, 1949 was even better. Ferrari cars won a total of 32 races, including the Targa Florio and Mille Miglia again. There was also a first F1 victory at the Grand Prix of Rosario— plus five more grands prix. These were somewhat hollow conquests because Alfa Romeo had withdrawn the Alfettas for the season. But they did show that Ferrari's new team was becoming ever more capable. Perhaps the most important win of all, though, was the 24-hour contest at Le Mans, the world's best-known sports car

race and one of the most famous races of any sort. That got the new marque noticed overseas. It was that same summer that the first Ferraris were sold in America.

Prime mover in bringing Ferrari to the United States was an Italian named Luigi Chinetti. An old friend of Enzo's, Chinetti was an experienced racer who had been a co-winner at Le Mans in 1932 and 1934, driving Alfa Romeos. It was he who had scored

that 1948 Ferrari victory at Paris, and the following year at Le Mans he marked his own third triumph by driving the winning 166 Ferrari more than 23 of the 24 hours himself.

By then he had become an Ameri-can citizen, with a garage business in New York. According to his own ac-count (Ferrari's mentions nothing of this), in 1946, soon after the end of the war, he had paid a visit to his old buddy in Maranello. In an *Auto Week* in-

Raymond Sommer, his 1.9-liter Ferrari 159 S sandwiched by a pair of 2-liter Maseratis, powers through a corner on the Turin Grand Prix circuit in 1947. Sommer's win in this race was an important milestone in establishing Ferrari's engineering and competition credentials.

51

terview with Denise McCluggage, Chinetti recalled that it was a typically bitter northern Italian winter, with fog in the air and snow on the ground. But there was no heat in the Ferrari office, nor any light. Chinetti remembers Enzo hugging himself in the dark, trying to keep warm. Luigi advised Ferrari to build racing cars for him to sell in America. Enzo retorted, "If you order five, I will." Luigi ordered 20—even though, he confessed later, he had no means of paying for them. With those cars and with the others that soon followed, Chinetti established Ferrari on some of America's best racetracks and put them in some of America's wealthiest driveways.

It's an appealing tale, and its absolute precision is less important than its illustration that the Ferrari car business lacked as smooth a genesis as the race record might imply. Indeed, for the first 20 years, Ferrari was almost always on shaky financial ground. There are all sorts of speculations as to where Enzo may have gained sup-

port, just as there are innumerable stories of sly dealings: cars sold as new that were later revealed to be well-used; cars sold just in time for the factory to make the next payroll.

Ferrari's story is no fairy tale. It didn't all happen automatically, with success written into the script from the beginning. Any number of similar automaking dreams have withered to dust. This one survived because of the personal qualities of its dreamer: Enzo Ferrari's ambition, determination, experience, intelligence, and guile.

Even his strong emotionalism was a component. Early in 1947, for instance, a Ferrari racer won a sports car "Grand Prix" in Turin's Valentino Park, near the Fiat factory from which the young Enzo Ferrari had years before trudged in utter despair. He described in his autobiography how he had slumped, sobbing, on a snow-covered park bench. Almost 30 years had gone by, yet on that October afternoon in 1947, the mature business-man sought out the same bench and

sat down on it. "The tears I shed that day, though, were of a very different kind!"

He cried again four years later, on July 14, 1951, when Ferrari's Argentinean driver Froilan Gonzalez beat the Alfa 159 for the first time in a fair fight at Silverstone, in England. "I wept with joy; but my tears of happiness were blended too with tears of sadness, for I thought that day, 'I have killed my mother!'"

Throughout these memoirs runs a tint of histrionics. Had he been gifted with a better voice, Ferrari might well have made a fine opera singer. But there is no reason to doubt that he had such feelings. What he was doing truly held great meaning for him.

Ferrari's type 166 engine in 2-liter form (*above*), seen here in the 1950 Formula 2 car. This V-12 was extremely successful in naturally aspirated and supercharged forms and it dominated its class in 1949 and '50. These racing victories established Ferrari's name with European sports-car enthusiasts and helped immeasurably the retail sales of Ferrari cars.

# Chapter 4:

# Building a Legacy

The construction of La Ferrari continued, car by car, race by race, year by year. The Tipo 166 engine grew again, several times. It became the 195, with 2341 total cc, in 1950; the 212 (2562 cc) in 1951; then the first 250 (3-liters) the following year. It ultimately grew into the 3.3-liter 275. This powerplant, still basically the original small-block V-12 that Colombo had designed as a 1.5-liter, was the engine that probably gained Ferrari more success and fame than any other, and he built many, many others.

In 1950, Lampredi enlarged the basic drawings and changed certain important details to produce the first of a new generation of physically larger motors. It started out at 3322 cc and grew in stages to the 4494-cc F1 motor (Tipo 375) that brought Ferrari's first GP victory. Eventually, it became as large as 4954 cc and won Le Mans. A derivative displacing 4963 cc powered the type 500 Superfast road cars.

Vittorio Jano, whom Enzo Ferrari had lured from Fiat to Alfa back in the '20s, also came up with his own V-12 for Ferrari. Other engineers contributed their own designs as the factory grew, as it became, indeed, an Italian national institution. There was a steadily expanding, ever more complex array of thoroughbreds in the horsepower stable.

Eventually, the engine list grew so long that the factory had to abandon the original cubic centimeters-per-cylinder model designation. One common replacement scheme gave the displacement in liters followed by the number of cylinders. For example, "512" meant a five-liter with 12 cylinders; "328," a 3200-cc eight. Counting the famous race winners and street engines, as well as experimental prototypes that never saw the public eye, several hundred different designs wore the Ferrari badge. There were V-12s, inline fours and sixes, V-6s, V-8s, even flat-12s. Ferrari built an experimental 2-cylinder engine and once considered building an 18-cylinder. There was also an air-cooled F1 design, and, many years after the early supercharged F1, a line of turbocharged models.

On one end of the size spectrum was a tiny, 850-cc four intended for a small street car. On the other, a 7-liter twelve for Can-Am racing in America. Revealing this behemoth, Enzo proudly jested, "Other Ferrari engines have cylinders like wine glasses. These are like wine bottles!"

Ferrari's early experience had been that "it is engine power which is—not 50 percent but 80 percent—responsible for success on the track." Of course he realized that whenever other teams built engines as strong as his, attention had to be paid to the rest of his cars to remain competitive. Still, it's clear that he just wasn't much interested in these other elements. That's why Ferraris in general are so well known for the magnificence of their powerplants—and for the relative backwardness of everything else.

The machines from Maranello were late in adopting such advances as independent rear suspensions, disc brakes, and fully monocoque chassis.

Even after his English rivals proved in the late 1950s that putting the engine behind the driver was the best way to build a racing car, Ferrari resisted. "The horse does not push the cart," he asserted, "it pulls." What horse carts have to do with racing cars was left unexplained, and Enzo probably made this famous pronouncement with a smile, but his basic turn of mind cannot be denied. His drivers had to soldier on for several seasons with increasingly obsolete, clumsy-handling front-engined racers. This innate conservatism was reflected in the road cars.

Enzo Ferrari's consuming passion was racing, so building roadgoing models was something of a necessary evil—the necessity being revenue to support his racing. But of course it was his team's exploits on the track that generated the aura of magic around his name and made his road cars so desirable. So perhaps in the view of some Ferrari customers the necessary evil was the racing.

In any event, the model generally recognized as the first purpose-built highway Ferrari was the 166 Inter. Introduced late in 1948 at the Turin auto show—Ferrari's first appearance at such an exhibition—it featured a smooth coupe body by Touring, the honorable old Milanese *carrozzeria*. Ferrari at that stage saw his role as sup-

Ferrari's Formula 1 car of 1951, the type 375 (*both pages*), boasted superb handling and helped end the rein of the supercharged Alfa Romeos. The naturally aspirated V-12 produced 380 horsepower at 7500 rpm in its 4.5-liter form. It also brought Ferrari his first Formula 1 victory, in July 1951, at Silverstone, when Argentinean driver Froilan Gonzalezit beat Enzo's mentor, Alfa. "I have killed my mother!" Enzo cried after the race.

plying the bare chassis. He left the bodywork to the customer.

For the next 25 years or so, development of the Ferrari road-car range generally paralleled that of the racing models. Whenever the V-12 was enlarged and proved a success in competition, a street version often followed, usually sharing much of the same drivetrain, suspension, and chassis technology. This was in some ways Ferrari's golden period, when he was setting the pace in exotic road machinery, creating the wondrous automobiles that are now worth, in some cases, millions of dollars.

Standouts include the 340 Mexico of 1952, a 4.1-liter with a striking Vignale body; 1953's 375 America, its mighty 4.5-liter V-12 clothed most gracefully by Farina; and, beginning the same year, a long line of 250 GTs, all of which incorporated various versions of the original Colombo engine in 3-liter form. Of the 250 GT series, some of the greatest were the so-called Tour de France model, a successor named the SWB (for Short Wheelbase Berlinetta), and the ultimate development of the line, the magnificent GTO (Gran Turismo Omologato).

Many of these were not, strictly speaking, everyday road cars. They were built to regulations that fostered

race cars usable on the road by enthusiasts who were skilled, committed, and wealthy.

Although it is sometimes said that Enzo himself had little interest in his bread-and-butter production vehicles, at this stage he definitely dealt with them on a fundamental level. It was he who decided, after reviewing the work of everyone else who had erected bodies on his chassis, that the best stylist was Battista "Pinin" Farina. "That singular man," as Enzo called him, was also a former race driver and at least as headstrong a personality as Enzo, so they spoke the same language. "Pinin has led the renaissance

A gathering of giants (*left photo*): Enzo Ferrari, drivers Antonio Ascari and Giuseppe Campari, designer Vittorio Jano, an unidentified man, and engineer Luigi Bazzi. The 375 Plus LM of 1952 (*below*). Pinin Farina with one of his designs, the 1964 275 GTB (*opposite page, top*). The seminal 166 Inter of 1947 (*opposite page, bottom*), Ferrari's first real dual-purpose road-and-racing car.

in Italian automobile styling....," Ferrari said. "His car bodies are simple and clean, being reduced to the essential lines...actually nothing sensational, but his style will always preserve its personality and will never look dated."

A professional relationship seemed logical, Enzo wrote, because "our interests were complimentary, for he, as it were, was seeking a beautiful woman to dress, and I was in search of a high-class couturier to dress her." But it wasn't as simple as that. There

ensued a childishly amusing little power game between these two willful men: each refused to come visit the other! They finally compromised on an intermediate meeting place at which was born a long, fruitful collaboration and a close friendship.

Ferrari also kept a sharp eye, and sometimes a firm hand, on the cars that went into the world bearing his name. There is a legend that he personally road-checked each car off the production line. If that were ever true, he didn't go quite that far in later

years, though for a long time he did take the time to try each new model in the prototype stage. As related to writer Griff Borgeson by designer Jano, Enzo was still checking up on the work of his development drivers at least as late as the early 1960s.

Jano, who did this same sort of work at Alfa, often rode along on these outings. He described Ferrari as "a terrific driver at speed." The Boss showed steadiness rather than fire and was capable of "that analytical, critical judgement that it takes to arrive at a really

refined result. A car that does not hold the road to perfection goes right back to the shop," Jano said. "If there is any shortcoming in high-level performance, if there is any defect whatsoever, if the car is not wholly sincere, Ferrari is capable of feeling the fault, and he commands that it be eliminated. This is why it takes no time at all for a good driver to learn to handle a Ferrari, right out to the limits and without fear of ugly surprises. There are some fast cars that take two or three months to learn to control. And

there are others that just leave the road and no one ever knows why. But a good driver is at home in a Ferrari from the word go."

These of course are the words of a company man. At least one outsider, writer David Owen—though an ardent admirer of the marque—speaks of "the old Ferrari surprises for unwary drivers."

Ownership of a production Ferrari also had its drawbacks in terms of practicality and, often, reliability in certain detail points. Even the purchase experience could be disagreeable. Enzo—who favored the royal color purple, notably in the pens with which he signed documents—maintained a thoroughly imperial attitude toward his supplicants. He frequently kept even the most high-born of his adoring public awaiting his pleasure in the cold before finally admitting them to his office. Sometimes he didn't admit them at all. And once a person stood across the desk from him, Ferrari might go through a little head-down theater, as if he were too busy to notice the visitor.

But his customers rationalized that cavalier treatment was just part of prancing-horse ownership. So were the mechanical quibbles, none of which seemed a serious threat to the sense of excitement, enjoyment, satisfaction, prestige, even beauty, that one felt behind the wheel of a *Ferrari*.

Production swelled from three in 1947 to nine the next year, and to 30 in 1949. The period after 1950 saw an average of 70 to 80 Ferraris per year go out the doors. By 1960, the number was over 300; by 1965, 750. In the 1980s, production soared well above 1000 annually. Staff swelled accordingly, topping 1000 by 1970, and the modest original factory had extensions built on in 1948, in 1962, 1970,

Ferrari's 340 Mexico of 1952 (*both pages*) was intended for racing. The name celebrated Ferrari's 1951 one-two triumph in the Carrera Panamericana, or Mexican Road Race, though the actual victory had been scored with a pair of Tipo 212 Vignale-bodied, Colombo-engined coupes. Giovanni Michelotti of the Alfredo Vignale *carrozzeria* styled the 340 Mexico. It had a Lampredi-designed 4.1-liter V-12 of about 280 horsepower at 6600 rpm.

and '78, '81, '82, and '85. Another major addition was Fiorano, the private test track just across Highway 12 from the main factory. In 1960, the company had a name change, from the old Auto-Avio Costruzioni to Societa Esercizio Fabbriche Automobili e Corse, or SEFAC. Five years later the wording was altered to FERRARI Societa per Azioni Esercizio Fabbriche Automobili e Corse, which it remains today.

Enzo himself became such a distinguished figure that in 1960, the University of Bologna conferred upon him a degree *honoris causa* in engineering. This was nice in itself; it also neatly solved the problem of what to call him—Cavaliere, Commendatore, what? Henceforth, Enzo responded to "Ingegnere."

Ingegnere Ferrari's degree was purely honorary, but it was suitable. He had an engineer's mind. It focused exclusively on the future. He simply did not care what happened yesterday, win or lose, beyond the lessons it could teach about winning tomorrow.

There was no sentimentality about past designs. He was once heard to express his puzzlement at the veneration—and the value—people attached to models that, to him, were simply obsolete old crocks. Indeed, the only museum at Maranello was a chamber of horrors, an upstairs room full of race-broken parts maintained for the edification of the errant engineers.

In the later years, especially, Enzo's devotion to his business was all encompassing. He usually was at work all day and for many hours into the night. He worked weekends. He wrote a column for *Autosprint*, the Italian motorsports weekly. He did enjoy convivial dinners with friends and he is known to have hosted strenuous, allegedly bawdy, drinking sessions at home. And he was an urbane host to an endless procession of the rich, famous, and powerful admirers of his cars. But he seldom attended formal entertainments. He did not take vacations. He avoided travel. When a personal business meeting was required, he insisted the other

party come to him. He didn't even go to races anymore—he said it hurt him to see his beloved *cavallini* put to the spur.

How could anyone keep proper tabs on a world-wide racing campaign without being in the field with the troops? Ferrari relied partly on reports from his lieutenants, which of course left him open to misinformation generated out of fear or other self-interest. Witnesses reported overhearing team managers and engineers phoning doctored lap times back to base, for instance. But wily Enzo Ferrari knew a thing or two about manipulation.

Two among many versions of the 250 GT, the car that first expressed the definitive Ferrari virtues of speed and style. A 1957 competition model of the Pininfarina-bodied car (*above*) sprints around the Ferrari test track at Modena. A more civilized sportster was the so-called 250 GT Boano/Ellena of 1956-58 (*opposite page*). Both cars used a 3-liter Colombo V-12, though the Boano/Ellena introduced such important refinements as bigger brakes and steering by ZF of Germany.

From his office, working through telephone and telex, and later with a TV and video recorder, he kept his finger on the pulse and his hands on the strings of international motorsport. As Doug Nye wrote in the British monthly, *Thoroughbred & Classic Cars,* "he remained at home, a spider central in his web, sensing its vibrations, manipulating, planning, attacking when need be."

There is plenty of evidence that Ferrari exercised abnormal control over racing's regulating body, the French-based International Automobile Federation (FIA). Nye describes Enzo "politicking feverishly behind the scenes to ensure the FIA's rule makers made rules to suit his plans!"

Ferrari didn't always get his way. It wasn't unusual for him to threaten to withdraw from the sport and close down his entire factory when the FIA didn't bend its rules for him. But some of his struggles with authority cut far deeper.

By now, Ferrari was well-used to the reality of fatal injuries in racing. His first racing friend, Ugo Sivocci, had died at the wheel of an Alfa in 1923. His first World Champion driver, Alberto Ascari, was killed in a Ferrari in 1955. There were others. The racing community seemed indifferent to driver protection in those days. But then death stepped beyond the racetrack bounds.

Just before the end of the 1957 Mille Miglia open-road race, the sports-racing Ferrari of a Spanish Marques, Alfonso de Portago, suffered tire failure and crashed at high speed. Killed were de Portago, Ed Nelson (his American navigator) and 11 roadside spectators. Though the crowd was unprotected by any sort of barrier, the Italian government blamed Enzo Ferrari for equipping the car with inadequate tires, and actually charged him with manslaughter. The Vatican, as it would on other such occasions, issued denunciations of its own.

Enzo had been raised a Catholic, and although he later wrote that he "lacked the gift of faith," one does not easily shrug off a Vatican reproach in Italy. Opprobrium cascaded in from other sources as well, and Ferrari was deeply affected. He announced that he was closing down both his factory and his racing operation. He insisted he would leave the country, though he might have had trouble at the border, in as much as the court had confiscated his passport. He would claim later that only touching pleas mailed by a loyal public caused him to relent.

The Mille Miglia case dragged on for years before the court acquitted Enzo. It was finally decided that the tires had not been faulty, but that one had been cut on a reflective "cat's eye" marker sunk into the road. Scarcely had the good news come down to

Enzo Ferrari worked hard, but always enjoyed the fruits of his labors. Here, he relaxes with associates (*below*). Enzo is seated second from the left in the photo. Alberto Ascari (*opposite page*) joined Ferrari in 1948 and won world driving championships in '52 and '53. He's shown here in 1952, a year in which he also raced a Ferrari in the Indianapolis 500. Alberto's father was Antonio Ascari, who had driven with Enzo at Alfa Romeo. Alberto died of injuries suffered racing a Lancia D50 at Monte Carlo in 1955. He was 37, the same age at which his father died in a crash while leading the 1925 French Grand Prix.

Maranello than the F1 Ferrari of Wolfgang von Trips, a German Count who was a full-fledged member of the 1961 Grand Prix team, crashed into a spectator fence at Monza. He died, and so did about a dozen people pressed against the fence. Enzo was hauled into court once again. And the Church railed against him once more.

Suddenly, the attacks by outsiders on his carefully managed empire were magnified by an assault from within. At the end of the '61 racing season a group of his top staffers staged a walkout—the famous "Palace Revolution." The conspirators apparently believed that acting in concert, they could pressure The Old Man into management revisions. They "felt they were offering Ferrari a faultless ultimatum," Nye recounts. "It backfired. He hardly said 'goodbye.'"

Ferrari had in fact nurtured a management style that equipped him to deal blithely with such a revolt. "He emerged as a practiced exploiter of other people's talents," Nye explains. "He spotted engineers and drivers, took them on, groomed them to his ends, wrung them dry and ultimately tossed them aside. But before he let them go he always had a ready-prepared replacement, strength in depth was the key, young lions were always being made ready, waiting in the wings should Ferrari's axe fall on their superiors. Nobody was safe."

He treated everyone, especially his race drivers, with a similarly iron hand. "All the time Ferrari was massaging and manipulating the press to publish what he wanted," Nye says. "After decades of practice he would sting drivers to greater effort by having calculated doses of poison published about them, often putting critical words of one driver into a teammate's mouth through tame journalists he cultivated....Ferrari kept the fire blazing beneath the bubbling cauldron into which any driver worth the title would willingly throw himself."

Not a pretty picture. But a portrait of the only kind of man Enzo thought capable of building La Ferrari.

All in all, this operatic autocrat doesn't seem to have taken much time for a personal life, at least not one as conventionally understood. Some of this came from the man's love of his "job." In his book, Enzo is both revealing and amusing about why he spent

so much time at the factory:

"Single-mindedness of purpose in pursuing one's ambition is, indeed, a force that can overcome many obstacles, although I do not, of course, consider myself unique in this respect. It is true that I have never met any man whom I thought altogether resembled me—but only because my faults are so enormous that I view them as something quite out of the common. I have known men, instead, who have borne a resemblance to me in the way in which I endeavor to sum up the facts rapidly and reach a speedy conclusion in discussions or negotiations. I have met others who undoubtedly loved cars as much as I. Perhaps, however, I have yet to meet anyone quite as stubborn as myself and animated by this overpowering pas-

sion that leaves me no time or thought for anything else. I have, in fact, no interests in life outside racing cars. I have never gone on a real trip, never taken a holiday—the best holiday for me is spent in my workshops when nearly everybody else is on vacation. That is the time when I and a few of my staff can really concentrate on new ideas, modifications and so on, subsequently enjoying the surprise of the rest of my people when they return to work."

But beneath Ferrari's devotion prowled personal demons of bitterness and bereavement.

For one thing, his marriage to Laura had turned acrid. In his autobiography, written about 40 years after he met the "pretty and smartly dressed little blond," he never once mentions her

Laura Ferrari married Enzo around 1920 and bore their only child, Dino. She played a vital role in the company, acting as Enzo's trusted eyes in the factory and his keen ears on the proving grounds. Here, she congratulates him after an early race (*opposite page*), and poses with a dapper-looking Enzo around 1914 (*above*). She remained his wife until her death in 1978, at which time Enzo brought into public Piero Lardi-Ferrari, the illegitimate son he had fathered by his long-time mistress, Lina Lardi. "...[M]arriage takes away from a man at least half of his freedom," Enzo once wrote.

name. In fact, beyond that first description he never has another nice thing to say about her—and this in a book containing a whole chapter about "The Woman's Role" in racing, most of it positive in tone. But he does feel a need to make several sardonic comments: "I married very young, somewhere around 1920; I cannot remember the exact year as I have mislaid the certificate." This from a man who could recall the winner's speed in a race held in 1908.

Women are the ones who choose their partners, not "we men," he wrote. "We think we have wooed and won, whereas in reality we are merely the slaves of our desire, on which the woman has played with consummate skill."

Enzo was poor when he married, but he had an impassioned feeling that "nothing else mattered where there was love. I later came to realize that the rest did matter and mattered a lot."

"I should never have married," he says at one point. "...marriage takes away from a man at least half of his freedom. Had I listened to my wife, I should have gone and got myself a job with the local tramway company."

Something somber and sad lurks here; it's as if Ferrari felt himself early and thoroughly wronged by women, and spent the rest of his life trying to build the ideal woman in metal.

Not that Enzo avoided all liaison with women. Not by any means. He and Laura remained together in law, and she took on a role in the family business. In fact, it was her negative reports to Enzo about some staffers' performance at races and in the factory that allegedly led to the Palace Revolution. But Enzo clearly felt few conjugal restraints. By all accounts, he roamed freely, a notorious womanizer. Carroll Shelby, himself a builder of specialty cars, once joked that the only reason Enzo built roadgoing GTs was so that he'd have something appropriate to drive to a rendezvous with his mistress.

For he did in fact keep a long-term mistress. She bore him his second son. Piero was born to Lina Lardi around the time Ferrari was changing his factory over from its wartime economy to his new racing enterprise. For more than three decades, no word of this birth was breathed in public—certainly none was printed in Enzo's autobio-

graphy. After Laura's death in 1978, the young man was brought into the firm openly and introduced as Piero Lardi-Ferrari.

The real tragedy of Enzo's life centered on his firstborn son, Laura's only child. Born in 1932, he had been named Alfredo, just like Enzo's father and older brother, although the formal name immediately became the affectionate Alfredino, and then its diminutive, Dino. Enzo's writing turns almost mawkish as he describes Dino's intelligence, good sense, and innate engineering ability. As his own father had hoped for a career in engineering for Enzo, Dino Ferrari was being groomed to inherit the house that Enzo built.

Dino proved a good student, with a fine head for automobile design. As a young man he was given the authority to develop a whole new breed of Ferrari powerplant. After weighing all the factors, he chose a V-6 configuration, and his father set the necessary wheels in motion. But Dino never heard the engine run. He died of kidney disease in June 1956, after a long struggle with muscular dystrophy. The V-6 went into production with his nickname scripted on its cam covers and, indeed, several models of car were officially called the Dino. In a bittersweet postscript, Ferrari V-6s won the World Championship in 1958 and 1961.

Dino's death crushed Enzo. He had immersed himself in details of his son's treatment and had harbored a false hope for recovery even toward the end. Enzo daily filled out a graph

plotting Dino's symptoms. "I was convinced he was like one of my cars, one of my motors; and I had drawn up a table showing the calories of all the foodstuffs he could eat...." But suddenly the boy was gone. In his notebook the stunned father made a single final entry: "The race is lost."

His grief was sharp and all-pervading. For many years he made daily visits to Dino's grave, and kept in his office what visitors described as an eerie shrine to the boy's memory. Though first published six years after his great loss, *My Terrible Joys* was written very much in this mood; it has bitter passages in which Enzo speaks of his life as a long and wearying travail devoid of hope for a future. He jabs at Laura "...the only perfect love in this world is that of a father for his son."

Perhaps it was only social convention, and not a cold heart, that compelled him to ignore Piero and mourn the departed Dino as his "one and only son."

Ferrari closed his autobiography with a chilling coda: "I feel alone after a life crowded by so many events and almost guilty of having survived. And I feel too a certain detachment, for in this arid earth that is myself, the plant of hope can thrive only if watered by a son's love."

Yet before him lay more than a quarter of a century of work. And work he did, constantly, unrelentingly, throwing his every hour into building La Ferrari still bigger. To a visitor remarking on how hard he worked, he replied that it was work, only work,

*(continued on page 70)*

Enzo named his first son Alfredo, after his father, then shortened it to the affectionate, Dino. Born in 1932, Dino was the light of his father's life, following him into the family business and showing early promise as an engineer. His death in 1956 cast a pall over Enzo's world. Ferrari preserved Dino's desk as a memorial and visited his grave daily for many years. Dino at nine years of age (*opposite page*) is shown after a midday bicycle ride with his father and (*above*) relaxing with his mother in 1954. "...[T]he only perfect love in this world is that of a father for his son," Enzo wrote in his autobiography six years after Dino's death.

Ferrari in 1943 moved his ball-bearing machine factory from the attractive military target of Modena to Maranello, a village about 10 miles south. He built a small complex of buildings around a tri-cornered, cobblestoned courtyard, and began assembling cars there as World War II ended. Over the years, the plant expanded to include additional shops, garages, offices, and a complete test track (*both pages*). The Modena region seemed to produce more than its share of automotive craftsman. Ferrari said its natives had what he termed a "psychosis for racing cars.... The union of blood and brain is such that the result is a type of man who is stubborn, capable, and daring—the very qualities that are needed for building racing cars."

that kept him from dwelling on thoughts of death.

Now that Dino was gone, much of Enzo's energy centered on an alternative line of succession for the factory, which even by then had become an enterprise of substance. In the summer of 1963 he conducted the famous, notorious, negotiations with Ford Motor Company of America that would have sold off 90 percent of the road-car side of Ferrari, but retained 90 percent of the racing department in his own hands.

The wily Enzo's motives and machinations in this affair have long been points of speculation. It's enough to say that it wasn't the right deal for the autocratic old man, but that it did show future-partner Fiat that Ferrari was serious about selling out. Fiat chief Gianni Agnelli immediately offered financial and managerial assistance. Six years later, in June of 1969, Fiat—which had once told Enzo it had no use for his talents—bought 40 percent of Ferrari's company with an option for another 49 on his death (Pinin Farina owned one percent, and

Piero had been given the last ten). Enzo remained president of the company and in charge of the racing department. Fiat installed resident managers to oversee the production lines, which were greatly expanded and modernized.

The actual agreement was built around something called *in vitalizio,* a sort of rental arrangement in which Fiat paid Enzo on a monthly basis as long as he lived. Enzo, crafty old devil, lived long enough to make a healthy profit on the deal. But Fiat was well served, too: it was able to tap Ferrari's advanced technology; it had linked its image with that of the single greatest name in auto racing; and it had saved a genuine national treasure. On Enzo's part, at one stroke of his purple pen he had solved his decades-old money problems while retaining full control

Ferrari opened the 1970s with the 365 GT4/Berlinetta Boxer (*opposite page, top*), a 2-seat coupe with 360-horsepower 3-liter flat-12 mounted midships. The engine was enlarged to 5-liters late in '76 (*opposite page, bottom*), and in 1981, got fuel injection, winding up with about 340 horsepower. The Boxer was supplanted in 1984 by the Testarossa (*this page*). It was larger than the Boxer, but used the same mid-mounted flat-12 layout. It had 390 horsepower, however, courtesy of all-new cylinder heads, which incorporated modern 4-valve technology.

Ferrari's final masterpiece was the F40 (*this page*), a mid-engine rocket that uses a twin-turbocharged 3-liter V-8 rated at 478 horsepower. Enzo introduced the car himself, at a moving ceremony in Maranello's civic center on July 21, 1987. Enzo remained the center of attention at every gathering (*opposite page*). He died on August 14, 1988, of kidney failure, at age 90. Piero and Lina Lardi were at his side. The man was gone, the legend lives on.

of what he really cared about. He retrenched more and more into his racing, exercising less and less interest in production cars.

To many ardent Ferraristi, 1969 marks a "sellout" to Fiat and the end of the period of "true" Ferrari road cars. Whether that position is justified by the merits of the later models is in the eye of the beholder. The magnificent Boxers and Testarossas, and even the mass-production 308s and 328s, are certainly the most sophisticated road vehicles ever to wear the prancing horse. And they're more satisfactory as "daily drivers" than anything Ferrari turned out in the old days of racer-based street cars. But in no longer sharing their engines, and in some cases their chassis and bodies, with championship-winning competition models, the "Fiat-Ferraris" have surely lost some of the glory factor present in the earlier cars.

An exception is the sensational F 40, a starkly beautiful, super-powerful, 201-mph coupe created in 1987 in commemoration of the 40th Anniversary of the Ferrari automobile. After four decades, Ferrari remained capable of springing a genuinely awesome car on his public.

Enzo was still active that year, still very much the "commander" of his racing team. As quoted by Nye, one of his staff described how Ingegnere Ferrari was still chairing meetings: "No question, only one man was doing the talking."

Journalist Quentin Spurring got the same impression that winter, when he was invited to a luncheon at the factory. Though obviously frail, Enzo conducted a wide-ranging press conference lasting several hours. "He showed us that his mind remains sharp," Spurring wrote in *AutoWeek*. "He can still hold his audience, amuse it, tease it, anger it even."

At one point, after enduring repeated questioning about professional and personal differences with John Barnard, a Britisher who designed racing chassis, Ferrari spoke sharply: "You are all besotted with the subject of Barnard. And you are living in the past. What counts in motor racing today is what can be achieved by a group, not by an individual as might have been the case with Vittorio Jano in the twenties. In those days, a project would begin when Jano sharpened his pencil and started to draw. Times have changed. Now we have so many

different factors involved that even someone as clever as Barnard has to rely on a great many other people. Every Formula One Ferrari is the work of a team. What about the contributions that our other people make? Listen to me: This is Enzo Ferrari speaking to you."

That was Enzo Ferrari speaking from the experience of some 4000 to 5000 racing victories, including 13 world championships, nine of them in Formula One.

A few weeks later, Enzo celebrated his 90th birthday, on February 18, 1988, by hosting a lunch for his 1750 factory employees. Later in the spring, he was too ill to participate in a long-scheduled visit by Pope John Paul II. He did spend time at his old farmhouse inside the Fiorano track, listening to his cars on test. His health worsened throughout the summer, and it became clear that time was short, but he remained lucid to the end. He died at seven in the morning, Sunday, August 14, 1988, officially of kidney failure. His surviving son and Lina Lardi were with him. His body was quietly interred before the world learned of the passing of perhaps the greatest figure in the history of motorsport.

# Chapter 5:

# Tipo 815: Ferrari's Hot Rod

"When I left Alfa Romeo, just before World War II, I was still bound by the clause that forbade my re-constituting the Scuderia Ferrari or engaging in motor racing activities for four years," admitted Enzo Ferrari in his autobiography. "...Although I did build one car for two young customers of mine in the old Scuderia Ferrari workshop in Modena."

In reality, there were two cars, not one. And he didn't just build them for "two young customers." Enzo Ferrari built for nobody but himself. Furthermore, it would be the rawest naivete to think he wouldn't have built others but for the outbreak of war.

Not that the two customers didn't exist. They were a local nobleman, the Marquis Lotario Rangoni Macchiaveli di Modena, and Alberto Ascari, the son of Enzo's old friend and team-mate, Antonio Ascari. Rangoni had been dabbling in car racing, and Ascari, then 21, was just beginning to move from motorcycles to four wheels. How easy it is to picture the two of them wandering into Enzo's machine shop one day late in 1939, the Marquis studiously not looking like a wide-eyed youth as his friend cere-moniously introduced him to the Commendatore, still one of the great-est personages in Italian motorsport even though he was, just then, a manufacturer of aircraft engine parts.

Many historians maintain that the project was all Ferrari's idea to begin with, and that he invited the wealthy Marquis to sponsor it. However, there

is evidence that it was Rangoni who broached the subject. This according to Enrico Nardi, a friend of Ferrari's who was interviewed by journalist Pete Coltrin many years later. Nardi (later known for his elegant steering wheels) remembered that the visit led to a dinner party on Christmas Eve, and that same night the agreement was made: Ferrari would build a couple of race cars for the young men to drive in the upcoming Mille Miglia.

Designing was not Ferrari's role, but primarily that of Alberto Massi-mino, another ex-Alfa man who'd come to join Enzo at his new firm, Auto-Avio Costruzioni. Another in-volved was one Vittorio Bellentani. Nardi served as test driver. Consider-ing it had to be done in haste—by April—it was a very ambitious project.

Partly because time was so short, and partly because Fiat was offering cash incentives, Massimino decided to use as many parts as possible from that manufacturer's 508 C Ballila sedan, a 4-cylinder, overhead-valve, 1100-cc model already popular with the Italian hop-up industry. Onto the basic chassis frame of the family car, complete with its independent front suspension and hydraulically-oper-ated four-wheel brakes, was put a light, open-cockpit sports-car body, a quite advanced envelope design by Carrozzeria Touring. It was painted red, of course, and was right-hand-drive like a real racer. A set of Borrani's spiffy wire wheels completed the racy appearance.

So far it was a straightforward cus-tom-car project, but what about the engine? Although the upcoming race had a class for 1100-cc cars, the col-laborators wanted to run with the 1500s. But the 508 C engine wouldn't stretch that far.

Here's where Ferrari came in—probably why he got interested in the project at all: His shop would join two four-cylinder engines together to make an inline-8.

It wasn't as simple as it sounded. He and Massimino saw they would be able to use some of the Ballila engine parts, such as the connecting rods, the pushrod/rocker-arm valve gear, and even a pair of cylinder heads. But most of the rest would have to be made from scratch. Ferrari didn't yet have his own foundry, so castings for the new aluminum block, sump, and valve cover had to be farmed out. New, smaller-bore pistons were needed, too. But A-AC handled everything else: machining the new crank and camshaft, fitting wet-iron cylinder liners, working out a new ignition sys-tem with a single eight-wire distribu-tor instead of the pair of stock units, making up a new, higher-capacity water pump.

Ferrari's first car saw the light of day in 1940 (*opposite page*). Enzo's legal agreement with former employer Alfa Romeo prevented him from putting his name on the roadster, so he called it the 815, for its 8-cylinder engine of 1.5-liters displacement. The 815 was painted red.

The new engine had a bore and stroke of 63 mm by 60 mm (2.48 × 2.36 inches) for a displacement of 1496.3 cc (91.2 cubic inches). Breathing through four single-barrel downdraft Webers, the energetic little eight produced a claimed 72 to 75 horsepower at 5500-6000 rpm, enough to show an officially timed 108 mph along a straight in the race. What a glorious sound it must have made.

"I could not bestow my name on it on account of my undertaking with Alfa," explains Ferrari. So he simply called the car the 815, after the number of cylinders and the displacement, and had a tiny yellow-on-blue badge with those numbers set into the nose trimwork. It's easy to imagine him stepping back for a moment to marvel how far automotive engineering had come in the 20 short years since he'd rattled down to Sicily atop that wood-wheeled CMN.

It was all done very quickly, and one car was already being tested in February. In the race on April 28, 1940, over a triangular course of public roads near Brescia, Ascari went right out to the head of the 1500 class and was still leading at the end of the first 103-mile lap—the first burst of light from a future star. Then something broke in the valve train. Rangoni took over with Nardi riding along as passenger. He set fastest lap and built up a lead of 33 minutes on the next 1.5 entry before his engine, too, failed—either bearing or cam chain trouble; accounts vary.

There it ended. Two weeks later Mussolini threw Italy into the war,

Ferrari had to forget about having fun with cars, and the twin racers were hidden away. They survived the hostilities, but their owner, the young Marquis, had been killed in a test flight of a new bomber. His car went to his brother, who kept it for many years but finally, sadly, allowed it to be scrapped.

Ascari's passed to another owner, who entered it in a 1947 race at Pescara, where it ran in company with Ferrari's first V-12 car. The 815 broke this time too, was set aside, and led a precarious existence in one wrecking yard after another until the mid-'50s when, Coltrin says, a collector rescued the forlorn little roadster literally on the day the axe was about to fall. Restored, it went to live in the safety of a small museum in the village of San Martino in Rio, near Modena.

"Despite a promising start," wrote Enzo Ferrari, his first car "was not a success" because it had been built in such haste. But such harsh judgment merely illuminates the loft of the man's own ambition and he did have pride enough to picture the pair of 815s on the cover of a brochure describing his grinding machines. In objective eyes, the 815 shines as quite an accomplishment. After all, its daring little homebuilt engine was stout enough to blow everything else in its class off the road in its first-ever race.

What plainer claim could any car offer for the right to be called the First Ferrari?

The 815 raced (*opposite page*), but with little success. One of the two 815s built survives in a small museum near Modena (*above*).

# Chapter 6:

# Tipo 125:
# "The Song of Twelve Cylinders"

To Enzo Ferrari, the born racer frustrated by half a decade of war, the end of European hostilities was a green flag. By the second part of 1945, he had launched a venture remarkable in its scope and vision. He was preparing to build sporting automobiles. But unlike so many with similar dreams, he wouldn't just build a hobbyist's plaything, nor was he simply making a statement. His ambition was no smaller than creating an empire to win world racing championships.

Being no trained designer or constructor himself, Ferrari began by assembling a team of his former racing colleagues and setting them to work on a brand new competition car. In harmony with his own primary interest in engines, it would carry a remarkable powerplant—a very high performance, all-aluminum, overhead-camshaft V-12. "I had always liked the song of twelve cylinders," said Enzo, explaining his audacious choice, although of course there were other, more technical reasons.

The man he brought in to draw up the new car, both chassis and powerplant, was Gioacchino Colombo, who back in the 1930s had been part of Enzo's Scuderia Ferrari. Colombo had assisted Vittorio Jano on the Alfa 12C, a car powered by a supercharged V-12 that won the 1936 Vanderbilt Cup with Tazio Nuvolari at the wheel. Then Colombo had been in charge of producing the straight-eight, 1.5-liter supercharged Alfa Romeo 158 (later 159) *voiturette* racer. As writer Griff Borgeson describes Colombo's post-

war situation, he was "something of a pariah" on account of his earlier enthusiasm for Mussolini's Fascist government. Although Ferrari himself had never been stained with that brush, he was "not exactly the man to blame anyone for loyalty to an iron dictatorship," Borgeson says. Enzo gladly rehired his former engineer.

Colombo's own memoirs say that he made his first sketches on August 15, 1945. They were translated into metal by a team that included himself working part-time, a young aeronautical engineer from Piaggio named Aurelio Lampredi, and two former Alfa Romeo engineers, Angelo Nasi and Giuseppe Busso. There was also the technician, Luigi Bazzi, who had been a valued Ferrari friend ever since Enzo had hired him away from Fiat in 1923.

Bazzi, in fact, emerges in Ferrari's book as the real key to the "daring and presumptuous" project. "There are initial difficulties with every engine," Enzo admitted, "but I never doubted we should win through, both because I had faith in Colombo's ability and because I once again had the trusty Bazzi with me and knew I could rely on his skill in designing engines."

Although the car as a whole was broadly similar to Enzo's 1940 eight-cylinder 815, the 125 was no Fiat-based hot rod that had taken a mere four months to create. This was an altogether more sophisticated, ambitious design. Virtually every part—engine, transmission, axles and suspension, steering mechanism, chassis

frame—was designed and made from scratch. Every part was also pre-planned for a long evolutionary life. A year of construction was needed before the little V-12 barked to life on a dynamometer late in 1946. It wasn't until March 12, 1947, that it ran in a complete car.

The Tipo 125, Ferrari's first Ferrari, had an engine displacing 1497 cc (91.3 cubic inches.) and in its original competition trim it produced a claimed 118 horsepower at 6800 rpm. It drove through a 5-speed gearbox to a beam rear axle. Both this and the independent front suspension had leaf-type springs, transverse in front.

As with the pair of pre-war 815s, Touring executed the aluminum envelope roadster body of the first Ferrari, although this time the styling showed less grace and more purpose. The second chassis was clothed even more purposefully, in a light, simple, cigar-shaped fuselage that left the wheels exposed, covered only by motorcycle-type fenders. Once again, the driver of each car sat on the right. For the first time, Ferrari's little *cavallino* emblem pranced boldly on the nose of a Ferrari.

Differing accounts of Ferrari's debut race have been published over the years. The facts seem to be that both brand new cars were entered for the event, which was held on May 11, 1947, at Piacenza, a town to the northwest of Modena.

One driver was supposed to be Dr. Giuseppe Farina, already an established ace who would one day become

history's first World Champion. However, either he or Luigi Bazzi crashed the cycle-fendered car on the highway the day before the race. Bazzi and crew toiled all night to get it ready again, but for some reason never fully explained, Farina decided he wasn't ready. It seems entirely possible that a canny, careful professional simply decided not to trust his life to a hastily repaired car.

Thus Franco Cortese, a local veteran and pre-war member of the Scuderia Ferrari, was the only Ferrari starter with the full-bodied car.

At first the 125's performance was disappointing, for it wouldn't pull its

peak rpm. During a pit stop partway through the 60-mile race, the mechanics realized they had put too much oil in the sump. That was fixed, and Cortese began to gain on the leaders. Some accounts—including Enzo Ferrari's—say he did take over the lead. But then the engine stopped dead. Its centrifugal fuel pump, a supposedly ultra-reliable aircraft part, had seized.

So ended what Enzo termed "at least a promising failure." The promise was fulfilled two weekends later, when Cortese and the second Ferrari 125, the cycle-fendered car, won at Rome on the so-called Caracalla circuit. This inaugural Ferrari triumph

was followed by several more during the course of that splendid summer, Enzo's first as an auto manufacturer.

A total of three of these Tipo 125s were built in 1947; number three had

*(continued on page 82)*

The aluminum V-12 that Gioacchino Colombo engineered in 1946 as the first real Ferrari engine was a design still in use in the 1980s. The ground-breaking powerplant ran in its first car, the Tipo 125, in 1947. It displaced 1.5 liters in its original competition trim and produced a claimed 118 horsepower at 6800 rpm. Enlarged to 2 liters (*above*) and installed in the Tipo 166, it went on to numerous racing victories in a variety of displacements.

Ferrari's first single-seater was the 125
Formula 1 of 1948. It was first raced at the
Italian Grand Prix in Turin, where Raymond
Sommer finished a credible third after a
thrilling battle with the more established
Alfettas and Maseratis.

another envelope body by Touring. Thanks to contemporary accounts, as well as to later evaluations by present-day journalists, a good idea of the road manners of these machines emerges.

One major impression would be that the steering was heavy, almost truckish. The steering wheel would judder in the driver's hands at low road speeds. The gearshift combined the faults of a long reach, stiff action, and the absence of synchromesh on first, second, and fifth gears—that's how Ferrari built it, for reasons now obscure. The clutch was heavy, too, for such a small engine, and compared to conventional passenger cars it was "in-or-out." The various pedals were

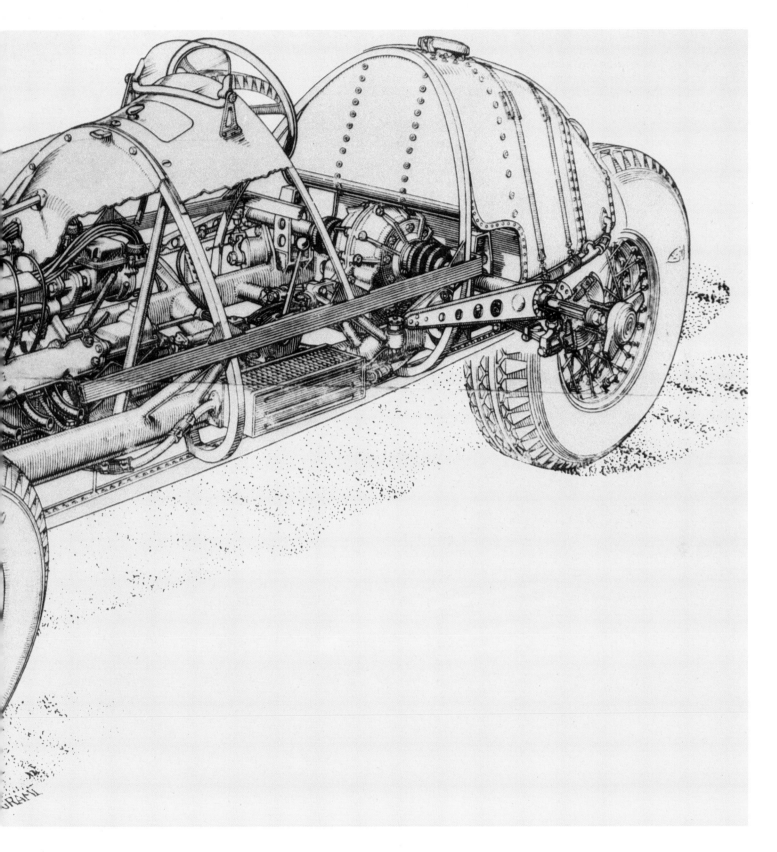

ill positioned for heel-and-toe down-shifting. Ride quality was stiff and harsh, and chassis rigidity was lacking, so there was a lot of shaking and leaping over the bumps. A curve at racing speeds would invite the rear wheels to slide very easily—this car had an anti-roll bar at the rear only, and was a decided oversteerer. A great deal of leg muscle was demanded by the drum-type brakes, which weren't very effective anyway.

The 125 Formula 1 had a supercharged version of the Ferrari 1.5-liter V-12, good for 225 horsepower. Its unusually short chassis featured an all-independent suspension. Engines in later versions used a dual camshaft and a twin-phase supercharger.

By today's standards, the magnificent little engine seems decidedly underwhelming. According to timing done by *Car and Driver* magazine in 1984, even a 2-liter version of the V-12 (Tipo 166) didn't make the original car very quick. Observing a 6000-rpm redline with a freshly rebuilt engine, and treating the notoriously fragile clutch with sympathy, tester Don Sherman recorded 0-60 mph in a not very impressive 13.1 seconds. This despite the very light 1490-pound curb weight quoted for the car, distributed at a rather nose-heavy 56.4 percent front/43.6 percent rear. The standing quarter-mile came up in a long 19.6 seconds at only 72 mph. Top speed was

not actually observed, but estimated to be no higher than 121 mph for this car, fitted as it was with a reproduction of the high-drag, cycle-fendered body style.

Of course, such a comparatively modest performance level by today's standards proved to be ample for the 125 to see off most any opposition it encountered in 1947. After all, Ferrari was one of the few racing anything but leftover pre-war equipment.

Ferrari's first Ferrari was the 125 S (*both pages*). It won its first race just two weeks after its debut in May of 1947. The utilitarian 2-seat roadster body was fabricated of aluminum and clothed an oval-section tubular chassis, 5-speed manual transmission, and a 1.5-liter V-12.

It was its personality, certainly, that proved to be the archetypical Ferrari's most endearing quality. As Sherman described it, the enchantment began the instant you fired the little aluminum engine: "The starter whines with a tired electrical moan as it clanks a dozen pistons up and down...there's a puff or two of blue smoke out the straight pipes, then automatic rifle fire. The Jaeger tach needle skips nervously...as the first Ferrari ever made lets out its familial battle cry—the sound of ripping canvas." Even at warmup rpm, all those explosions from all those cylinders made the engine seem to be racing.

Out on the track, Sherman found, "the throttle response is strong and sure above 3500 rpm, and above 4000 rpm the rampant stallions break into full stride. The cockpit is a heady blend of engine heat, hot-oil vapor, and hang-on-for-dear-life. Since there is little bucket to the seat and nary a shred of seatbelt, only those strong of arm need apply. It's easy to see why it took a he-man like the blood-spitting Nuvolari to win in this car."

No wonder that the name Ferrari quickly became magic to most anyone who saw and heard the 125.

Ferrari and engineer Luigi Bazzi aboard an Alfa Romeo P2 (*below*) during their days with Alfa. As Alfa's racing manager, Enzo had hired Bazzi away from Fiat in 1923, then brought him to the new Ferrari operation in 1945. Enzo believed Bazzi's arrival gave him the confidence to create an all-new V-12 "I once again had the trusty Bazzi with me and knew I could rely on his skill in designing engines," Ferrari said. Testament to the enduring quality of that original 1946 Colombo design is the fuel-injected 4.8-liter descendent used in the 400i Automatic of 1979 (*opposite page*).

ZAGARI

# FERRARI ENGINES

## The Colombo V-12

The first engine to bear Enzo Ferrari's name was a V-12. Romantics might suggest Enzo was infatuated with the intoxicating sound made by a engine of that configuration. "I had always liked the song of twelve cylinders," Ferrari confides in his autobiography. And he acknowledges great admiration for the Packard V-12 owned by Antonio Ascari and for the Delage V-12 Grand Prix racer.

But Enzo's decision to stake his reputation on a V-12 was more likely a bow to the engineering dictum that horsepower is directly related to piston area: For a given displacement, the more cylinders, the more piston area, and therefore the greater power potential.

Additionally, twelve cylinders proved a good balance between maximum power and minimum complexity—both important factors in racing. A V-12 engine is almost perfectly balanced, and its greater number of cylinders puts lower pressures, and therefore less loading, on crankshaft, rods, and bearings.

Ferrari brought Gioacchino Colombo to his Maranello factory in 1946 to design his new engine and out of that effort came a V-12. The cylinders were arranged in a 60-degree Vee. There was a 20-mm offset be-

tween cylinder banks so side-by-side rods could be used. The engine had a bore of 55 mm and a stroke of 52.5 mm, with a displacement of 1496.7 cc.

Cylinder block, heads, and crankcase were cast of aluminum alloy. Cast-iron wet cylinder liners were shrunk into the block, and a flange at the top of the liners was held in compression by the cylinder head.

The connecting rod big-ends were cut at a 40-degree angle so that the rod and piston assembly could be removed through the relatively small bore and out the top of the block. This eliminated the need to remove the crankshaft to get them out through the bottom. The crankshaft, turned from a solid steel billet, ran in

seven plain bearings. At least one 166 MM engine, however, is on record as having roller-bearing mains and rods.

A single, chain-driven overhead camshaft on each bank operated two valves via short rocker arms and finger followers. The valves were set at a 60-degree included angle per cylinder. Each valve was closed by a pair of hairpin-type valve springs. These springs allowed the valve stems to be short, thus reducing reciprocating weight and making for a more compact engine.

There were 12 exhaust ports, but only six, siamesed intake ports on these first engines. This layout is contrary to any engine designer's theories, at least when ultimate power is desired. But these engines were planned to be supercharged for Grand Prix racing, so individual intake-port tuning wouldn't be critical. The normally aspirated sports-car engine would just have to suffer.

The engine was designated the 125 S because each cylinder had a 125-cc displacement. With an 8.0:1 compression ratio and three Weber 30 DCF carburetors, it put out 72 horsepower at 5600 rpm.

Three Ferraris were built in 1947, all with 125 V-12 engines, but two were subsequently bored to 1902.8 cc and gained the Type 159 label. They were enlarged once again in 1948, to 1995 cc, and redesignated Type 166.

These Colombo-designed engines continued with numerous displacement increases: to 2.3 liters (Type 195); to 2.6 liters (Type 212); to 2.7 liters (Type 225); to 2.95 liters (Type 250); to 3.3 liters (Type 275); and to 4.0 liters (Type 330 and 400 Super-america).

Little change was seen in these Colombo

V-12s until 1958. That's when the 250 Testa Rossa engine received the most drastic changes to date. Coil valve springs replaced the hairpin, or "mousetrap" springs. This allowed a fourth cylinder-head stud to be used near each cylinder. In addition, roller followers replaced the old finger followers; intake ports were no longer siamesed; spark plugs were moved from inside the Vee to the outside of the head just above the exhaust ports; two distributors and four coils made up the ignition system; and connecting rods were cut straight across instead of at a 40-degree angle. The compression ratio went to 9.8:1.

The result of all this was 300 horsepower at 7200 rpm and one of the best examples of a powerful yet reliable racing engine ever conceived. This engine was also used in the 250 GT long- and short-wheelbase competition *berlinettas*, models that dominated the Tour de France. They finished 1st in 1956; 1st, 2nd, and 3rd in '57; 1st and 3rd in '58; 1st, 2nd, and 3rd in '59; 1st, 2nd, and 3rd in '60; and, in '61 were 1st, 2nd, 3rd, and 4th.

The Testa Rossa version, which had six

A 2.6-liter version of the Colombo V-12 powered the first Ferrari styled by Pinin Farina (*opposite page*), this 1952 212 Inter. New cylinder heads and a trio of Webers gave the elegant cabriolet 170 horsepower. By 1958, the engine was producing 300 horsepower in the nose of one of Ferrari's most dramatic cars, the original 250 Testa Rossa (*above*). This original "red head" was one of Ferrari's most successful sports-racing cars, winning the World Sports Car Championship in 1958, '60, and '61. Several 250 GTs also used this engine.

38 DCN downdraft Webers, started out with wet-sump lubrication, but switched to dry-sump in 1959 after Le Mans. This engine was put into the 250 GTO in 1962. It retained its dry-sump lubrication when it moved from the front of the car, in the 250 GTO, to the mid position, in the 250 LM. Interestingly, only one 250 LM actually had a 250 engine. Subsequent models were 275-powered, but still were called 250 LM for homologation reasons.

Colombo's original 1946-47 design, though modified by other Ferrari engineers after Colombo left the firm, was in use in some form for more than two decades, powering the majority of Ferrari road cars during that time. It was, and is, a superb engine. As long as it's not abused, it can be driven hard and long with incredible reliability.

No other single engine design contributed more to the fame of Ferrari cars than the Colombo V-12. There were later Ferrari engines with more power, but none served so long, or in so many models, with such continuing success.

Few cars embodied the Ferrari spirit more than the 250 GTO of 1962 (*above*). Its heart was the same basic Colombo V-12 used in the early Testa Rossas, including its six 38 DCN downdraft Weber carburetors. The GTO's engine, however, used dry-sump lubrication. It's 3-liter made about 300 horsepower at 7400 rpm. The compression ratio was 9.8:1. A well-tuned example could reach 170 mph. Britisher David Clarke owned a GTO and wrote that above 6000 rpm, the engine emitted a "spine-chilling howl."

# Chapter 7:

# Barchetta:
# The Beautiful Little Boat

Ferrari's Tipo 125 may have been rather a crude device, but it proved to be an effective instrument for the competition conditions of its place and time. And it was only the beginning. One of the significant points about the early Ferrari engine is that, from the first stroke of the pencil, it was planned for progressive increases in displacement and, therefore, power.

The Colombo V-12's long career began in 1.5-liter form—precisely 1496.77 cc, or 91.3 cubic inches—with a bore and stroke of 55 mm by 52.5 mm (2.17 × 2.07 inches). But, with a spacing between cylinder bore centerlines of 90 mm (3.54 inches), there was obviously plenty of room to grow. The first spurt of growth occurred as early as the summer of 1947, when master technician Luigi Bazzi made up new pistons, liners, and crankshafts, increasing both bore and stroke. The new measurements were 59 mm × 58 mm (2.32 × 2.28 inches), which took the displacement to 1903 cc (116 cubic inches) and power to a stated 125 at an elevated 7000 rpm.

To Ferrari, that change was enough to constitute a new type number, 159 (1903 divided by 12). In fact, the two cars built to this nomenclature were little more than existing 125 chassis with the enlarged engine installed and certain minor revisions to the bodywork. They raced a few times in the late summer and fall, and it was one of them, the cycle-fendered version, that won the October sports car race in Turin at which Enzo Ferrari paid an emotive visit to his old park bench.

Over the winter, Bazzi took the next step in making the V-12 into a full-scale 2-liter, which was the upper limit of several important racing categories. Actually, he made the new engine in two steps. First, he enlarged the bore to 60 mm (2.36 inches) for a displacement often erroneously rendered as 1992 cc, but really 1967.892 (120.1 cubic inches). Then Bazzi found he could add a trifle to the stroke, up to 58.8mm (2.32 cubic inches), to bring the total cylinder capacity to 1995 cc (121.7 cubic inches). That bumped horsepower up to as much as 160, by the factory's reckoning, and the type number to 166.

The 2-liter engine was successful during 1948, particularly as installed in a model called the Spyder Corsa, which can be translated as "roadster-for-racing." This still had the cycle-fendered body style, antique to modern eyes, but which retained the traditional look of a real racer to the eyes of 1948. It also had a major practical attraction: the fenders and lights could be removed easily, thus making the car eligible for open-wheeled Formula 2 races as well as for sports car events. Maserati was another manufacturer offering the same arrangement at that time. There were additional 166 Ferrari models, such as the Inter and the Sport, plus proper single-seater F2 cars, all of which continued the same utilitarian cigar-shaped body. Only a handful of each was built.

At the Turin auto show in November, 1948, however, Ferrari presented a version with a fully enveloping body. As with the pair of 1947 sports cars, the styling was by Touring again, but this time the lines were as pretty as they were advanced. Italians called the style *barchetta*, meaning "little boat." The formal model designation was Tipo 166 MM, for Mille Miglia, the grand old "thousand mile" race around Italy, which that summer Ferrari had won for the first time.

Up to now, the new marque had been pretty much an Italian national phenomenon. The 166 MM Barchetta was destined to become the first of the world-famous Ferrari road cars.

What did it was Luigi Chinetti's iron-man performance in the first post-war Le Mans 24-hour endurance race. He drove almost the entire distance by himself in one of Ferrari's appealing little *barchettas*. If there had been any doubt about the prancing horse's basic soundness, this victory went a long way to erasing it. True, Ferrari had begun winning F2 and even F1 single-seater sprint races around Europe. But Le Mans, watched by the world, demonstrated that the complex V-12 would last as well as go.

Suddenly the Ferrari was a car that sports-car lovers everywhere could realistically dream about owning. Many realized that dream. "The 166 MM can be considered Ferrari's first series-built automobile, and the first one intended to serve both touring and competition purposes," wrote

Dean Batchelor in *Automobile* magazine. "Since the real heart of the Ferrari mystique has always been that blurry distinction between racer and road car, the 166 MM may be called the model that started the magic."

Of course, "series-built automobile" as applied to early Ferraris is a relative term. There were only a few dozen cars in all, and many variations were incorporated as each of these essentially hand-built "little boats" was launched.

For one thing, two different wheelbases were available: 86.6 or 88.6 inches, both substantially shorter than the 95.3 typical of the 125 models. There were two different trim levels offered, too. One was a stark, stripped machine intended purely for racing. The other was a *lusso* ("luxury") version civilized somewhat with leather and carpeting—but not so civilized that it couldn't wade into a nice scrap on the track. Other changes

were rung among such particulars as instrumentation, windshields, body shape and trim details, even fuel tankage. Weights ranged between 1500 and 1600 pounds, according to Batchelor. Horsepower was on the order of 125, and top speed perhaps about the same number.

"Although Ferrari built the 166 MMs in both street and racing versions," Batchelor wrote, "driving a 166 reminds one quickly that it was first a competition car and second a street car.

"Insert the ignition key, turn on the magneto switch, hit the starter button on the dash, and it's instant bedlam. That tiny V-12, with its light reciprocating mass, can hit 5000 rpm before you react.... [The Barchettas are] tractable in traffic and can survive stop-and-go situations without overheating. Their handling at racing speeds is predictable, with just a bit of oversteer. And the brakes are excel-

lent. The steering is somewhat heavy but not bothersome, and a good driver can 'dirt-track' the car around corners if he wants to. Unfortunately, the rather skinny tires, which are made with a hard rubber compound, don't offer the best traction. The 166 MM driver knows that he should get the car straight on the track before getting on the gas too hard or he's going to go sideways. But isn't that the fun of driving a car like this?"

It was fun that had to be tempered with prudence, however. Sometime owner of several vintage Ferraris himself, Batchelor had learned that "a Ferrari is not indestructible, but it is rugged and durable if the engine, the transmission, and the rear axle assembly are warmed up to operating temperature before being driven hard. Ferrari clutches are another matter. Engagement is smooth and usually stays that way as long as it lasts, but the driver of one of these

early Ferraris never, but never, uses a drag-racing start."

His meaning: Let the clutch out gently with the engine pulling only hard enough to avoid a stall, and don't open the throttles wide until the clutch is fully engaged.

The Ferrari driver of the late 1940s also had to learn to cope with other characteristic quirks. As several contemporary observers noted, it took time to accustom oneself to a Ferrari. Enzo had no intention of making a driver feel at home immediately; the

driver had to work at being accepted by the car. The owner also had to work at finding someone he or she could trust to work on it. Weather protection on most Barchettas was equivalent to that of a motorcycle. The soft, hand-hammered aluminum body could be dented by a careless elbow. The chassis design was essentially identical to the original 125's, and gave the same bone-shaking ride at everyday traffic speeds on rough surfaces, though it would have smoothed out at the open-road speeds

for which it was intended. And the gearbox still had that odd lack of synchros on all but third and fourth—when it was new, that is. After some hard miles, there was a tendency to lack any synchronization at all. It was

The 1948 166 MM Barchetta spread the Ferrari name beyond Italy and to the sports-car world (*above*). It was powered by a 160-horsepower, 2-liter version of the original 1.5-liter 125 V-12 (*above and opposite page*). The simple body with its strong lines reminded Italians of a little boat, or a *barchetta*, and the MM tag was in honor of Ferrari's Mille Miglia victory.

all part of the charm for drivers who had learned to pause for a moment in neutral while shifting up, and to blip the throttle while double-clutching for downshifts.

This red-hot new roadster may have suffered lapses in what auto de- signers would come to call Human En- gineering. But its immediate appeal was to something called human na- ture. Ferrari very rapidly muscled its way to the top of the sports-car enthu- siast's must-have list.

The good folks at Carrozzeria Touring, recognizing a roll when they were on one, did everything they could to aid and abet Enzo's grip on his grow- ing public. Building on the *barchetta's* successful lines, they evolved an equal- ly pleasing little fastback coupe—a *ber- linetta*, or "small sedan." Still called the

166 Mille Miglia in factory sales literature at first, and later the 195 Sport when the engine was enlarged, it was substantially heavier than its topless sibling. Batchelor quotes 2125 pounds. But it had, and has, a lean, efficient, purposeful grace that gets the blood pumping. In fact, Touring's Ferrari *berlinetta* of 1949 was the stylistic genesis of the most covetable coupes made by anyone for the next 40 years.

Of course, Ferrari was not responsible for bodywork. Following the automaking procedures he had learned on his introduction to the business in 1919, when he drove stripped chassis from Turin to a coachbuilder in Milan, he saw his role as producing a soundly-engineered springboard for someone else's flights of styling fancy. In the late 1940s and early '50s, Ferraris were dressed by several *carrozzeria* other than Touring: Allemano, Bertone, Ghia, Stabilimenti Farina (not the same as Pinin Farina), Vignale. Some of these turned out some lovely cars, some did not. Touring itself produced a few small Ferrari sedan-like 2+2s. Enzo was serving his public as he found it, and some of his less adventurous customers were perfectly happy with a detuned, single-carburetor model called the Inter. Naturally,

bodywork for the Inter chassis tended toward boring practicality.

Meanwhile, to the racers in the Ferrari audience, the original *barchetta* body style was such a hit that variations of it remained in production for several years, fitted to a succession of chassis models marked by ever larger engines. One of the nicest Barchettas was the 1951 Tipo 212. The number signified a further increase of the Colombo V-12's displacement: leaving the

*(continued on page 100)*

Variations on the 166 theme: Vignale's coupe interpretation (*opposite page, top left*) and a *berlinetta*, or small sedan, by the 166 Barchetta's original styling house, Touring (*opposite page, bottom*). Both these cars are Inters, which means they have a detuned single-carburetor 2-liter engine of about 114 horsepower (*opposite page, top right*). In 1950, a 2.3-liter version with about 170 horsepower, called the 195 S, was introduced (*this page*). Ferrari's prancing horse emblem in these years sported the "SF" initials of Scuderia Ferrari.

# FERRARI CHASSIS

## The Early Cars

Ferrari's first cars emerged from his engineering office as all-new designs made with all-new components. Though some pieces had to be farmed out for manufacture, Enzo resisted using proprietary elements from other marques.

While the engine Ferrari produced was considered a bit radical for the time, the chassis he made was not. It was a simple, straightforward design that was relatively easy to build and maintain—desirable qualities for a high performance car.

Manufactured from high-carbon steel tubing, 2 millimeters thick, the chassis side rails were oval in shape, 60 mm wide in plan view, and 90 mm deep in side elevation. The X-member of the early cars also was oval—at least as seen in Ferrari brochure illustrations. The one early car (No. 002C) we've examined closely had a round tubular X-member about 75 mm in diameter.

At the front, a fabricated box-section cross member was incorporated to carry the suspension and steering box. On some cars the side members kicked up over the live rear axle; on others, the side tubes ran "underslung" beneath the axle. The frame was gas-welded to Ferrari design by Gilberto Colombo's firm, Gilco Autotelai SRL, into an extremely rigid and rather sturdy structure.

Front suspension was independent with parallel but unequal-length A-arms and a single transverse-leaf spring under the front cross-member. The first few Ferraris had Dubonnet shock absorbers incorporated into the upper A-arms, but these were soon abandoned in favor of Houdaille Vane-type lever-action units that could be removed separately for service.

At the rear, two semi-elliptic springs supported the car on its live axle. On the first cars, the springs and upper triangulated arms of the Dubonnet shock absorbers positioned the axle. An anti-roll bar was fitted inside the rear tubular cross-member and connected to the axle by short trailing arms and links.

As the cars got into more serious competition we find that racing really did improve the breed. The basic form of the chassis was not abandoned, but important refinements were made. Rear-axle positioning, for example, was accomplished by twin parallel (upper and lower) radius arms on each side of the chassis that supplemented the springs.

While altered in detail, this basic frame

design was used for all early Ferraris, regardless of the engine used. It was employed by the 4-cylinder Mondial, 500 TRC, and Monza; the 6-cylinder 118 and 121 LMs; and both the Colombo and Lampredi 12-cylinder 125, 166, 195; 212, 225, 250, 340, and 400/410 Superamerica models.

As a result, wheelbases of these early cars ranged from 2200 mm to 2800 mm (86.6 inches to 110 inches). Tracks varied from 1200 mm to 1455 mm (47.2 inches to 57.3).

All Ferrari competition cars and most of the road cars up through 1953 had right-hand steering. This was common for cars

built for competition, but was unusual for cars intended for use on Italy's public roads, where drivers sat on the left side of the vehicle, but drove on the right side of the road. The predominance of right-hand drive Ferraris suggests that Enzo's early cars, regardless of suggested use, were intended to be dual purpose vehicles.

Brakes remained aluminum drums with iron liners until 1960, when the 250 GT received Dunlop disc brakes. Also in 1960, tubular shock absorbers were made stan-

Ferrari capitalized on the versatility of the basic 166 MM chassis (*opposite page, top*) by using it as a foundation for numerous cars, including the 121 LM of the mid-1950s (*both pages*). This handsome sports-racer was one of only two models to employ an inline-6.

dard, replacing the Houdaille lever-action units that had been used since the first cars. New cylinder heads with individual intake ports and spark plugs on the outside of the heads were fitted. A single-disc clutch replaced the twin-disc, and overdrive was added to the four-speed transmission.

In 1955, the 250 Europa became the first Ferrari in which coil springs replaced the front transverse leaf. Rear suspension remained the familiar live axle with semi-elliptic springs and twin parallel radius arms on each side to position the axle and absorb the torque reaction. At the front, unequal-length A-arms and coil springs were standard, as they had been since the 1955 Europa GT.

When the 250 GT Lusso came out in 1962, it retained all the typical Ferrari features, but incorporated some new ones borrowed from the competition-oriented 250 GTO: The rear tubular shock absorbers had concentric "helper" coil springs, and the axle's lateral location was by a Watt linkage.

The chassis and suspension of the 250

GT Lusso and GTO marked the end of the development of this original Ferrari ladder-type chassis. The design survived and worked very well from 1947 to 1964, the end of 250 GT production. While many rival road cars, as well as his own racing cars, had gone to all-independent suspension, Ferrari clung to his archaic suspension design. For this he was chided during the late 1950s and into the '60s by customers, press, and competitors.

It is a legitimate criticism and one that's difficult to rationalize. It is important to note, however, that the GTO was quite successful through 1964, even with the live rear axle. Perhaps it was a case of the well-developed old design working better than an underdeveloped new design.

The 212 Export of 1951 (*opposite page, top*) continued the *barchetta* bloodline in an aggressive 2.6-liter roadster. Chassis development continued with the 1953 250 Europa (*opposite page, bottom*), Ferrari's first car in which coil springs replaced the front transverse leaf. The chassis of the '52 Mille Miglia-winning 250 S (*above*) was the basis for the 250 Europa.

stroke at 58.8 mm, while taking the bore out to 68 (2.68 inches), brought the swept volume to 2563 cc (156.4 cubic inches) and the quoted horsepower to 170 at 7200 rpm. Note how, even as its size and power increased, so did the marvelous little motor's appetite for revs.

American sports-car racer Phil Hill, later to become World Champion driving for Ferrari, owned a 212 Barchetta and in 1952 let *Road & Track* magazine have its instrumented way with it. The account demonstrates that the bloodline of the prancing horse was growing ever more refined. Once truck-like, the steering was now "light and positive." Formerly awkward, the cockpit layout was now described as comfortable and roomy—although the pedals had no space wasted between them. The once iffy braking ability was now the best ever tested by *Road & Track*. And by now

synchromesh had spread to all gears but low.

Hill himself had improved the handling, at least by his lights. He'd added an anti-roll bar to the front—the car had come with a rear bar only—and changed the shock absorbers. The result was that his car exhibited understeer through the corners now and had less of a tendency to lift its inside rear wheel (this was before locked differentials). The changes allowed the driver to feed in more power sooner coming out of a turn. That made for a faster package in Phil's hands. "However," *Road & Track* opined, "the car demands more driving ability in its present form.... The Ferrari as originally delivered would unquestionably suit better the average driver's limitations."

The little roadster was still built on the 88½-inch wheelbase, and over time had gained gratifyingly few

pounds. *Road & Track* stated the curb weight as 1975 pounds, but then cast doubt by breaking down the distribution as 1040 front/865 rear. Seventy pounds had gone missing somewhere in the calculation. But performance was definitely up: 0-60 mph in 7.05 seconds, and the quarter-mile in 15.0. No trap speed was given, but it would have been in the low 90s. Observed top speed was 123 mph. The magazine's testers believed a properly set up 212 would have been capable of 140 mph. But in what is getting to be a familiar Ferrari test story, the engine in this car wasn't running at its best and wouldn't pull cleanly over 6500 rpm. In addition, it had short U.S.-track

gearing of 4.28:1 overall in the overdrive top gear. Plus, noted a photo caption, wind pressure had broken the plastic windscreen!

The road test illuminates one usually overlooked driving condition with which this Ferrari had to contend: The poor quality of the fuel available in its day. This racing machine had a compression ratio of 7.5:1, far below that of 1960s-era American muscle cars, and less even than most of today's passenger-car engines. The magazine's test, incidentally, was carried out using "90 octane aviation fuel."

There was one further increase in Barchetta engine sizes, to the 2715 cc (165.7 cubic inches) of the Tipo 225 of

1952, which had a 70-mm bore (2.76 inches). From the displacement point of view, though, the Barchetta story ended a couple of years earlier, in a muscle car of Ferrari's own.

In 1950, work that Aurelio Lampredi had done to give Ferrari a large-displacement, non-supercharged Grand Prix engine was extended to

Two examples of the venerable 212 type, circa 1951. The 212 Inter (*opposite page*) was the more civilized version and had a 102-inch wheelbase. The 212 Export (*this page*) was competition oriented and ran on a wheelbase of 88 inches. Both could be ordered with a trio of 32 DCF Weber carburetors. Both of these cars have bodies by Touring, one of several styling houses to design skins for the 212.

the sports car world. Lampredi constructed a physically larger V-12 with a bore spacing of 108 mm (4.25 inches), which resulted in a block about five inches longer overall. One of the homes it found was the 340 America, a competition-oriented model built in limited numbers, seven of which wore the familiar Touring Barchetta body shape on a 95.3-inch wheelbase.

From the model designation, the displacement can be calculated: 4.1 liters (250 cubic inches), from a bore of 70 mm (2.76 inches) and a stroke of 68

(2.68). The compression ratio was 8.0:1, and the stated horsepower 220 at 6000 rpm. Top speed was supposed to be 149 mph. Without actually verifying this, an excited *Road & Track* labeled the 1950 340 America sports racer the "fastest passenger car in the world!"

The Lampredi and Colombo engines continued through many notable Ferraris. The story of the pretty Barchetta body ends here, except for one final note.

Carroll Shelby's venomous struggle to defeat Enzo Ferrari on the race

tracks of Europe with his Ford-powered Cobra ranks among the most monumental battles in the annals of motorsport. The victorious Cobra was derived from the British-built AC Ace, a lovely little open 2-seater with

Giovanni Michelotti, a young stylist with the Alfred Vignale coachworks, developed the elliptical radiator opening and eggcrate grille that was to influence Ferrari design for many years. His work is shown on a 1952 Vignale 212 Inter coupe (*this page*). A Touring 212 Export spyder of 1951 (*opposite page*). A 212 Export *barchetta* with a Touring body won the first Tour de France.

an aluminum body very much of the Barchetta type. In fact, the original front-end styling of the Ace, before it took on its Cobra guise, had a largish grille-mouth with a down-and-outward-curling "moustache" under the headlights remarkably similar to Touring's design.

It *was* Touring's design. Not directly, but AC derived its Ace under license

from a sports-racing car built in 1952 by a British cottage-industrialist named John Tojeiro. And Tojeiro did, boldly and unabashedly, copy the essential lines and feel of the Ferrari Barchetta.

So in an oddly circuitous and convoluted way, it could be said that, at least in the Cobra matter, it took a Ferrari copy to beat a Ferrari.

This 1952 212 Export *berlinetta* has a one-off body by Vignale/Michelotti (*both pages*). It was raced in the United States in the late '50s. Vignale went on to use this design—including the two-tone paint scheme—for the Cunningham C-3, a grand touring car conceived by American Briggs Cunningham and produced from 1952-55. With a wheelbase of 105 inches, however, the C-3 was much larger than the 88-inch wheelbase Ferrari, and used a 5.4-liter Chrysler V-8.

# Chapter 8:

# The Lampredi Cars: Ferrari's Big Bang Theory

Any other specialty automaker setting up at about the time Enzo Ferrari did might have been entirely content with a product line built on the the likes of the sweet little Gioacchino Colombo V-12. Indeed, any number of fine and famous marques have soldiered on for decades with one basic engine. But Enzo Ferrari had scarcely begun his power game.

His first motor was a 1.5-liter, but enough structural beef had been designed in to handle a lot more work. The additional output would come either by means of supercharging, to meet the contemporary Grand Prix formula, or through a succession of displacement increases allowed by a variety of racing classes. In fact, the little Colombo eventually did yield an astonishing number of cubic centimeters; 4-liters' worth and more. For many years it remained the definitive Ferrari powerplant.

However, as a supercharged Formula 1 engine, Colombo's twelve proved unable to beat the supercharged Alfa Romeo straight-eight he'd designed in 1938. Ferrari's team only scored its first F1 win during 1949 because Alfa's had taken the season off.

For 1950, Alfa was back and stronger than ever. Horsepower figures for racing engines are always questionable data, particularly looking back several decades, but published material indicates that the highly developed Tipo 159 Alfetta now was pumping out as many as 350 horses. Even

with experimental twin-cam cylinder heads and dual-stage supercharging, the Ferrari fell short of that by 70 to 120 horsepower, depending on the data's source.

So the Maranello motorheads tried another tack. The F1 regulations also allowed non-supercharged engines up to 4.5 liters (274.5 cubic inches). Historically, this option had never shown the power potential to match the blown 1.5s on straight speed, but Ferrari decided it was worth a fresh try. For one thing, such an engine would present fewer maintenance problems for his still-small company; for another, it would offer the potential benefits of much lower fuel consumption.

Colombo left Ferrari at this point and Aurelio Lampredi, who had assisted Colombo with the first engine, now enlarged the basic design. The essential point was the increase in overall engine length by a little over five inches—from 94 centimeters to 107, or 37.01 inches to 42.13. This gave a cylinder-bore spacing of 108 mm (4.25 inches) rather than 90 (3.54), thus allowing larger-diameter cylinders.

Externally, the two engines looked very much alike. To tell the Lampredi V-12 from the Colombo at a glance, count the number of studs holding down the lower edge of a camshaft cover. The bigger unit has seven; the smaller, six. A tape measure reveals a four-inch difference in the lengths of the covers themselves: 27 inches versus 23.

Ferrari abandoned the 1.5 partway

through the 1950 season. Working in careful steps from an initial displacement of 3.3-liters, his engine technicians developed both the new "long block" V-12 and a single-seater chassis to carry it. By the time they reached the full 4.5-liter displacement, they are said by some historians to have been seeing 350 horsepower at 7500 rpm.

Ferrari's new Tipo 375 hadn't yet beaten Alfa's 159, but there was obviously a real chance of it. In 1951, the Alfa was further refined and Alfa reportedly had as much as 385 horsepower in track trim—and 405 on the dyno. But the Ferrari, with new dual-ignition heads and compression ratios ranging as high as 12:1 (F1 cars then used alcohol-based fuel), had improved to 380.

The two completely different designs were functionally equal and had some tremendous, 190-mph battles that summer. In July, at the British GP, the big 4.5 scored Ferrari's long-awaited triumph over the firm he called his "mother."

It would be naive to think that Enzo didn't have his eye on additional uses for this bigger engine from its very inception. For one thing, it suited the

Aurelio Lampredi's big-block V-12 saw its first widespread use in the 340 America of 1951 (*right*). It had a 4.1-liter version of the long engine with 220 to 230 horsepower at 6000 rpm. Some 25 were built, a hodgepodge of open and closed cars, of racers and tourers, 2-seaters and 2+2s, with styling spread among three different bodymakers. This *barchetta*'s coachwork is by Touring.

Indianapolis 500 regulations of the day, and Alberto Ascari did drive a Ferrari there in 1952. This adventure was not a success. Despite its claimed output of 400 horsepower, neither the car nor the effort behind it had really been competitive from the beginning, and a wire-spoked wheel collapsed during the race. Sadly, despite what Enzo once described as annual plans for a return, that remained the only time during his lifetime that his *cavallino* raced at Indy.

Planting the big-block in sports cars bore more fruit, although it took a while to nurture. The first appearance of a Lampredi-engined 2-seater was early in 1950, when two examples of the engine in its 3.3-liter displacement were shoehorned into a pair of Barchettas with the 88.6-inch wheelbase.

In April, these type 275 S cars ran in the Mille Miglia. Both subsequently retired and never raced again.

The Tipo 340 America was introduced in October. This model was in production during 1951, and involved a longer wheelbase (95.3 inches) carrying a 4.1-liter version of the long engine developing 220 to 230 horsepower at 6000 rpm. Some 25 were built, a hodge-podge of open and closed cars, of racers and tourers, of 2-seaters and 2+2s, with styling spread among three different bodymakers. Two of these cars were the year-old 275 S chassis, revamped but not renumbered. An attempt to trace the 1951 340 America variations would be a good illustration of why Ferrari-tracking can be so difficult.

Ferrari's 340 act was more polished

for 1952, with a more distinct split being made between racers and road-going cars. Four examples of the former were called the 340 Mexico. The name celebrated Ferrari's 1951 1-2 triumph in the Carrera Panamericana, or Mexican Road Race, as the Americans called it. In point of fact that long-distance, open-road victory had been scored with a pair of Tipo 212 Vignale-bodied, Colombo-engined coupes, but Ferrari did prepare Lampredi-powered machines for the 1952 event. All were styled—rather startlingly so—by the talented Giovanni Michelotti of the Alfredo Vignale *carrozzeria*. One, an open spyder, did not actually make the Carrera Panamericana, but the three Berlinetta coupes did. One of them, driven by iron-man Chinetti, finished third.

The engine of the 340 Mexico had a bore and stroke of 80 mm × 68 mm (3.150 × 2.67 inches) for a displacement of 4101.66 cc (250.2 cubic inches)—so the capacity of one cylinder was actually almost 342 cc, not 340. Quoted horsepower output was 280 at 6600 rpm, on a compression ratio that was either 8.0, 8.1, or 8.5:1, depending on the authority. The transmission was still a 5-speed, but the wheelbase had been increased yet again, to 2600 mm or 102.4 inches. Curb weight of a coupe was said to be 2200 pounds.

Dean Batchelor owned the ex-Chinetti 340 Mexico for several years, and wrote about it lovingly his 1974 book, FERRARI, The Early Berlinettas & Competition Coupes: "It is cramped inside, steers like a truck, rides like a brick wagon, has dodgy brakes until those large drums are thoroughly warmed up, is hot in the summer and cold in the winter, but at the same time gives more personal pleasure per mile than just about any conveyance one could name.... hit the starter button and zowie! Instant bedlam. There is absolutely no insulation in this car any-

Competition versions of the Type 340 cars for 1952 were called the 340 Mexico, in honor of Ferrari's 1-2 finish in the '51 Mexican Road Race. This is one of the three Berlinettas built (*this page*); the fourth was a spyder. All were styled by Vignale. The engine is a 280-horsepower 4.1-liter. "...[H]it the starter button and zowie! Instant bedlam," wrote one 340 Mexico owner. A 4.5-liter Lampredi powered the only Ferrari to race at Indianapolis (*opposite page*). Alberto Ascari's drive in the 1952 500 ended when a wheel collapsed.

where, and every sound from the engine compartment is immediately part of the passenger compartment."

The multi-plate clutch—originally with seven discs, later with five—and the totally unsynchronized transmission made this a demanding machine. But once the technique had been mastered, "fairly smooth changes can be made," Batchelor wrote. "The big Lampredi engine pulls reasonably well from anything over 1000 rpm, but if you wait until it's turning 3500 or so it really gives a belt in the back." Speeds over 100 mph were "easy riding in a 340 Mexico," but the vintage brakes made such velocities feel "just a bit insecure."

Another 340 Vignale racing coupe, though not a Mexico, was tested by *Road & Track* in 1952. Reputedly a car that had led the Le Mans race that year before retiring, it came with a factory letter stating its output was 260 horsepower at 6500 rpm. The magazine's data panel gave this car's wheelbase as 96.0 inches, and estimated its weight at 2050 pounds—or 2390 pounds carrying driver and test equipment.

Top speed was another estimation—150 mph—but genuine acceleration times were taken: 6.1 seconds 0-60 mph, and 15.39 for the best standing quarter-mile. The young *Road & Track* had never seen better numbers, though once again, here was a Ferrari road test noting that the clutch had been treated gently. The engine had

been babied, too, with upshifts made at 6000 rpm, 500 below peak power.

As for the car's road manners, "It would be absurd to say that the 4.1 Ferrari offers handling powers, cornering ability, and steering qualities to match its fantastic performance," *Road & Track* said. "What it does offer is a combination of qualities which, in the hands of an experienced driver... makes it possible to drive safely over all types of roads far faster than any average driver (like us) would ever

dream could be possible."

The ride was described as firm, with little pitching and "absolutely no roll." The steering was quick at 2.3 turns lock-to-lock and, not surprisingly, was heavy and lacked feel at low speeds. "Above 30 mph the steering becomes light and is very accurate. However, at around 60 mph on slightly rough surfaces the entire steering column sometimes vibrates viciously—a fault which all Ferrari owners seem to accept without complaint."

Lampredi's engine (*this page*) was about five inches longer than its Colombo counterpart and had seven studs visible on the lower-edge of its camshaft cover; the smaller engine had six. The engine shown is from a 340 America. A larger, slightly more sedate alternative to the Type 340 cars was the 342 America. Six were produced, including this Pininfarina cabriolet delivered to the King of Belgium in 1952 (*opposite page, top*). More aggressive bodywork by the same *carrozzeria* was featured on one of the 375 MMs (*opposite page, bottom*), suiting its harder performance edge.

Batchelor's feeling about this oft-mentioned early Ferrari steering judder is that it occurs only in examples that have been poorly maintained or run very hard. But there's no doubt about the interior sound levels of these raw competition coupes. As *Road & Track* remarked about its 4.1 test car, "The engine and transmission make a lot of noise—a racket which one unkind soul likened to a threshing machine. The first time we took off hard through the gears it sounded like the whole works was coming apart."

Going through those five gears, all non-synchronized in this box, still demanded real skill, and the non-assisted drum brakes still took "more pedal pressure to stop the car than might be expected." Even moving the short gearshift lever called for a surprising amount of muscle.

Such were the little drawbacks of trying to use a Ferrari racer as a road car. Still, many enthusiasts would happily put up with them. However, for those of his customers burdened by an insatiable taste for civility, Enzo offered the concurrent 342 America model. This had basically the same engine, though in a softer state of tune, with 200 horsepower at 5000 rpm. It also had a "softer" 4-speed, all-synchro transmission. A longer wheelbase, at 104.3 inches, and slightly wider track dimensions, plus its much heavier weight of about 2650 pounds, made the America a much softer-riding car than the Mexico. Their sedanish Pinin Farina bodies were rather ponderous looking, however, and only half a dozen were built.

For the 1953 racing season, Ferrari came up with the Tipo 340 MM, a model designed to meet the challenge of the inaugural World Sports Car Championship, which combined seven famous events into one series. By now the 4.1 engine was up to 300 horsepower at 6600 rpm, but the wheelbase was down to 98.4 inches. The combination was immediately effective, winning the championship's first round, the Tour of Sicily, and then the Mille Miglia soon after. At all-important Le Mans, though, the best finish was fifth. By now some cars had the 4.5 engine and longer wheelbases, and this marked the functional end of a series of about ten

340 MMs. Most were finally converted into 375s.

There were in fact two different versions of the 375 MM engine. Seen first at that 1953 Le Mans was a stroked 340, its 80 mm × 74.5 mm dimensions giving 4494 cc (274.5 cubic inches) and 340 horsepower at 7000 rpm. This output was below that of the F1 engine, at least partly because the compression was down to 9.0 to suit gasoline. This first 4.5 Ferrari sports car set fastest lap during the race, and although it retired of clutch failure, it was obviously the way of the future.

By the end of the season, about 30 of the 375 MM had been constructed, some out of existing 340 MMs. Quite a few were sold to private racers. The "customer" cars had a slightly different engine, with a larger, 84-mm bore and a shorter, 68-mm stroke, for a capacity of 4522 cc (376.8 cubic inches). Once again, there was a bewildering variety of body types and styles, including several competition coupes, many of whose bodies were adaptations of Farina's lines for the 375 roadster shell.

All this playing around with bores and strokes was showing the way to the ultimate Lampredi-engined sports racer, the so-called 375 Plus of 1954. Combining the largest cylinder dimensions, 84 mm × 74.5 mm, gave 4954.338 cc, or 302.332 cubic inches. The 375 Plus—nobody knows why it wasn't called the Tipo 412—became another immediate winner. It took the first race of the season, at Agadir in North Africa, then another at Silverstone. It followed up by winning both Le Mans and the Mexican Carrera, Ferrari's second triumph in both these world-famous events.

The 342 America (*opposite page*) was introduced during the winter of 1952-53 to take the place of the 340 America street cars. It was larger and heavier than the 340s, and unlike those competition-oriented cars, the 342 had right-hand drive. It's 4.1-liter Lampredi was rated at 200 horsepower. This coupe has the extended grille characteristic of Pininfarina's 342 Americas. The 1953 340 MM (*above*) was built to contest the first World Sports Car Championship. **Its 4.1 was rated at 300 horsepower and it had a 5-speed transmission to the 342 America's 4-speed. This 340 MM is by Vignale.**

The 375 Plus was a brute of a sports car, one that foreshadowed Shelby's massive 427 Cobra of the next decade, being all engine and only enough car to hold the sump off the road. A number of older accounts credit the 4.9, as it was called, with merely 330 hp at 6000 rpm. A more recent issue of *Cavallino* magazine gives it 344 at 6500. Either way, the big V-12 was similar to the 4.5 in terms of peak power. Torque, though, was up markedly (to 348 pounds/feet, says *Cavallino*) and the horsepower curve had been re-shaped for a more effective mid-range.

It was almost too effective. The 375

Plus was a rocket on the straights—it was allegedly clocked at 180 mph at Le Mans—but its snaky antics coming out of turns quickly gained it a reputation for difficult handling. Picture the generally narrow, highly crowned and bumpy open-road courses of the day, all of them lined with trees and stone walls and houses. It's little wonder that some racers are said to have chosen to drive the non-Plus "little" 375 whenever they could invent an excuse.

Ferrari's new monster motor actually forced his chassis people to advance the hitherto somewhat somnolent state of their art. To improve weight distribution, they moved the 4-speed gearbox to the rear of the 375 Plus, mounting it as a unit with the differential. Obviously this transaxle had to be affixed to the frame, so they replaced the normal beam-type rear axle with a Grand Prix-style de Dion rear suspension. This, in turn, required raising the fuel tank and spare tire positions, so the Plus cars are easily distinguished by a prominent hunchback in the rear deck. Rear track was narrower than the front, at 50.6 inches compared to 52.2, while wheelbase was, again, 2.6 meters, or 102.4 inches. Listed weights range from 900 kilos to a suspiciously even, but more likely,

During the 1953 racing season, Ferrari concocted the 375 MM by enlarging the 4.1-liter twelve of the 340 MM and by stretching the 340's wheelbase. Displacement of 375 MM engines ranged a few cubic centimeters either way of 4.5-liters and generated about 340 horsepower. As with the 340 types, the MM suffix once again applied to the sports/racing variant of the 375, while the 375 America, with its 300 horsepower, was the street version. Vignale designed a few spyders on the 375 MM platform, but most were styled by Pininfarina, including this 375 MM coupe (*both pages*).

1000 (2205 pounds.).

To one way of thinking, this exercise, successful as it was, turned out to be a dead end. Ferrari's racing technology chose other avenues, and only five of these 375 Plus cars were built in their Pinin Farina-bodied, factory competition form; the line never led directly to any later racing or road car of importance.

But Enzo's heart was in the right place. He did make a stab at building a road car out of his Le Mans racer. Sort of. This project was announced in a brochure for a "410 Superamerica" model. Illustrated was that incomparably evil-looking roadster with its shark-mouthed grille very slightly tamed by small chrome bumperettes. A low, full-width windscreen sheltered a young rake dressed nattily in suit and tie, obviously a person of substance, who was trying to entice a smartly dressed woman in beside him. Never mind that there wasn't a passenger-side door for her, or side windows to keep her hair neat, or a top, or any luggage space; as every sports car

aficionado of the time understood, the very lack of such amenities was the acid-test of a date. The male fantasy held that any woman who complained was immediately crossed out of the "little black book."

According to the brochure, the "410 Superamerica" was built on a long, 2.8-meter wheelbase—110.2 inches—and wider track measurements—57.3 inches front, 57.1 rear. Instead of the 5-speed transaxle and de Dion rear suspension, it had an all-synchro 4-speed gearbox in the traditional location and a live axle. Its front suspension was also unlike the Le Mans racer, having the coil springs to which Ferrari was moving. Similarly, the engine was an individual piece. The Lampredi block was fitted with a new bore/stroke combination: 88 mm × 68 mm (3.465 cc × 2.677 cc), giving 4963 cc (303 cubic inches). On a compression ratio of 8.5, it was supposed to make 340 horsepower at 6000 rpm for its lucky owner to play with.

Alas, only the one vehicle pictured in the brochure was built. And in

truth it wasn't a 410 at all, but had only the 4522-cc "375" motor. Neither did it have that long wheelbase, nor those coil front springs. Dean Batchelor knows the car well and explains that it was nothing more than a box-stock 375 MM racer converted—very sketchily—for street use at the re-

The dozen or so 375 Americas produced between 1953 and 1955 hosted a wide variety of bodies, including this classic 1954 cabriolet fashioned by Pininfarina for King Leopold of Belgium (*this page*). It was the styling prototype for the California series 250 Spyders. The one-of-a-kind body is on a 375 MM chassis and is the only left-hand drive version of this platform. The car has a 5-liter 375 Plus engine of factory-racing specification, rather than the traditional 375-series 4.5-liter. Aimed at the American market, the handsome 410 Superamerica (*opposite page*) used a 4.9-liter V-12. The shift pattern of the 4-speed was unusual, with first gear forward and to the right.

quest of an American customer, a California woman. It was painted bright yellow, had green leather upholstery, and was driven frequently by its owner on the public streets of Monterey, California. Such a raw, raucous, four-wheeled motorcycle might have its daydreamy appeal for hard-core enthusiasts, but most people who could actually pay for such a confection were accustomed to more comfort in their carriages. Inevitably, Ferrari sprang to their service.

For those of his clients who were merely fabulously wealthy, Enzo started up something of a production

model, a follow-up to the 340 America called the 375 America. Using the 84 × 68 engine on a compression ratio of 8:1, it made 300 horsepower at 6300 rpm. Its transmission was the synchronized 4-speed, and its wheelbase that long 110.2 inches. Bodies were made by Pinin Farina, Ghia, and Vignale. Only a dozen or so were produced in the period 1953-55.

Enzo made an even smaller number of even more special chassis for the upper crust of his clientele. The cabriolet created for Leopold, King of the Belgians, in 1954 by Pinin Farina is still regarded among the most grace-

ful Ferraris ever. Ingrid Bergman, the Swedish movie star who was then scandalizing American society by her affair with Italian director Roberto Rossellini, ordered a coupe of advanced aerodynamic lines from the same *carrozzeria*. In 1955, Rossellini himself went to Scaglietti for another, the muscular shape of which recalled the Mercedes-Benz F1 streamliners of the year before. Under his hood throbbed a 375 Plus engine.

At the Brussels auto show in January 1956, Ferrari displayed the first example of the car that would replace the 375 America. At last there was an actual 410 Superamerica, a closed car that in concept as in appearance owed nothing to the stark original bearer of the name.

Under the elegant skins of these latter-day 410 Superamericas, however, was to be found a good deal of that racy old roadster: the long, 2800-mm wheelbase was the same at first, though it was reduced to 2600 mm on some later cars; the forward-mounted 4-speed gearbox was similar, although the shift pattern was strangely "reversed," with first to the right and forward, and fourth left and back; there also was a coil-spring front suspension. The engine was the 4963 again, tuned to the same 340 horsepower at 6000 rpm, later to 360 at 7000.

During four years of availability, through 1959, there were three "series" of this model totaling 37 known examples. The last, Series III, received the most mechanical changes. These included the uprated engine, with 9.0:1 compression; spark plugs moved to the outsides of the heads, which improved both combustion efficiency and mechanics' access; and bigger brakes.

On these exceptional foundations were erected some of the most elegantly exciting bodywork ever seen. It was as if the stylists let their creativity run free of the constraints of the conventional, workaday world.

That feeling certainly embraced the string of Superfast show cars created by Pinin Farina. The first Superfast appeared in 1956. It was a wild, gaudy thing, with Yankee-style tail fins and no structural A-pillars at the corners of the windshield. Power was by a dual-ignition engine, with a total of 24 spark plugs.

This very special Superamerica eventually came to America, where it

reduced august *Road & Track* to abject servility: "... one of the most beautiful cars in the world, with a performance which is so fantastic as to be almost beyond all comprehension." What really lit the editorial fire was the engine. It would light up the rear wheels on dry concrete in third gear at 100 mph, gushed *Road & Track*. Thus, "acceleration from a standstill to 100 mph be-

comes primarily an exercise in the driver's skill, to prevent excess wheel-spin. We made no tests on this car, but 0 to 60 should come up in under 5 seconds. ..."

The quoted price was a scandalous $18,500 in big, fat 1957 dollars and to those harboring doubts about the value of such an extravagant beast, the magazine offered this balm: "Driv-

An example of one of the 10 or 12 "Series III" 410 Superamericas produced in 1959 (*opposite page*). These cars got an uprated engine with spark plugs moved to the outsides of the heads. Ghia's Mario Savonuzzi penned one of the most unusual Ferrari bodies ever with this exercise on a 410 Superamerica chassis (*above*). It recalled two styling studies he had done earlier for Chrysler, the Dart and the Gilda.

ing a car such as this is a relief from boredom, a challenge to one's driving skill and a never-ending source of satisfaction through pride of ownership."

By the time *Road & Track* was fawning over Superfast I, Farina had produced a successor. It was called the 4.9 Superfast, though the chrome script on the car itself read Super fast. The car was obviously derived from Superfast I, but Farina had wisely installed

A-pillars and lost the tailfins. It soon fell into the hands of another U.S. publication, *Sports Cars Illustrated* (later known as *Car and Driver*). This ultimate Ferrari road weapon also conquered the colonies. Steve Wilder began his Driver's Report by confessing how he had been unable to resist unleashing all 380 horses—and the Marchal air horn—in low gear on a hapless pair of "checkered cap collegiates" in an inno-

cent MG TD. The deed done, "we fled the scene at full throttle, rending the air with not-so-quiet thunder and leaving a faint trace of abused rubber on the concrete."

It was the Ferrari devil that made him do it. "A bit theatrical perhaps, but in a car which can do 0-60 in first gear alone, a car which roars from under 30 in fourth to a maximum way over two miles per minute, a car

which excites the eye of every beholder, well, in such a car as this, complete restraint is nearly impossible for us."

The reporter did settle down enough to provide some hard numbers. Price: $16,000. Wheelbase: 102 inches. Track: 57.5 inches front, 57.2 rear. Overall length: 188 inches; width 68; height 54. Wilder didn't weigh it, but the steering took 3.4 turns lock-to-lock, the fuel capacity was 29 U.S. gallons,

and the tire sizes were 6.50 × 16 on 5-inch rims. The rear-axle ratio was 3.44, which gave 24.4 mph per 1000 rpm in top gear.

Acceleration to 60 mph took 5.6 seconds; to 100 mph, 12.1 seconds. It turned the quarter-mile in 13.9, at which point the speed was an estimated 108 mph. Once again, these figures were "the fastest ever recorded" by the testing publication. Top speed

For the 400 Superamerica (*opposite page, top and lower left*), Ferrari abandoned the long-block Lampredi for a development of the Colombo V-12. The wheelbase was also down, to 95.3 inches, from the 410's 102.4. Pininfarina's Superfast series explored several themes, including an aero-inspired shape and hidden headlamps. The Superfast Series III (*above*) was shown at the 1962 Geneva Salon. A production 400 Superamerica that adopted Superfast styling (*opposite page, lower right*).

was not observed, but had the car pulled its 6500-rpm power peak in top (fourth) gear, that would have been 158.6 mph. Fuel consumption worked out to 11.8 mph.

All very commendably scientific. Then Wilder confesses: "Coming upon a large rotary, apparently undiscovered by the rest of the motoring public, we commenced making fast laps, followed by still faster ones... the Ferrari is a genuine understeerer, requiring more and more steering lock to maintain the same radius as the speed is raised. With the increase in lock is a corresponding climb in force required at the wheel rim. And then, when you really think you're second only to Fangio, another crack of the throttle will induce the rear wheels to start their slide to the outside in a smooth transition to a power-controlled final-oversteer. That's really living!"

Wilder also raved about the engine's "supple" low-speed manners: "We were able to use full throttle as low as 900 rpm, even in top gear." Ride quality was "firm, which endows it with a healthy sort of comfort." The superb build quality and "sumptuous" interior were appreciated, too. On the debit side, he noted that it was difficult to move off from rest smoothly because of the small, lightweight engine flywheel and the delicate, do-not-slip-me-at-all-costs triple-plate clutch. On rough New York City streets the steering would sometimes shimmy badly. Also, footroom was cramped, due to this big Lampredi engine being stuffed into a chassis really intended for the shorter Colombo block. And the gearshift pattern was still "backwards."

But none of the problems overshadowed the joys. "Quick and beautiful, and occasionally awkward, the 4.9 Super fast is like a woman; she demands something in return from the man who would enjoy the best she has to offer."

Three years after the 4.9 Superfast, in 1960, Farina followed up with Superfast II, then Superfast III and, in 1962, Superfast IV. By this time the glorious Lampredi engine, Grand Prix and Le Mans winner, was considered obsolete, and Ferrari's big-bore road cars were getting their power from a development of the Colombo design taken out to almost 4 liters.

But in 1964 there was a final car in the Big Bang series, the 500 Superfast. This again carried a "4.9" Lampredi long-block, although one redesigned with detachable cylinder heads (one of the main points of Lampredi's original was prevention of cylinder leakage by means of barrels screwed into the heads, aircraft-style). Horsepower appears to have been about the same as its ancestors, some authorities saying 360 and others 400, either number achieved at 6500 rpm. Something of a production run of this unique model ensued, amounting to three dozen cars up through 1966.

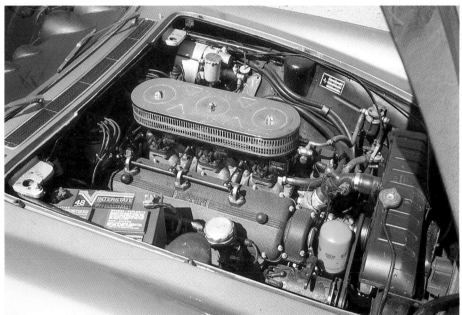

Then it really was time to go. By the mid-'60s the high-performance automotive scene had changed drastically, and a big, slow-turning, single-cam-per-bank powerplant must have seemed antediluvian even to Ferrari's most mature customers. When the *cavallino* again pranced forth in five-liter form, it would be as modern as tomorrow's starting grid.

(*Opposite page, from top*): This blue production 400 Superamerica borrowed much from the Superfast family; Built on the longer 400 Superamerica wheelbase, this Superfast was displayed at the Turin Show in 1962; A '62 Superfast VI with quad headlamps and sans fenderskirts; Another long-wheelbase Superamerica coupe, this one a '63. Note the different door handles and the absence of air exits behind the rear wheels. Pininfarina styled this 1962 GT coupe (*this page*) in the spirit of the 400 Superamericas.

# FERRARI ENGINES

## The Lampredi V-12

While Gioacchino Colombo was creating the first Ferrari V-12 engine, he had as his assistant a young technician named Aurelio Lampredi. Lampredi had only a technical-school education, but he had worked for Piaggio, the Italian aircraft firm that also made Vespa motor scooters, before joining the Ferrari organization. It was with the Maranello firm that he proved his engineering ability.

The Grand Prix formula at that time allowed supercharged engines of 1500 cc or naturally aspirated engines of 4500 cc. Colombo had designed the Ferrari V-12 to be a Roots-blown 1500 cc engine, quite likely with Ferrari's approval. Scuderia Ferrari,

in fact, had created a 1500-cc Roots-blown engine for Alfa Romeo in the late 1930s. That Alfa 158/9, though, was a straight eight.

In contrast to Colombo's plan for a new blown Ferrari 1500, Lampredi campaigned for larger displacement. He argued that he could get more power with less fuel consumption from an unblown 4500-cc V-12. Ferrari gave Lampredi the go-ahead to design the larger engine. This led to a rift between Lampredi and Colombo that caused Colombo to leave Ferrari in 1949 and return to Alfa Romeo.

Lampredi's new engine had much in common with Colombo's original V-12 beyond the obvious 60-degree Vee, single-overhead chain-driven camshafts, and inclined valves. But there were differences not so evident from a cursory look at the engines. Due to the displacement increase,

the bore centers of the Lampredi engine were 108 mm apart instead of 90 mm, as in the Colombo powerplant. This made the Lampredi "big block" V-12 27.5 inches long, four inches longer than the Colombo "small block" unit. A quick visual identification is the number of studs at the lower edge of the valve covers: six in the Colombo engine, seven in the Lampredi design.

Inside the Lampredi engine, wet cylinder barrels screwed into the heads, eliminating any possibility of gasket failure. Also, the offset between cylinder banks was 22 mm, reflecting the 1-mm increase in connecting-rod width. Inasmuch as Lampredi designed the engine for Grand Prix racing, there was no provision in the block for a starter; it was mounted in the lower left side of the clutch housing.

Hairpin valve springs were continued, as on the Colombo engines, but roller cam

followers were used from the beginning in the Lampredi design. Because the engine was not planned to be supercharged at any time, there were 12 intake ports for better breathing and, if needed, for individual port tuning.

Lubricating oil was fed to the main bearings through passages in the block on the Colombo small-block; on the Lampredi big-block, an outside, separate bolt-on pipe did the job.

Though it was designed for the 4.5-liter

During its five years of production, the Lampredi-designed V-12 was turned out in displacements ranging from 3.0-liters to 4.9-liters and in road and racing forms. Here is the 375 MM's 4.5-liter (*opposite page*) and the 4.1-powered 340 MM of 1951 (*above*).

Grand Prix formula, the first Lampredi V-12 was a 3.3-liter unit that appeared in the 1950 Mille Miglia in cars driven by Luigi Villoresi and Alberto Ascari. The same size V-12 then powered a Grand Prix car driven by Ascari at Spa-Francorchamps, Belgium.

The first road car to use the Lampredi big block was the 340 America, which was shown at the 1950 Paris Salon with a Carrozzeria Touring Barchetta body. The Lampredi engine had begun to appear in all manner of Ferraris by 1951. These included the 340 and 342 America; 340 Mexico and 340 Mille Miglia; 375 America and 375 Mille Miglia; and even a 250 Europa.

These early Europas were an exercise in marketing. Ferrari realized the need for export sales and he knew that America was a prime target for his cars. It was a

country with cheap gas and wide, long stretches of open road suited to a skillful driver in a fast car. Even more important, America was a country with lots of money.

By contrast, European roads didn't lend themselves to big engines in big cars with tall rear-axle gearing. The European market also suffered from high fuel prices and from high taxation based largely on engine displacement. Ferrari's answer was to build the same basic car—in this case the 250 Europa and 375 America—with a choice of engines: a 3-liter for Europe, a 4.5-liter for America. Both engines were of the big-block Lampredi design so the weight balance, installation, and appearance were virtually the same for each car.

For all practical purposes, the big-block Lampredi period ended at Ferrari after 1955, when Lampredi went to Fiat. During the five years of its existence, the Lampredi V-12 was produced in 3.0 liters (250 Europa); 3.3 liters (275 Sport and Grand Prix racers); 4.1 liters (340 Mexico, 340 Mille Miglia, 340 America, and Grand Prix racers); 4.5 liters (375 Mille Miglia and Grand Prix racers); and 4.9 liters (375 Plus and 410 Superamerica).

All 410 Superamericas, series I, II, and III, used the Lampredi V-12, while the 400 Superamerica had a 4-liter version of the Colombo engine.

The Lampredi big-block V-12 acquitted itself well in competition, winning Le Mans, the Mille Miglia, and the Carrera Panamericana. It didn't do as well at Indianapolis; Ascari's Lampredi-powered Ferrari was running in the middle of the Indy 500 field in 1952 when a collapsed right rear wheel put the car out of the race.

**Ferrari's Series III 410 Superamerica of 1959** (*opposite page*). **No more than 15 were built, all with bodies by Pininfarina. Note the vented metal sail panels. Under the hood was a 4.9-liter Lampredi with three 42 DCF Webers good for 400 horsepower at 6500 rpm** (*opposite page, bottom*). **Ferraris are commonly associated with the color red, but Pininfarina's touring cars, such as the King Leopold cabriolet** (*above*)**, were often a dignified blue or gray.**

# Chapter 9:

# The 250 GTs: Achieving Maturity as an Automaker

Every sports-car enthusiast has a vivid memory of the first Ferrari that made a personal impact. For the author it was the 250 GT Berlinetta "Tour de France," a stark competition coupe whose lean lines one day pierced his heart and staked him in his tracks like a butterfly on a pin.

The year was probably 1958; the occasion, the Sebring 12-hour race in Florida, where an adolescent who had only just learned to drive had gone to pay homage to the most exciting driving machines in the world. Some crazy fortune brought him to the expansive grounds of Harder Hall, the finest hotel in the area, where he was transfixed by the sight of not one, but five or six glistening *gran turismo* Ferraris strewn artfully across the manicured lawns under the royal palms. He wandered among them in a daze, feeling them weave a spell that would remain unbroken for more than 30 years. He didn't realize that at the time. All he knew was that he might not have learned much about driving yet, but here's what he wanted to be driving!

He was not alone. Born out of some mysterious, magical marriage of technology and taste, the race-bred coupes that Enzo Ferrari sent out into the world of the late '50s were seeds of automotive passion. The early Ferrari 250 GT was not a perfect Grand Touring car. But it was seminal.

For the factory, it marked a growing maturity. There had been a turbulent half-dozen years in which the fledgling manufacturer tried seemingly every type and style of car, restlessly seeking some true Ferrari form. That would continue, and there would still be cars that only marque specialists have heard of. Maranello also was turning out small numbers of highly desirable vehicles built around the big Lampredi engine, while racing, of course, brought its own developments. But this was the period when the GT car powered by the Colombo V-12 began to emerge as the definitive vehicle for enthusiasts keen to experience Ferrari performance in everyday driving.

The Colombo itself, from its initial capacity of 1.5-liters up through many progressively larger variations, had made Ferrari's reputation as an automaker. But it really wasn't until it reached a cubic capacity twice its original size that this brilliant powerplant earned its undying fame.

A good place to pick up the story of the 3-liter, or 250, series is with the 225 S, a 1952 model of 2.7-liters. This was built around another of the Colombo engines. The stroke remained at the 58.8 mm of the two-liter Tipo 166, while the bore diameter was opened out to 70 mm (2.76 inches) for an exact capacity of 2715.5 cc (165.7 cubic inches). So far, so familiar, but this time there were new cylinder heads featuring individual intake ports, 12 in all, for better breathing. They replaced heads with the original two-by-two siamese arrangement.

Additionally, the updated Colombo enjoyed the roller cam followers of its big sister, the Lampredi, for less mechanical friction; it retained Colombo's hairpin-type valve springs, however. Stated horsepower was 210 at 7200 rpm. About 20 cars were made, mostly bodied by Vignale. In the phrase of automotive historian Stanley Nowak, as a competition machine, the 225 S was "very fast and beautifully balanced."

Even as the 225 S was going out into the world, though, Ferrari was developing its successor. In the spring of 1952, one of these newly revised engines had its bore increased yet again, to 73 mm (2.874 inches) for a displacement of 2953.2 cc (180.2 cubic inches). That brought output to 230 horsepower at 7500. Note another rpm increase for this remarkable design. The compression ratio was up to 9.0:1, so gas was getting better, too.

One of the seven 225 S Vignale coupes received this engine and was entered in the Mille Miglia that year. Thanks to inspired driving by Giovanni Bracco, this first-ever Ferrari 250 won the "thousand-mile" event outright. It beat not only numerous Ferraris and other fast contenders, some with much bigger engines, but also a trio of 3-liter 300SL gullwing Mercedes-Benz factory prototypes. It was an enormously popular home victory and Ferrari had an instant classic automobile.

The follow-up was swift. Before 1952 was out, there was a 250 MM in production, the "MM" in honor of the Mille Miglia victory. However, this

was not an exact duplicate of Bracco's car. Available data suggests the engine was changed enough to give more horsepower, 240, but at lower rpm, 7200. The transmission, too, was different, being a fully-synchronized 4-speed instead of the prototype's 5-speed "crash-box." Wheelbase was a nimble 94.5 inches.

This proved a deservedly popular model, and Ferrari-watchers count between 31 and 36 made in 1952 and

1953. Some were open-cockpit roadsters—spyders in factory nomenclature—and others were competition coupes, or *berlinettas*. Both Alfredo Vignale and Pinin Farina worked their magic on these chassis.

The 250 MM is an obvious favorite of historian Nowak, an ardent Ferrari specialist who has owned, repaired, restored, sold, examined, and driven countless prancing horses. In a "salon" piece in the marque publication, *Caval-*

**Welcome to the machine that for a decade defined Ferrari performance and Ferrari style, the 250 GT. Powered by the Colombo V-12 in its enduring 3-liter displacement, the 250 GT held sway with racers and enthusiasts from its introduction in 1954 to its retirement in '64. It cemented the Ferrari mystique of a single car at home on the track and on the road. The 250 GT "Tour de France" (*above*) is a fine example of the *gran turismo*'s lithe, yet muscular character.**

*lino*, he writes lyrically of a drive through the rural lanes of Connecticut in a Vignale spyder:

"Driving a 250 MM is a rare treat. Like all Ferraris the heart of the car is the engine. Don't believe the stories of these cars as harsh, demanding, finicky, and unreliable beasts. They are pussycats. The Ferrari V-12 engine, even in racing tune with three 4-barrel Weber carburetors, is surprisingly tractable. They start at the push of the button and can be driven on the street with a minimum of fuss. Shifting is easier than on the earlier semi-synchromesh boxes but still can benefit from double clutching for smooth maximum speed down shifts. The power is more than ample and owners have reported a standing start quarter-mile time of 15 seconds flat. The ride is stiff but not inflexible and on American main roads it is truly comfortable. The excitement is in the roar of the V-12 engine—like ripping 50,000 sheets of calico—and in the challenge of mastering the extraordinary cornering power. I had the pleasure of driving the salon car on the back roads of Connecticut between Lime Rock and Sharon and it was an experience I will not forget: the firm ride, the vivid acceleration, the pinpoint steering and the noise—the glorious noise. This is a car that requires the utmost concentration to drive really well. It is this continuous challenge to your driving ability that heightens the overall effect. How fast can I make this machine go? Fantasy emerges as one pushes toward the limits of this car's capabilities. The road is between Florence and Bologna and the goal is Brescia. And you are Bracco—pressing harder and harder—trying to stay on that fine line that separates genius from madness."

Another 250 MM Vignale spyderman was Phil Hill, who campaigned his in California during 1953 and '54. *Road & Track* managed to talk him into a

The 250 MM of 1953 (*right*) was the competition counterpart to the 250 Europa touring car. Note its hood-mounted auxiliary windscreen, designed to protect the windshield from road debris. Both the 250 MM and the 250 Europa were adopted from the 250 S, which was the first Ferrari powered by the 3-liter Colombo engine. Giovanni Bracco won the '52 Mille Miglia in a 225 S powered by this engine, a victory commemorated by the MM suffix on the racer that followed.

130

performance test that second year. The stopwatch showed that this "2.9 Ferrari," as the magazine called it, "proved itself a better performer than the 4.1 coupe" it had tested the year before. Once again, a Ferrari delivered the best times and speeds the magazine had yet seen. Sixty miles per hour came up from rest in 5.1 seconds, 100 mph in 13.7, and the quarter-mile in 14.4. Top speed was actually measured for once, but due to short 4.25:1 gearing it was a disappointing 135 mph. The factory claim was 158; *Road & Track* reckoned a true 150 might be possible.

Such stunning performance did not come easily in 1954. "Gunning a Ferrari from a dead stop is always a tense business," the test explained, "for it requires perfect coordination to ob-

tain a perfect take off. Too much throttle creates rear wheel spin, too little and the engine stumbles and there is always the danger of dropping the clutch in too suddenly and wiping out vital portions of the rear axle assembly." Hill once demonstrated this last achievement at the start of a race.

The reporters believed the synchronized 4-speed was a definite improvement in Ferrari transmissions. They said it coupled much quicker, surer shifts with a reduction by more than half in shifting effort compared to the 340 of their prior experience. They also noted that the steering column no longer shook on rough roads. At top speed "the car held a true steady course and other than the telephone poles suddenly looking like a close-

coupled picket fence, there is no terrifying sensation of great speed." Braking power was even more impressive: "It is impossible to imagine the sensation. At 100 mph, a passenger slides forward in the snug fitting seat and cannot force himself backward. It seems impossible to be slowing at that rate...."

Clearly, Enzo Ferrari's little band of merry car crafters had been making great strides in mechanical civility. "The 2.9 seems more of a dual purpose car than rumor and speculation has established," wrote *Road & Track*'s reporters, obvious thoughts beginning to stir in their heads. "The 2.9 Ferrari rides firmly, steers a little heavily at low speeds (2.5 turns lock to lock) but is not one of those traffic 'beasts'...."

It seemed to the testers that the addition of a complete windshield and fiberglass top might make this car a completely acceptable dual purpose vehicle."

They were right. Dean Batchelor has recorded that at least two U.S. owners of *berlinetta*-bodied 250 MMs used theirs in everyday traffic—one owner put over 100,000 street miles on his.

With the world at his feet, turning out a car that everybody seemed to love, Enzo chose this moment to take a step backward. Despite its name, the next 250 to appear was not part of the successful new series at all. Ferrari's 250 Europa of 1953-54 was built on the longer, 110.2-inch-wheelbase chassis of the 375 America introduced

at same 1953 Paris show. The body was very similar, too. It even had the same engine as the America—not a Colombo, but a Lampredi with the downsized cylinder dimensions of 68 mm × 68 mm (2.68 inches) giving 2963.4 cc (180.8 cubic inches). Horsepower was a soft 200 at 6000 rpm. Clearly this was meant as a tax dodge for Europeans who wanted to be seen in the mighty 375 without paying stiff levies for the big-bore engine. The ploy was not a major commercial success, as the discerning Ferrarist soon realized that the heavy engine, low horsepower, and long wheelbase made this car a lifeless understeerer. Only about 18 250 Europas were produced.

Ferrari got back on track the next

Between 31 and 36 250 MMs were built before production ceased in 1953. Pininfarina's bodies were on all but one of the *berlinettas.* His taut lines and purity of form are evidenced in this example's strong face (*opposite page*) and in the tucked-in grace of its tail (*above*), all on a 94.5-inch wheelbase. Lots of power, little weight and a taut suspension made for a responsive *cavallino.* "This is a car that requires the utmost concentration to drive really well," wrote automotive historian and Ferrari authority Stanley Nowak after slicing up the back roads of Connecticut in one.

Vignale styled the 250 MM cabriolets (*above*). Its V-12 (*left*) is fitted with a trio of 4-barrel carburetors. One driver likened its roar to "ripping 50,000 sheets of calico." This cabriolet (*opposite page, top*) is a first-series 250 Europa GT, with the long-block Lampredi V-12 and a 110-inch wheelbase. Subsequent Europas had the 102.3-inch wheelbase and the Colombo short-block engine. By 1960, the 3-liter Colombo V-12 (*opposite page, bottom*) was pumping out 250 horsepower and redlined at 7400 rpm.

year. Although the 250 GT Europa of 1954-55 was an apparent successor to the porky 250 Europa, and is sometimes called the Series II Europa, it really was more in the spirit of the original 250 GT. It returned to the Colombo engine, still with the 73 mm × 58.8 mm dimensions that would become so well known in Ferrari lore, but tuned now for 220 horsepower at 7000 rpm. This, and the well-liked 4-speed transmission, were installed in Ferrari's new-design chassis. This

chassis used the mid-range 102.4-inch wheelbase, but now featured coil-spring front suspension and frame tubes that rose over the rear axle. All this added up to better performance and more satisfying handling, plus a better ride and roomier interior. Not surprisingly, production ran to numbers twice those of the "Series I" 250 Europa.

Incidentally, Ferrari's first use of the terminology GT, for *gran turismo*, was with the 250 GT Europa. The original purity of this expression has long since suffered corruption. But to enthusiasts of the '50s and '60s, "grand touring" meant a true dual-purpose sports car, one that genuinely

combined the best attributes of a racing and a luxury vehicle. A difficult blend to achieve, obviously, but a well-done GT was a machine enthusiasts yearned to drive hard and fast—not for just a few hours on a Sunday, but for long days over arduous routes. Ferrari had been learning how to build authentic *gran turismos* and was now fully justified in applying the mystic term to his *berlinettas*.

This development coincided with a shift of emphasis in international racing regulations. An outcry had arisen—not for the first time, not for the last—that the super-powerful sports-racing cars based on Grand Prix technology, including Ferrari's 375 Plus, had grown too fast. So racing authorities decided to bring about heavier, slower, theoretically safer cars by instituting a championship for dual-purpose GTs. This began in 1956. Ferrari was well prepared for the consequent surge in demand from privateer racers, for he and his favorite coachbuilders had been refining the 250 GT series concept right along.

In September 1956, one of these coupes gained first place in the Tour de France, a multi-stage timed endurance event that covered 3600 miles of open roads all around that country. The competition includes a variety of track races and hillclimbs, and even a drag race. This specialized contest was not in the mainstream of conventional racing, but Ferrari's turned out to be an important victory from the image standpoint: a GT that could do all that must indeed be a real GT!

Ferrari never officially assigned the event name to the car; his public took care of that for him. The line of high-performance, two-seater fastback coupes built from 1957 through 1959 came to be widely known as the 250 GT Berlinetta "Tour de France."

These TDF *berlinettas* wore a variety of sleek Farina-designed and Scaglietti-built aluminum bodies. Beneath the skin, almost everything was familiar to those who knew their Colombo-engined Ferraris. The engines themselves, though, were treated to numerous detail refinements. The most obvious difference was the pair of cylinder heads, which had reverted to the siamesed intake ports of the very first Colombo designs. This meant that instead of three four-barrel carburetors, the V-12 could wear only a trio of two-barrel Webers. Nonetheless, horsepower began at about 230 and during the car's production life rose to an alleged 280, always at 7000 rpm. The power claims were bolstered by the car's performance. The Tour de France won its namesake event again in 1957, and a large number of pure speed meets that year and afterwards.

Of course, the pace of technological development in racing rapidly makes obsolete even world-class equipment. Dual-purpose GTs enjoy longer lives as street machines, and there's evidence that Ferrari's TDF made a delicious, if demanding, road car.

Batchelor has this to say in his book, *FERRARI The Early Berlinettas & Competition Coupes*: "Although built for competition, these 250 GT *berlinettas* make

ideal touring cars if one could stand the possibility of damage to the relatively fragile aluminum body. Careless door opening in parking lots which does minor damage to a steel body, will do far more to an aluminum body, and with only minimal bumpers, the front and rear are virtually unprotected as well.

"If the owner is willing to risk this aggravation the 1956-1959 long wheelbase *berlinettas* are some of the most tractable and most enjoyable Ferraris to drive of all the now accepted 'classic' Ferrari designs."

*Sports Cars Illustrated*'s 1959 view of the 250 GT Berlinetta Tour de France was slightly less sanguine. Perhaps because he simultaneously tested a 250 California roadster—a similar but distinctly more civilized Ferrari— Steve Wilder was reluctant to describe the 250 GT Berlinetta as an ideal daily driver. "Today's competition sports cars are no more suitable for shopping trips than a Caterpillar tractor," is the way he put it.

Well, they were not intended for "shopping trips." In fact, this particular race-bred GT survived Greater New York traffic surprisingly well— even when Wilder mistakenly started off his test in third gear. The magnificent V-12 simply pulled the car smoothly and uncomplainingly, if a bit sluggishly. Only when Wilder noticed the tach showing a mere 2000 rpm at 40 mph did he realize that this was a conventional transmission, one without the reversed shift pattern of the previous Ferrari he'd sampled. He was embarrassed, but impressed: "What manner of car is this Gran Turismo that it can be so docile despite its violent Grand Prix lineage?"

Like so many of his colleagues, Wilder had no end of praise for the Ferrari V-12. "Ferrari Automobili seem to do a singularly fine job on the engine above all other components," he wrote. "The fabled plug changes of early models are now a thing of the past, and it is no longer necessary to

A first-place finish in the 1956 Tour de France long-distance competition by a 250 GT earned subsequent 250 GT coupes the TDF label. Most 250 GT TDFs had Pininfarina bodies, but this '57 (*both pages*) wears coachwork by Zagato. It shared the other cars' Colombo V-12, with its siamesed intake ports (*opposite page, lower right*) that dictated a trio of two-barrel Webers instead of three four-barrel carburetors.

carry twelve spare spark plugs, ready to be changed as soon as the city limits are reached." And, "How rare and refreshing...to find this ex-racing engine turned into a sweet-tempered, responsive engine for touring. All this and four horses for every three cubic inches."

But, he added, "Tractable engines do not by themselves make tractable cars...." His complaints about those other components were numerous: a taller driver couldn't find a comfortable seating position; the seat itself wasn't very supportive; the beautiful steering wheel was set so high that its wood rim blocked the view of the front of the car. The clutch also was touchy, requiring considerable finesse to engage properly. And braking was disappointing, both in terms of stopping power and in the way the big drums seemed to set up a wiggle through the steering wheel. Finally,

the steering quality was "frankly disappointing," for it was so heavy and stiff that "the torque required put blisters on our hands." There was also play in the steering mechanism, but the tester did mention that this car had seen many hard miles on the race track.

Probably it was all the racing that caused the clutch to slip if too much power went through it. That, plus taller gearing, seems to have made the timed acceleration runs a little worse than those of the California roadster. Half full of fuel, but with nobody aboard, the Berlinetta scaled 2520 pounds, which was exactly 200 pounds lighter than the steel-bodied street car. However, the aluminum racing coupe was six-tenths of a second slower to 60 mph, at 7.8 seconds. It was a half-second slower in the quarter-mile, at 16.1, though at the end it was traveling 100 mph, three

mph faster than the street car. The magazine found no place to measure top speed, but the car was geared for 143 mph at its 7000 rpm redline. The California's tighter gearing gave 125 at the same rpm.

Ferrari's speedometer calibration proved to be wildly off, by the way, showing 60 mph at a true timed speed of 51, and indicating 100 at a mere 85. Other interesting specs: compression ratio, 9.57:1; horsepower, 260 at 7000 rpm (the red line); torque, 195 pounds/feet at 5000 rpm. But the set idle speed was only 900 rpm. The steering took a moderate three turns lock-to-lock. The tire sizes were 6.00 × 16—narrow tires on a car with a narrow track of only 53 inches. Overall length was 173 inches; width, 65; height, 55. The gas-tank capacity was 37 U.S. gallons. As tested against the stopwatch, the car carried 2840 pounds, distributed 49.3 percent

front/50.7 percent rear.

On the road, the Berlinetta's ride was on the hard side, and *Sports Cars Illustrated*'s Wilder accepted that as being in the nature of the beast. At a place it was made for, the Lime Rock race course, he found the handling to be so responsive as to be almost twitchy. "The Berlinetta is set up for racing, and no matter how well camouflaged their bodies nor how docile their engines, racing cars, like freedom, demand constant vigilance to ensure that they don't get away from you."

Not among the most famous Ferraris, the so-called 250 GT Boano/Ellena of 1956-58 was nonetheless a significant step in the civilization of Enzo's grand tourers. Reminiscent of the contemporary Ford Thunderbird, this cabriolet (*this page*) shows some of the styling adopted by subsequent 250 GTs, like this 1960 coupe (*opposite page*).

He did love the gearbox and its short shift lever, which was topped by a black plastic knob with delicate little finger-flutes. "The feel of the shift lever in action too is without peer... the entire motion feels superbly precise. It's a joy to shift, especially since all four speeds have Porsche-type synchromesh."

All in all, the assessment was this: "Briefly, we thought the bodywork, the engine and gearbox were great, and that the handling was good; but that the steering as well as the brakes and seating were awful....Our criticism of the Ferrari 250 GT is that it seems to be still too much a special; as it were, a pseudo-road car designed to cash in on the Grand Prix reputation. It's a lovely reputation, but in some respects we can't say the same for the car."

As the report pointed out, the Sports Car Club of America also concluded that Ferrari's 250 GT was pri-

marily a competition design. The club classed it with the 550 Porsche Spyder and D-type Jaguar as non-production for racing purposes. However, the owner of the test car, George Arents, kept the *gran turismo* faith, proving that this really was a multi-mission machine by running the same car in races, on cross-country trips, and in New York City traffic. "It's obvious, then," acknowledged *Sports Car Illustrated*, "that as dual-purpose sports cars, the Ferrari 250s are a success."

Had the magazine sampled this veritable supercar on the sorts of wide-open roads for which it was conceived, instead of thinking about taking it shopping, it's likely the overall tone of the report would have been more, well, excited.

For the Ferrari Tour de France was an exciting car in its day. To many, TDF meant "GT." For evidence, search no farther than the first Ford Mustang fastback. It is impossible to look

at this 1964 Detroit product and fail to see the lines drawn half-a-dozen years earlier in Pinin Farina's studio. It's just as inconceivable that anyone could gaze at this wondrous *gran turismo* and not long to go speeding off in it, over marvelous roads to somewhere splendid, with someone very, very nice alongside. The GT dream.

The trouble with dreams, of course, is that they often clash with reality. Not even for hardcore driving enthusiasts can every journey be a personal Mille Miglia, and in many people the vein of enthusiasm for arduous motoring is thin. Like every manufacturer, Ferrari had to serve his market as it came. He soon recognized that for every customer eager to race about in a competition-ready *berlinetta*, there were many potential buyers unwilling to part with their money for an automobile that reminded them of the other meaning of the Italian root word, *berlina*: "pillory." As Webster's

puts it, a pillory is "a device for publicly punishing offenders."

So, as he had done with his early "Inters," and as he was doing at the same time with his big, Lampredi-engined cars, Enzo expanded his 3-liter product line to include models of wider appeal. Inevitably, in the pro-

They weren't the fastest Ferraris of their era, but the 250 GT California Spyder, Cabriolet, and Coupe are among the most timelessly stylish *cavallinos* of all. This Spyder California (*both pages*) is a '57 one-off displaying the same Pininfarina lines of its 1958-62 namesakes. Though built on a wheelbase just slightly longer than that adopted in 1960, the black cabriolet retains the steel body and superb proportions that qualified the 250 GT Spyder among the sweetest driving and most desirable of Ferraris.

cess, the hard-muscled meaning of GT gradually softened.

The so-called 250 GT Boano/Ellena was the first of these more civilized sportsters. Built from 1956 through 1958, there were some 130 cars in two series, thus proving the concept's popularity. It was a very smooth-lined, entirely rational-looking road car originally designed by Pinin Farina. Farina ceded production to Carrozzeria Boano due to plant incapacity. Mario Boano later handed his firm over to his son-in-law, Ezio Ellena.

The Boano/Ellena was never counted among the most famous Ferraris, but historians note that it introduced such important refinements as bigger brakes and a steering system by ZF of Germany. Horsepower ranged from 220 to 240 at 7000 rpm, on compressions that rose from 8.5:1 to 8.8:1. The transmission was always a 4-speed, although some cars came with the curious "backwards" shift pattern. All were built on the 102.4-inch chassis with front coil springs.

Ferrari followed this concept to its logical next step, or steps, with his 250 GT California Spyder, Cabriolet, and Coupe. Cloaked in timelessly sleek Farina styling themes, all were primarily intended for road use, although some owners did prove the Spyder to be a useful weekend warrior. It was, after all, mechanically very similar to the Tour de France. The Spyder, Cabriolet, and Coupe all had heavy steel bodywork, however, in keeping with their highway orientation.

There were numerous detail changes and refinements to these lovely cars during their production lives. The Spyder moved to a shorter, 94.5-inch wheelbase, for example, and all three received engine and styling

variations. This group of cars was the closest Ferrari had yet come to mass production, with the total output eventually topping 600.

They were popular because they were by far the sweetest Ferraris yet for everyday street driving. In its 1960 road test of a 250 GT Coupe, *Road & Track* could find no fault. "In fact, about the only real objection we could find is its price: we can't afford it."

Buying one that year cost an American $12,600. This delivered a Ferrari that *Road & Track* found "not only comfortable, responsive without being temperamental, and agile, but also one of the easiest cars to handle we've ever driven." Timed performance was brisk, with 0-60 mph achieved in 7.1 seconds, and the quarter in 15.5 at 94, Top speed was not tested, but the manufacturer quoted a believable 126. The steel-bodied Coupe scaled 2700 pounds without fuel; it was tested weighing 3020, distributed 49 percent front/51 percent rear. Fuel consumption ranged from 13 mpg to 16 mpg.

One of the very few negative remarks concerned the optional electrically-operated overdrive fitted to the test car. It lowered engine rpm by a substantial 22 percent for more re-

Coexisting with the 250 GT Spyder California in the late '50s and early '60s was the more stolid-looking 250 GT Cabriolet (*above*). Where the Spyder California evolved from competition berlinettas, Ferrari provided this roadster with such street-oriented amenities as an upright windshield to increase cabin space. Both open versions of the 250 GT shared the 3-liter Colombo V-12, though the California Spyder had more horsepower, about 280 versus 260. The influential Bona/Ellena 250 GT in another view (*opposite page*).

laxed highway cruising, but the testers were reluctant to use it—and rec-
ommended against buying it—because
it had earned a reputation for unreli-
ability.

The test car still had drum brakes,
which were judged "adequate." But
the magazine also briefly tried a brand
new example with Dunlop discs, and
termed them "just great."

Ferrari made further use of the
102.4-inch wheelbase chassis and 3-
liter engine for the 250 GT 2+2, sometimes also known as the 250 GTE.
Here continued the debasement of the
"GT" terminology, for this was by no
stretch of the imagination a raceable
car—unless the race refers to that for
sales.

Ferrari saw firms such as Maserati
and Aston Martin as rivals, and their
customers were happily buying
models with a tiny rear seat that
would accommodate two passengers
on at least an occasional basis. To
make room for the additional legs in
the 250 GT 2+2, the Colombo engine
was moved forward something over
half a foot—published figures range
from 6.5 inches to 12 inches. And
Pinin Farina drew up a steel bodyshell
that gracefully enclosed all the heads
without really looking like a sedan.

A 250 GT 2+2 was the subject of a
1960 road test carried out in Europe
and published in *Sports Cars Illustrated*.
The car had a curb weight of 3280
pounds, showed a top speed of 136
mph, and achieved 14-16 mpg. Exact
acceleration numbers were not
printed. But from the description of
the reporter, Jesse Alexander, here
was a Ferrari smoother, quieter, and
more comfortable than any before,
yet it was still a Ferrari—very exciting
to drive.

"The responsiveness of the V-12 is
thrilling," Alexander wrote. He found
it "sensational" to plant his right foot
at 5000 rpm in second gear and feel
"the insane way the car moves out."
Again Ferrari had a hit. Three series of
these 2+2s were offered and more
than 900 were sold.

Ferrari's first production 4-seater was the
250 GT 2+2 of 1960-63, sometimes also
known as the 250 GTE (*right*). Based on the
2-place 250 GT Coupe, the GTE had its
Colombo V-12 moved forward about six
inches to make room for two supplemental
rear seats. Pininfarina fashioned a new body
that didn't betray the car's grand touring
heritage and it shared the 240-horsepower
engine from the 250 GT Coupe.

All of these "civilized" 250s were worthy road cars and deservedly popular. They obviously helped Enzo pay a lot of his racing bills. But business is one thing, art another. In the minds of most Ferrari fans, the one version of this first 3-liter, "long-wheelbase" Ferrari that will live forever in the popular fancy is still the true Grand Tourer—the racing-oriented/road-usable 250 GT Berlinetta Tour de France.

Another view of the '57 250 TDF Zagato coupe (*above*). This car does not have the convex roof bulges or uncovered headlights of previous Zagato coupes, but it does share with many other Tour de France Ferraris a history of competition victories.

# Chapter 10:

# SWB:
# The Last True GT

Ferrari's brochure for its "250 granturismo berlinetta" of 1959 to 1962 was a spare, four-page publication that described the exquisite coupe in these few words:

"The design of this new Berlinetta by Pininfarina had as the main object a streamlined body particularly suited for high speeds. We also took into account the requirements of comfort, so that this can be used as a Granturismo as well as for racing. It provides a sufficient space for luggage, has a heating system, doors giving easy access, comfortable seats, there is plenty of visibility. The 250 GT Berlinetta, therefore, can be used both for touring and racing without any particular modifications."

The brochure text was translated from the Italian by Richard F. Merritt in his *FERRARI: Brochures and Sales Literature-a Source Book*. The appeal of the car itself needed no translation. It was red hot in any language.

This was the Ferrari that would become known to history as the SWB, for Short Wheelbase Berlinetta. It was a direct development of the beloved 250 GT Berlinetta Tour de France. But it was even better: tighter, lighter, faster, prettier.

It appeared in prototype form at the Le Mans race of 1959. Though built on the now-familiar GT chassis with its 102.4-inch wheelbase, the body represented a new direction by Pininfarina (who had legally changed his name from Battista "Pinin" Farina in 1958). The shape wasn't particularly stream-

lined, despite the brochure's claim. Uncovered headlights, a blunter "face," and a glassier cockpit did make it seem like a more practical everyday car than the Tour de France, however.

And it was indeed fast on the track. The two cars entered in the Le Mans 24-hour enduro of '59 finished 4th and 6th overall, though a TDF finished third. Later that year, one of the new models asserted itself—and incidentally proved its highway suitability—by winning Ferrari's fourth consecutive Tour de France event.

Only six or seven of the 102.4-inch wheelbase cars were built. They are now known as an interim design because that same October, Ferrari and Pininfarina presented the first of the definitive SWB cars at the Paris auto show.

Here was a masterpiece. Its form remains aesthetically simple, clean, and balanced, even after 30 years. The lines are reminiscent of Farina's forward-thrusting "shark-mouth" concept seen a few years earlier on many of the 375 models. But these are much more refined, an uncanny combination of aggression with restraint that expressed perfectly the new GT's dual purpose.

Its wheelbase had been shortened by 7.9 inches, to 94.5. This achieved the twin benefits of more agile handling and less overall weight. Although the chassis itself was essentially Ferrari's 12-year-old conventional twin-tube design, it did exhibit more of the welded-in superstructure the factory

had begun incorporating to stiffen the chassis/body package.

The "interim" prototype and the SWB were also the first street cars from the conservative house of the prancing horse to benefit from two significant bits of advanced technology: Tubular shock absorbers replaced the old lever-type shocks; and Ferrari finally installed 4-wheel disc brakes. The brakes were the Dunlop items that were then sweeping the European industry. There also was a limited-slip differential.

Under the SWB's lightweight, lift-off aluminum hood was basically the old Colombo V-12 in its 2953-cc, 73 mm × 58.8 mm form. It had been updated significantly, however, with new cylinder heads on a suitably revised block casting. The heads were now held down by four studs per cylinder, rather than three, for more secure pressure sealing. Space was found for the extra fastener by switching from the traditional hairpin-type valve springs to coils, which also improved valve control.

These new heads had individual intake ports for better breathing. It was an arrangement seen on an earlier 250 model, but the new heads themselves were taken from the contemporary Testa Rossa sports-racing car. Using individual intake ports caused the spark plugs to be moved to the outsides of the heads. This improved access to the plugs, and some believe it also created superior combustion-chamber geometry.

All SWBs came from the factory
with only three carburetors, though
the 12-port heads were capable of taking six two-barrel Webers, as on the
Testa Rossa. Many SWBs were later
converted to the six Webers.

Despite Ferrari's brochure boast
about a single, dual-purpose GT,
almost from the start there were two
quite different versions of the new
"250 granturismo berlinetta." One,
with all-aluminum bodywork, was in-

tended primarily for racing. Its more
highly tuned engine had a compression ratio of 9.5:1. Some sources credit
it with as much as 295 horsepower,
though 280 is the figure more commonly seen.

The second variant was called the Lusso by the factory, a word that means "luxury" and which more commonly applies to a different car that wouldn't appear until 1963. The engine of this softer SWB was basically the same as its racier sibling's, but had a bit lower compression, smaller carbs, different cams, a quieter exhaust system, and lacked perhaps 40 horsepower.

This Lusso came paneled mainly in

The competition-oriented 250 GT introduced in 1959 (*above*) used a 94.5-inch wheelbase six inches shorter than its Tour de France predecessor's. The resulting performance gains and ready-to-pounce stance made for a coveted race-winning Ferrari *gran turismo* known as the Short Wheelbase Berlinetta.

steel, but with aluminum hood, doors, and trunklid. There was glass in the side windows, rather than plastic, and chrome trim generally appeared in places like the hood-scoop opening. Sound and heat insulation were included, as well as a more sumptuous interior. To further deaden noise, the gearbox case was cast iron, instead of aluminum. Ferrari authority Dean Batchelor estimates these modifications added about 100 pounds to the curb weight. To round out the package, the suspension springs and shocks were softer, and the brakes had more servo assistance. Even the gas tank was smaller in an attempt to increase luggage space.

The Lusso specification obviously made for a more durable, more docile highway vehicle with a more amiable personality. Nothing prevented one version from "invading" the other's sphere, however, and such crossover usages were common. Short of changing the main body panels to aluminum, the owner of a street SWB could create a virtual race-ready car by bolting on all the hard-core competition hardware. Many did so.

Ferrari itself produced a short run of 22 supertuned SWBs for the 1961 GT racing season. They were known as "SEFAC hot rods"—SEFAC being the initials of the company's formal name—and were even more specialized for track work than the original competition version. The SEFAC cars packed more power at the top end, an improvement that probably is the source of the 295-horsepower figure. They also had stiffer suspension settings, larger gas tanks, fatter rear tires, and a distinct tail-up stance to improve high-speed aerodynamic stability.

How the SWB was received by the automotive world is reflected in a 1960 report by John Bolster in the British weekly, *Autosport*.

"The Berlinetta is a superb competition car, but it is almost ideal for fast touring," Bolster wrote. "Its small size is a great advantage.... This is an outstandingly easy car to drive and the short wheelbase renders it noticeably handier on corners...one can remain totally relaxed while really sliding through the bends."

His test car was a steel-bodied, 240-

horsepower version, and he found the engine a sheer delight. "It is ... amazingly smooth for such an efficient piece of machinery, and just as flexible as the average touring engine." He found a real advantage in having so many pistons: "The 12-cylinder engine, even when really 'hot', is smooth enough to render this one of the fastest and most desirable of road cars."

That same year, the American magazine *Sports Cars Illustrated* conducted a Road Research Report on an all-aluminum car. After some 1200 miles on both track and road, the testers were agog over the 280-horse engine: "Right now we want to establish, without equivocation, that it's powered by the greatest automotive engine in the world today. There's no en-

gine that begins to compare with it, that deserves mention in the same breath with the Ferrari V12."

Just why did they love it so? Let them count the ways. First and foremost, there was the splendid music. "When it's running this ultimate engine is exhilarating, electrifying. Twelve pistons, 24 valves and roller-tipped rockers, two cams, a few yards of chain and an assortment of pumps combine to produce the most wonderful racket ever to reverberate in an eager enthusiast's eardrums....[a] soul-stirring cacophony...."

*Sports Cars Illustrated* also admired the Colombo V-12's staying power as a class-leading powerplant after 13 years of production. It noted that the same basic engine was used in a vari-

ety of Ferraris, and marveled that it could win races and also power "a silky-smooth, Lincoln-Continentalesque touring coupe." It had "astounding versatility" that combined a "wild" state of tune with perfect manners. The editors drove it in dense city traffic and not once did it overheat or foul its spark plugs as many super-tuned engines of the day would have. Yet,

Most SWB bodies were steel with aluminum doors, hood, and trunklid (*opposite page*). Popular with both enthusiasts and racers, this true dual-purpose GT came in both left- and right-hand-drive versions. Its 240-horsepower 3-liter Colombo V-12 (*above*) had cylinder heads taken from the contemporary Testa Rossa sports-racing car. This one has the factory tri-carb setup, but the 12-port heads were capable of taking six two-barrel Webers.

they found it ready at any instant to "project you so violently into another speed spectrum that you have to re-orient yourself completely."

An acceleration graph showed the SWB reaching 60 mph in a bit less than seven seconds. It covered the quarter-mile in under 15 seconds at a shade below 100 mph. Top speed was an estimated but entirely believable 145 mph with a rear axle ratio of 4.00:1. This car tipped the scales at 2380 pounds with its 31-gallon fuel tank full; 54.5 percent of its weight was carried by the rear tires. Fuel economy ranged between 10 and 16 mpg, giving a generous maximum range of 400 miles. The price as listed by Luigi

Chinetti Motors, the American importer, was an even $14,000.

Despite the rearward weight bias, cornering behavior on the skid pad was resolute understeer that simply increased the faster the circle was driven. Yet, said *Sports Cars Illustrated*, "the Ferrari didn't have the logy, slow response that often accompanies this kind of understeer. With quick steering and an embarrassing amount of power available the car was ready at any instant to have its radius tightened/opened or speed lowered/raised, at a rate of transition just as fast as you like."

As for that steering, "Ease and precision...was a great improvement

over last year's cars, making the latest version sheer delight to handle. The steering's never hypersensitive, but has just enough self-centering action and reversibility to give you a direct wire to those all-important front tire contact patches." The car was "always working with you, offering you the tools with which to do the job."

It also demonstrated Enzo's progress with suspensions. Although the springs and shocks were stiff, the ride was comfortable, "softer, more flexible, deeper-kneed" and more "modern" than earlier Ferraris, *Sports Cars Illustrated* said. Despite the short wheelbase, the test car was notably free of pitching. It did heel over when corner-

ing, however, which slowed progress through S-bends taken at racing speed. The disc brakes were judged good, though there was some caliper flex and the pedal was heavy.

The cabin was larger than the TDF's, and though the testers found plenty of head room, larger people still felt their legs cramped for space. Luggage volume was almost entirely eaten up by the larger fuel tank, and cockpit ventilation remained only "adequate." As for outward visibility, "Slim (1¾-inch) corner pillars, the high roof line and sloping hood account for a great improvement in vision forward. There's no more 'Berlinetta Hunch' from peering through the old shallow windshield."

For all its dynamic virtues, the SWB wasn't sensational in the fit-and-finish department. "Pininfarina's design is executed by light-body expert Scaglietti, in Modena, which produces a coupe of remarkable lightness but not of impressive durability," wrote *Sports Cars Illustrated*. Though the doors were ill-fitting, "the bodywork is generally well-done, and the interior is especially successful in avoiding the 'assembled' look that has always been typical of the G.T. Ferrari. It looks, and feels, much more as if it was designed as a whole and not just added later to give the driver someplace to sit."

As it turned out, the SWB was one of the higher-volume Ferrari supercars. Historians believe 163 were built during its 1959-1962 production run.

Not all were built alike. There were constant restless evolutionary changes to the body line, including alterations to the grill, cowl, roof, trunk, window shape and operation, vent windows, rain gutters, side outlet vents, side-

Ferrari offered an SWB with all-aluminum bodywork and a hotter engine of around 280 horsepower. But they couldn't match a "SEFAC hot rod" (*both pages*). This is one of 22 supertuned SEFAC SWBs produced for the '61 racing season. It had 295 horsepower, better aerodynamics, a stiffer suspension, larger gas tanks, and fatter rear tires. SEFAC was an acronym for Ferrari's formal company name.

mounted turn signal repeaters, gas cap position, external brake ducts, even the jacking points. Ken Gross, in his book *Ferrari 250GT, The definitive road-race car*, says some of these short-wheelbase cars were even built on a slightly longer wheelbase!

Given two, perhaps three, variants of the one basic design, defending the SWB as a paragon of the *gran turismo* ethic would be walking a very fine line. The "SEFAC hot rods" in particular were raspy things, just barely driveable on the street and satisfactory only if the driver worked to keep the rpm above 4500.

On the track, of course, a race-tuned SWB would eat a standard street model alive. Yet for all the qualifications that must be attached to the claim, this great and well-loved Ferrari remains one of the few genuine Grand Touring cars—in the classic, dual-purpose sense—that anyone ever built. And it was the last ever built by Ferrari. From this point on, the company's products became ever more specialized, designed for road *or* track, not both.

Ferrari's "250 granturismo berlinetta" SWB thus represents a sort of automotive Camelot, one brief and shining moment when fantasy merged with glorious reality.

Ferrari's race-bred SEFAC hot rods had a nose-down attitude to improve high-speed stability. This factory-raced car (*above*) recorded the fastest time by a 250 GT SWB at Le Mans in 1961. The SWBs were the best-balanced sports cars of their time and the SEFAC was their ultimate expression. Produced from 1959-62, the SWB was the last true dual-purpose Ferrari. From this point on, the company's cars would be designed for road *or* track, not for both.

# Chapter 11:

# GTO:
# Enzo's Masterpiece?

Auto racing's unwritten rule is that its *written* rules are not there to be broken, but to be beaten. Most manufacturers who make an end-run around a regulation aim to win races by it. That's what Ferrari did in 1962, when he made the GTO out of the SWB. In the process, he created an automotive masterpiece. If there's a quintessential Ferrari, it could well be this sensational racing coupe.

GTO stands for Gran Turismo Omologato, and the last word means "homologated." In racing parlance, a homologated car is one recognized by the relevant regulating body as a production-line vehicle. The manufacturer must prepare an official document describing the car in detail and certifying that a certain number of identical examples have been produced as street cars for sale to the public. At each competition where these rules apply, race inspectors compare every entry with the homologation papers. The purpose is to prevent a manufacturer from slipping a modified racer into a field of standard cars.

International racing's regulatory body, the FIA, made a change in 1962 that put unprecedented pressure on manufacturers to increase the performance of their fastest production cars. It decreed that the World Manufacturers Championship was to be contested with homologated Grand Touring cars. Enzo Ferrari knew that meant the pace of GT development would be stepped up, and that even his SWB "SEFAC hot rods" were going to

have to go faster.

So he began hopping up the hot rods. The main problem was aerodynamic. The SWB's design was practical enough on the road; few, if any, journalists ever found a place on the highways of the early '60s to safely measure its top speed. But on the race track, the bluff-nosed *berlinetta* ran into a wall of air at about 155 mph.

It so happened that the FIA's new homologation rules allowed an evolutionary variation in body style. As would any good racer, Enzo Ferrari saw his loophole: He could evolve a whole new body shape.

Aerodynamic experiments with the SWB had begun as early as 1960, when at least two SWB chassis were streamlined with new sheetmetal—and in some cases with chicken-wire covered in plaster. Actual race testing began at Le Mans in 1961, when a body shape taken from Pininfarina's streamlined-looking 400 Superamerica was built onto an SWB chassis. The car didn't finish the 24-hour, but the following February at Daytona, Stirling Moss brought it home fourth overall in a three-hour sprint.

The shape still wasn't right, however. It suffered too much of the front-end aerodynamic lift that had troubled drivers of the Pininfarina SWBs at very high speed.

Even before the Daytona sprint, Ferrari had decided to bring the job in-house, to take the styling out of the hands of the stylists. The project was conducted under the more scientific

direction of Ingegnere Giotto Bizzarrini, who had access to a wind tunnel at his alma mater, the University of Pisa. The nose of the new GT body was lowered and sharpened still further, and its tail was raised and cut off like the back of a boat-tail bullet. Though still very rounded, the body foreshadowed the "racer's wedge" profile that would emerge later in the decade to reshape virtually every form of racing.

Underneath the sleek new skin remained the basic SWB chassis. It retained the same 94.5-inch wheelbase and wishbone-front/beam-rear suspension, albeit with certain evolutionary improvements. Some of the frame tubing was lighter, but there was more of it, thus forming a very rigid structure that was nearly a space frame. Some suspension and body-mounting points were altered. A new, Porsche-patent, all-synchro 5-speed gearbox replaced the 4-speed. And a full-out, six-carburetor, dry-sump Testa Rossa racing engine was plugged in. This superb V-12 was state-of-the-Ferrari art. Its block was cast of a new aluminum alloy and it featured such goodies as magnesium cam covers. Almost every detail in this "Grand Touring" machine represented front-rank Grand Prix technology.

In one respect, however, Bizzarrini wasn't permitted to go as far as he wanted. Instead of an all-independent rear suspension, as used on other Ferrari racers by this time, the traditional live axle was retained. This was less a

scientific move than a political one: The factory had to be able to stand in front of the FIA and claim this substantially new car was merely a variant of the SWB.

Ferrari succeeded in this smooth ploy. He had no intention of producing 100 examples of the sophisticated, expensive new racer, even though that was then the requirement for its homologation. The FIA nonetheless agreed to list the new car as a production GT on grounds that it was nothing but an "evolution" of the SWB, and there were already more than 100 of those in existence.

But what to call it? Carrying over the designation "SWB" wouldn't do because everybody knew this was really a new vehicle. Historians tell different tales, but apparently on a piece of paper one day the car was referred to as "GT-O," to mean it was a GT that now was officially *omologato*. The press picked that up, it stuck, and as with the Tour de France years earlier, Ferrari's public had once again named one of its cars.

The first 250 GTO was revealed to the world in February 1962, at Ferrari's annual press conference and open house. Invitees considered these

fetes among the great and glamorous events of the journalistic year. They were held at the Maranello factory to display racing hardware for the coming season. There, sharing the spotlight with all of the new pure-racing models, including the open-wheeled Formula 1, was the GTO. Such showcasing was a strong clue that Ferrari didn't consider this a dual-purpose car.

Further proof of Ferrari's intentions was the absence of a provision for bumpers, and the lack of cockpit insulation. The side windows were sliding plastic panes. The backlight was plastic, too. A bulky battery, a

frame brace, and an oil tank that quickly grew hot trespassed on passenger space. There was room for a spare wheel in the trunk, but only just barely for that, and there was no hope of cramming in anything else. No air filter covered the lovely long row of Weber carburetors, though sketchy mufflers were fitted to the graceful, free-flowing exhaust system.

The GTO clearly was no everyday highway machine. But what a splendid driving machine!

Though wider and longer, its body was significantly lower and weighed less than the all-aluminum SWBs. The GTO had much better aerodynamic penetration, and its full-race engine screamed out even more power at higher rpm. Figures as great as 310 at 7500 have been given for horsepower, and it is said the racing rev limit was 8500. Such data are to be taken with as much salt as any other Ferrari number of the times, but suffice it to say the GTO was significantly faster than the SWB around corners and out of them, and a well-tuned example might poke through 170 mph on a long straight.

Handling was better, too. Part of the credit went to the superior aero-

No *cavallino* is today more desired than the 250 GTO (*above*). Voluptuous, uncompromising, and very fast, it's the last of Ferrari's front-engine competition cars. Only about 39 were produced from 1962-64. The name stems from its role as a GT that's *omologato*—homologated—or sanctioned for racing. Thus, GTO.

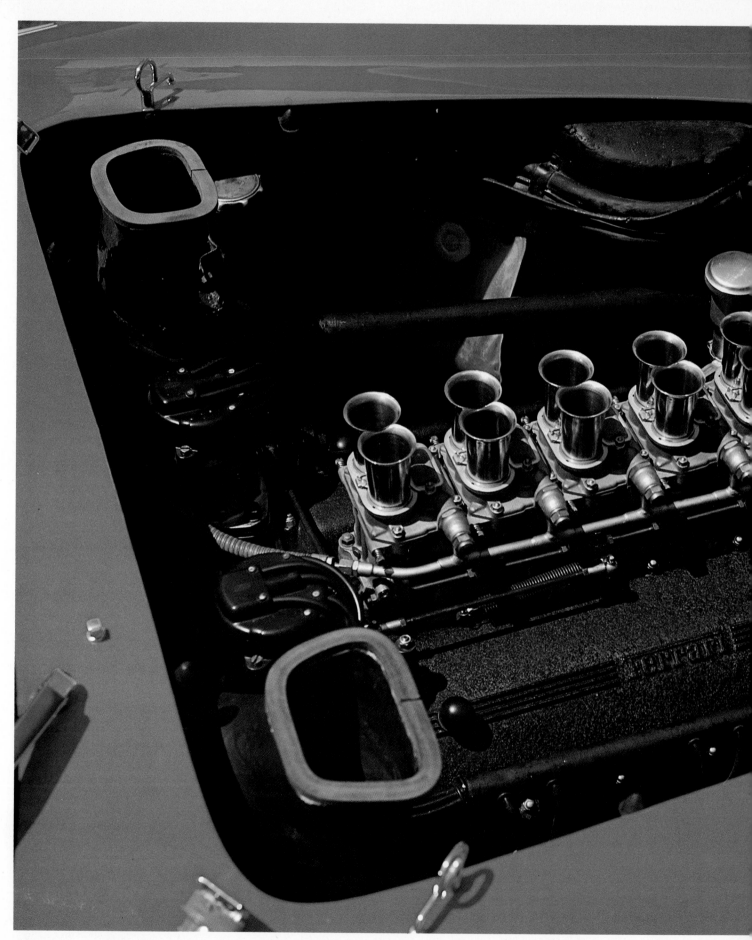

dynamic package, which balanced the anti-lift nose shape with one of the new tail spoilers just invented by Ferrari's American test driver, Richie Ginther. Also, the behavior of the rear suspension, already well tied down with quadruple traction rods, was improved with a Watt linkage to positively locate the axle laterally. (An early Bizzarrini experiment with "compensator" rear coil springs, which appeared on the GTO prototype, seems to have been quickly abandoned.) The whole car sat lower, too, at least partly because of the dry sump.

Success on the track was immediate. The month following the GTO's unveiling, new Grand Prix World Champion Phil Hill and his co-driver, Olivier Gendebien, won the GT class and finished second overall (to a Ferrari sports-racer) in the 12-hour race at Sebring, Florida. At Le Mans, the drivers were different but the results were the same.

The GTO scored numerous class and overall wins throughout the rest of that first season, and duly took the Manufacturers Championship for Ferrari. The following season went

From 3-liters of aluminum Colombo V-12, six twin-throat Weber 38 DCN carburetors, dry-sump lubrication, and a hot camshaft, Ferrari extracted 300 horsepower at 7000 rpm and a top speed of around 170 mph. The 250 GTO's engine (*both pages*) was the mechanical tour de force at the heart of a ferocious competitor.

substantially the same way, as did 1964. Oh yes, GTOs also upheld the Italian *cavallino's* domination of the long-distance, rally/race Tour de France.

Despite their competition achievements, GTOs remained very rare. Not that these *gran turismos* were undesired by Ferrari's general public; quite the contrary. But they were never meant as street cars, though some came to be driven on public roads. The "Pope of the North" had decided that the GTO was really too much the racing car for more than a handful of very competent privateers. Besides, he was getting all the value he needed out of the few he did make.

Ferrari is believed to have built no more than 39 250 GTOs. Of those, three were equipped beginning late in 1962 with 4-liter engines to be run in a so-called Prototype class. These had about 100 more horses and can be identified by their more prominent hood bulges. Five other cars were fitted in 1964 with a longer, lower, leaner Series II body style. And there it ended.

Their beauty and performance, his-

tory and quality, and certainly their rarity, have made these few great automobiles the most coveted of all Ferraris. Their value has risen to dizzying heights, and they typically are at the cutting edge of Ferrari price speculations. The auto world was stunned when a GTO seized by U.S. authorities in a drug action was auctioned off at $1.6 million in 1988. The same vehicle soon changed hands for a reported $2.1 million. The new owner subsequently turned down $4.1 million. This for a car that sold for a slightly more than $20,000 when new. What's more, neglected GTOs could be picked up for as little as $6000 in the 1970s.

Wildly escalating values have generated a lively cottage industry that Ferrari created a few 4-liter GTOs to race in the prototype class in 1962. The cars are identified by a pronounced hood bulge (*below*). The engine was a 3967-cc V-12 from the 400 Superamerica that had been brought up to Testa Rossa sports-racer standards. Horsepower was estimated to be in the 375-400 range.

produces "new" GTOs. These cars are generally built on genuine Ferrari chassis, and they can be considered in keeping with the marque's long and honorable tradition of supporting outside coachbuilders. But they are not real GTOs. Confirmed Ferraristi are disturbed. And the factory has on occasion brought legal action in an effort to stop what it views as counterfeit Ferraris.

What's it like behind the wheel of a genuine Ferrari 250 GTO? "Thrilling" only hints at the feeling.

A passionate Ferrari fan in Britain, David Clarke, bought one, restored it, and drove it on both road and track for more than a dozen years. He chronicled the experience in his book, *Ferrari 250GTO*. Clarke civilized his car a little by adding some cockpit heat insulation, by replacing the harsh racing tires with street rubber, and by jury-rigging a speedometer as required by law. In most respects, however, he retained its original competition configuration.

Contrary to the dire predictions of some of his friends, Clarke found this racing Ferrari a perfectly delightful supersports road car. It would idle smoothly at 800 rpm and not overheat in city traffic. Steering and clutch were much lighter to operate than he'd anticipated, though brake effort was heavier than he might have predicted. The ride was acceptable on all but the worst bumps. And of course, the performance was shattering.

Above 6000 rpm, he says, the engine emitted a "spine-chilling howl." He apparently never approached the

car for a drive without feelings ranging from excitement to awe, and afterwards he'd sit in the silent cockpit reliving the run.

Taking the GTO out was no simple, casual, jump-in-and-go experience. Clarke's description of his elaborate pre-start, warmup, and shutdown drills—not to mention the seemingly endless maintenance—recalls the attention required by a private aircraft.

Twenty years after the GTO's debut, *Motor*, the English weekly, had the good fortune to be allowed to attach a fifth wheel to one. Jeremy Sinek's test was handicapped by a damp track and winds gusting to 35 mph. Driving with due respect for the car's age and value, he still recorded 0-60 mph in 5.9 seconds and 0-100 in 14.1. "Perhaps most impressive of all," Sinek said, was the 0-120 mph time of 21.7 seconds. No trap speed for the quarter-mile was given, but it was above 100 mph because the finish line was crossed in 14.5 seconds. Sinek was impressed: "They really don't come much quicker than that, even today, least of all from just three liters without the benefit of turbo power."

The precise GTO tested by *Motor* once finished third at Le Mans, and later achieved the same placing in the Tour de France. Sinek's 1982 drive to

and from the test site in it involved a long slog across London in rush-hour traffic. But the veteran race car coped amazingly well.

"Mixing it on the North Circular with the commuter hordes on their dreary daily drive to work ought to have me champing at the bit, hemmed in and frustrated by urban speed limits and the sheer weight of traffic. But in-

From its racing debut in '62—where it won Sebring's GT class and finished second overall to a Ferrari sports-racer—the 250 GTO was always a winner's-circle threat. Its rear spoiler (*right*) evolved directly from racing. The car is still an eye-opener at vintage events (*below*), such as this '88 outing.

stead the experience is almost an end in itself: the sense of unreality is heightened....The engine idles reliably at the lights, and come the green it pulls cleanly from tickover speed upwards provided you're gentle with the throttle. In a slow crawl you can trickle along at 1500 rpm. You don't need a weight-lifter's left leg to depress the clutch pedal, and its engagement is as gently cushioned as a baby saloon's."

Sinek did find the transmission less than pleasant to operate. The tall, meaty gearshift rose up boldly out of its massive, machined gate, its big knob almost on a level with the steering-wheel hub. Its action was positive, but a long day of driving left his palm "bruised and tender." This difficulty may well have been a peculiarity of this car. While Ferrari gearboxes do have a reputation for stiffness, they aren't famous for raising blisters.

As did Clarke, Sinek found GTO steering to be "precise and direct, but also unexpectedly light." He too discovered the ride was rock-hard, at least at traffic speeds. When he finally found roads clear enough to bring the engine up to a "glorious howling cre-

With 100 horsepower per liter from its 3-liter V-12 (*right*), a 250 GTO tested in 1982 and driven conservatively recorded 0-60 mph in 5.9 seconds and 0-100 in 14.1. Yet, it was docile in traffic to and from the test site. Nose vents could be opened or closed depending upon conditions (*above*).

scendo," either the ride smoothed out or he was too enchanted to notice the bumps.

As for handling, "it feels every bit as taut and balanced as you'd expect from its pedigree, mild understeer giving way under power in low gear to easily controlled power slides. Even in the wet it is not intimidating, and feedback from the steering and chassis is all you could ask for."

Two years after that test, in 1984, *Car and Driver* brought racer Dan Gurney together with a 1964 GTO for some serious data gathering. On a dry track, this rare, last-of-the-breed front-engine screamer turned excellent numbers: 0-60 mph in 5.8 seconds; 0-100 in 12.7; the quarter-mile in 14.4 seconds at 108 mph. Fitted with the tight 4.25:1 axle ratio, it topped out at 144 mph at the 8000-rpm redline. Rated horsepower was 300 at 7400 rpm; torque, 250 pounds/feet at 5500. The compression ratio was 9.8:1. Despite being 20 years old and wearing moderate-sized 185-mm-wide front tires and 205-mm-wide

rears, the GTO circled the skidpad at an impressive 0.85 g. It took a rather long 218 feet to haul it to a stop from 70 mph, however. *Car and Driver* takes pains to weigh its test cars accurately, and always with a full gas tank, 35.1 gallons in this case. So the GTO's 2474 pounds, distributed 46.4-percent front/53.6-percent rear, can be taken as given.

So can the comments of one of America's greatest racers and a former Ferrari factory driver. "You can tell it's a race car, something meant to be driven hard," Dan Gurney said. "It's happy in that environment, particularly the engine. It will rev to eight [8000 rpm] with ease. It feels smooth as the dickens most of the time, but occasionally the carburetors aren't really giving it what it wants."

Big Dan's drive was at the Laguna Seca course, and he ran hard enough—an 85-mph lap average—to find some flaws in yesteryear's technology. "Cooling ducts would help the brakes a lot. The gearbox is nice, but sort of slow. The shift lever and its

throws are way too long. Aerodynamically, the bodywork is wrong. When you're going fast and put on the brakes for a turn, you've got to get back on the gas to settle it down. There isn't any understeer. A few minutes with some tin shears to make a larger rear spoiler and I'd have that fixed!"

*Car and Driver* staffers got a chance in the car and one of them, Don Sherman, reported their impressions. "...[W]e find the Ferrari to be an honest and forthright piece of machinery. The steering is light, direct, and devoid of kickback. The brakes require a heavy foot on the pedal, but they're quite effective. The long, tall shifter glides through its gate like a magic wand: let the synchros do their

164

duty, and it's all sweetness and light. The rigidly mounted bucket seat ties you to the car with the efficiency of a trailer-hitch ball. Cornering dynamics are telegraphed from the chassis up through the blue-leather upholstery with an accuracy that Western Union couldn't match. The pedals are high enough and far enough to the left that one's knee gets jammed beneath the

steering wheel during heel-and-toe downshifts, but get it right and it feels as if you were fending off the big guys at Le Mans (where this little Ferrari came home fifth overall in 1964). Engine heat wafts up through gaps in the floor, and there's a bouquet of hot oil vapor from the tank behind the passenger's seat. The sound is mechanical music. Whining gears, whirring

chains, and crackling exhaust tips beg for more throttle. Twelve unfiltered carburetor throats roar for air at 4000 rpm; by 6000, the 'ripping canvas' shriek from the exhaust drowns out every other sound in the world."

Clearly, the GTO was a racing car. Yet, Ferrari prepared it with a firm nod toward its pose as a grand tourer. The interior was styled and finished

with a neatness and completeness alien to strictly functional track missiles. Ferrari's gauges were trimmed with chrome bezels, and the instrument panel, finished in tasteful black crackle paint, left no wires or other hardware in sight. There was ample shoulder room, too. Only a scant few pounds of trim would have made the cabin look perfectly civilized.

It would be easy to go on and on about this Ferrari; it arrests the day-dreaming mind. The maestro of Maranello created many other fabulous, memorable automobiles. But in terms of sports cars usable by ordinary, if committed, drivers on ordinary, if open, roads, in the GTO Enzo Ferrari may have achieved his masterpiece.

Born of a loophole in racing rules, the 250 GTO was homologated under regulations calling for cars that could be driven on the street, though this coupe was quite clearly a pure competition car. Its form was determined by its function as a racer, with little consideration for occupant comfort. Ferrari put its styling in the hands of engineers, who proceeded to fashion one of the most arresting shapes in the history of the motor car (*below*).

# Chapter 12:

# Goodbye Colombos:
# 250 Lusso and 275 GTB

Enzo Ferrari's factory existed for his racing and grudgingly coexisted with most everything else. From nearly the very beginning, Enzo knew his racing depended on income from sales of Ferraris intended primarily for the street.

For years, many of these road-going Ferraris were built on the foundation of a contemporary racing model. Basic engines, chassis, running gear, even bodies were shared. Thus it was possible, if not always practical, for an owner to convert a tourer into a credible weekend warrior. Those who never did were still free to relish the fact that they could. Of such fantastic possibility was the Ferrari mystique sown.

But Enzo's world was changing rapidly. Success in competition, as well as with the beautiful people who bought Ferraris, was transforming his simple blacksmith's name into an

image of power, wealth, and excitement. Soon it was enough for the fashionable to be seen in a Ferrari; for them, the reality of the car under the nameplate dwindled in importance.

At the same time, the rift between racing and road travel was widening. Once twins, the two inevitably diverged under pressures of their own growing sophistication. Just as competition and highway driving had less and less to do with one another, street-going Ferraris were evolving ever further from the pure-speed models.

So it was that with the 250 GTO supercoupe safely launched in 1962, Enzo turned to draw up what in former years would have been a highway counterpart. But now, neither traffic conditions nor the tastes of Ferrari's maturing clientele would countenance the roaring racers-with-license-plates that had made the upstart marque's reputation. True, some highly enthusiastic owners did occasionally drive their GTOs on the street, but it was always a stunt. An era had ended.

The new age had to be dealt with on clean drafting paper. So to succeed the 250 GTO, Ferrari drew the 250 GT Berlinetta Lusso of 1963-64. The new car visually resembled Ferrari's Short Wheelbase Berlinetta of 1959-62; the SWB, however, was a genuine touring *and* racing GT. The 250 GT Berlinetta Lusso was designed for no other duty than enjoyable public-highway operation.

Ferrari had made street-oriented, 250-engined "GTs" before, of course. Some of them even had their long V-12 moved forward in the chassis to accommodate 2+2 seating. The 250 GT Berlinetta Lusso, though, was built strictly for two, and it was built on the now very familiar 94.5-inch wheelbase chassis. Its engine, too, was pushed forward a few inches; the front couple of cylinders were actually ahead of the front-wheel centerlines. The purpose was to increase leg room and to improving luggage space behind the seats. But the engine's positioning also was revealing: In a car with track aspirations, this deliberate imbalance would be unacceptable. It was clear right from the start this was to be a *lusso*—a deluxe car.

Though the doors, hood, and trunk-lid were of weight-saving aluminum, a heavier steel body was favored for durability. The 250 GT Berlinetta Lusso also had glass windows all around, and was crammed with heat and sound insulation, carpeting, leather trim, big seats, and all the creature comforts expected by the clientele of the day. It outweighed any race-ready *berlinetta* eggshell by some 500 pounds.

The new Lusso's chassis was very similar to that of the steel-bodied Lusso version of the SWB, though there were revisions at the front to accept the forward-mounted engine. At the rear, the leaf springs were assisted by coil springs similar to those tried and then abandoned on the GTO. Also like the GTO, the Lusso's axle benefited from a Watt locating linkage. The new car's 4-speed, all-synchro gearbox came from the steel-bodied SWB, and it had a cast-iron case without cooling fins.

Ferrari's grand-touring triumvirate of the mid-1960s poised for delivery to the discriminating enthusiast (*both pages*). From left: The 275 GTB short-nose, single-overhead cam berlinetta; the 275 GTS spyder; and the 275 GTB/4 long-nosed, twin-cam berlinetta. Introduced at the 1964 Paris Salon, the models were mechanically similar, but the coupes had more power.

The 250 GT Berlinetta Lusso of 1963-64 (*both pages*) confirmed Ferrari's move away from dual purpose road and track cars and toward a more civilized character for his street machines. Its *lusso*, or luxury, aspirations were evident in the positioning of the engine—forward for better cabin space at the expense of racer-like balance—and in the use of durable steel instead of lightweight aluminum for the body shell. With 200-250 horsepower, its 3-liter V-12 (*right*) was no screamer, but it did move the alluring 3000-pound 2-seater briskly enough to demonstrate its Ferrari pedigree.

The engine was virtually the same as the SWB unit and featured the 12-port, outside-plug heads with four hold-down studs per cylinder. Here was one Colombo engine, however, with five, not six, cam-cover fasteners along each edge.

Engine output was at the soft end of 3-liter Ferrari horsepower, with 250 at 7000 rpm a common quote. A dyno test sheet for one particular 1964 engine escaped the factory, however, and it shows a precise peak figure of 222 brake horsepower at 6750 rpm. Maximum torque occurred at 5500 and was 36.8 kg/m, or 266 pounds/feet. Those numbers come from Kurt H. Miska, an American owner of a Lusso and another Ferrari customer who loved his car so much that he wrote a book about it. In *The Berlinetta Lusso, A Ferrari of Unusual Elegance*, he explains that this car combines everything of

importance to him: race-proven reliability, everyday practicality, comfort, exciting performance, and great beauty.

Miska also reprinted results from a *Road & Track* test, which showed brisk acceleration for a car weighing very nearly 3000 pounds full of gas: 0-60 mph in 8.0 seconds and the quarter-mile in 16.1 seconds at 91 mph. Normal driving netted 14.5 mpg.

As for the Lusso's lovely lines, Miska had the novel idea of soliciting professional analysis of Pininfarina's work. He queried General Motors stylist Charles Jordan, who also was a Lusso owner. Jordan was effusive: "The Ferrari Berlinetta Lusso is an excellent example of timeless design.... The voluptuous feeling of the Lusso body design expresses grace and motion in a way which had not been accomplished before, nor has it been equalled since....It says power and

speed in capital letters without being brutal."

Sculptor Richard Lippold compared the car to classic art, specifically "...Fra Angelico's paintings, Brancusi's sculpture and Mozart's music. The Lusso shares their informal sensuality, their precise formal relationships, and their warmth of feeling, derived from the accurate equation between shape and function." Added Lippold, "This is a totally three-dimensional sculptural form of four perfectly united elements, impossible to criticize from any view (angle). The delicate accents of window frames, lights, spokes of the classic wire wheels and slender bumpers are like discrete jewels adorning a faultless body."

Faultless it may have been, but the 250 GT Berlinetta Lusso's lifeline was short. Just 350 or so were produced over a two-year span.

According to some, the Lusso's early demise came about because Enzo Ferrari himself thought it was too pretty. He is supposed to have said that a Ferrari should look more aggressive. But what of all the other Ferraris with merely beautiful bodies? In any case, there were other reasons to sharpen the drawing pencils: Automotive technology was changing rapidly, particularly on the race track, Ferrari's wellspring.

These changes materialized at the Paris auto show of October 1964, where Enzo introduced a new model designated the Ferrari 275. Its badge signaled the first time in more than 12 years that the evergreen Colombo twelve had undergone a displacement increase. Leaving the stroke at 58.8 mm, but taking the bore from 73 mm

to 77 mm (3.031 inches), gave a new swept volume of 273.8 cc per cylinder, and 3285.7 cc (200.5 cubic inches).

But that was only the beginning. When mechanically minded eyes roamed to the area behind the engine and clutch, they saw nothing but a slim propeller shaft. What had happened to the transmission? As on Ferrari racers, including the 375 Plus that won Le Mans a decade earlier, the gearbox had been moved to the rear of the car, where it formed a transaxle in unit with the differential. That shifted some weight to the rear, but more significantly for the new 275, it made the most of Ferrari's adoption of independent rear suspension (IRS).

On the old 375 Plus, as on numerous other racers of its era, the rear wheels had been located by a de Dion

system. This is a kind of beam axle that keeps the rear wheels parallel, as does Ferrari's conventional axle. But a de Dion system relieves the wheels of the weight of the differential and axle shafts and thereby improves roadholding. A de Dion axle had never appeared on a Ferrari street car and with the new 275, the company was leaping straight to a fully independent layout.

Following experience gained on the factory's race cars over the previous few years, the new 275 had a rear suspension system made up of A-shaped wishbones sprung only with coils. The arrangement was similar to that at the front and allowed each wheel to follow the contour of the road without upsetting its opposite number. IRS also enabled the chassis designers to alter camber and toe with wheel

Ferrari built roughly 350 250 GT Lussos and with cessation of its production closed a chapter on the 250 GT family. With about 2500 built over 10 years, it was perhaps the most successful high-performance exotic sports-car line ever. This blue '64 Lusso (*both pages*) is a fine example of the breed. Stylist Pininfarina deftly gave the car an aerodynamic sweep and a truncated tail that became important design influences. Inside, gone was the black-crackle paint and thinly padded seats of previous 250 GTs; the Lusso was slathered in leather, its seats were genuine buckets (*top*).

movement. If done properly, both advantages gave improved handling. This was quite an advance for conservative old Ferrari, a firm that had always reflected the founder's view that the source of more performance was more power. But vehicles that—by Maranello's lights—were lesser sports cars, such as Jaguar, Corvette, and Lamborghini, had already adopted IRS.

The Ferrari 275 appeared at its Paris debut as two very different models outwardly. The 275 GTS (S for spyder) was a refined, elegant convertible. Its overall shape looked almost rectangular next to the bullet-shaped 275 GTB, a fastback *berlinetta* that harked back to the wildest *gran turismos*.

The two were identical underneath, however. Both were built on the familiar oval-tube chassis frame, still with a wheelbase of 2.4 meters (94.5 inches). They shared the same transaxle, now featuring five speeds, the new independent rear suspension, and they each carried the new 3.3-liter engine in the same state of tune.

On a compression ratio of 9.2:1 and drawing through three two-barrel Webers, the GTS engine supposedly gave 260 horsepower at 7000 rpm.

Variations on the 250 GTO theme: the 250 GTO 64 (*opposite page, top*), a successful racing exercise; and the odd-looking "Breadvan" (*opposite page, bottom, and this page*), a racer built on a 250 GT SWB chassis and powered by a 3-liter Colombo V-12 modified to GTO specs. Former Ferrari engineer Giotto Bizzarrini and body designer Piero Drogo were responsible for the Breadvan, which they sold to privateers.

The GTB was marketed as the more aggressive car and its horsepower was rated a bit higher: 275 at 7500. A knowledgeable Ferrarist independent of the factory, Dyke W. Ridgely, puts the true horsepower of the 275 engine at 240 to 250. In an article he wrote for *Cavallino*, Ridgely adds that an optional six-carb setup would add 20 to 25 horsepower, albeit at a cost of reduced low-end performance. Ridgely noted,

however, that, "A new camshaft design and the larger displacement had eliminated the low-speed stumble which characterized the earlier 250-engined cars."

The GTB was indeed intended as a road car, and it was mechanically identical to the Spyder, which had no pretensions beyond street use. Still, it would be unfair to call the GTB a mere poseur's GT. It was in fact a seriously fast road burner, one much lighter than the Lusso. The engine offered crisp power along with lots of smooth torque, its body had a sleek aerodynamic shape, and the new, all-independent suspension system was technically superior to any previous road-going Ferrari's. That the GTB was designed from scratch to suit the new realities of the road, rather than

the romance of a dying era of racing, should not count against it.

Ferrari's new road missile certainly struck an anonymous *Car and Driver* writer straight in the heart. One moonlit midnight after a dinner party, he was given the keys to his host's glistening silver *berlinetta*. "Sitting in the GTB is pretty exciting all by itself, because the interior layout is exactly like that of the old GTO racing coupes. You sit very low, wrapped in a round, firm bucket seat that reclines very sharply—just like all your favorite heroes, arms and legs out straight, head cocked, the whole bit. The shift lever is close by, but on top of the drive line tunnel, and unusually high. All of the controls are extremely light and positive in operation, while all the instruments are large, legible and well-

VOLKSWAGEN

placed. There is a very definite World War II fighter plane feeling...."

The GTB's ride turned out to be much smoother and more pleasant than that of any Ferrari the *Car and Driver* writer had yet sampled. He said it suffered "little trace of the harshness and road shock that used to be standard equipment. But civilization of the suspension hasn't hurt the handling a bit—this latest Ferrari will corner with the best. We drove it hard, winding it tight in all five gears, banging on the brakes, throwing it into corners, really trying hard to disturb its calm and composure without success. It always did as bidden, and it always did it so well that the driver's silliest gaffes were kept secret." The only nits he found to pick were a lack of luggage space and seats that had to be adjusted with a wrench. Some speed and specification data were published with this story, but they are dubious.

French journalist Jose Rosinski, known as one of the best high-speed drivers among his profession, also wrote warmly of the 275 GTB in *Sport-Auto* magazine. As quoted by Antoine Prunet in his book, *The Ferrari Legend: The Road Cars*, Rosinski summed up the car as "a superlatively vigorous, very agile and quick automobile....It is a thoroughbred, with luxury devoid of excess, and a fiery temperament...." The performance figures published with the story showed a quarter-mile time of 13.8 (no trap speed was given) and a top speed of 148 mph.

Rosinski discovered a downside to the new suspension. The IRS glued the rear tires to the road on acceleration and almost completely eliminated any tendency to spin the wheels. But at high speeds on bumpy roads the car was nervous. Rosinski put this down to the steering, which was "extremely direct and reacts instantly to the smallest corrections by the driver." The front end of the GTB chassis included ball-jointed suspension arms for the first time, and the traditional Borrani wire wheels had given way to more

The 275 GTS, upon its unveiling at the 1964 Paris Salon (*left*). The car originally came with a passenger seat large enough to hold two occupants for short trips, but that was quickly abandoned and the car became strictly a 2-seater. It was powered by a Colombo V-12 enlarged to 3.3-liters and recorded 0-60-mph times of 7.2 seconds. Top speed was 144 mph.

rigid cast-alloy Campagnolos. Therefore, the steering may well have behaved differently from earlier Ferrari models, which were never accused of this instability.

Because the rear suspension was totally new, however, it is logical to suspect something wrong there, as well. Rosinski's *Sport-Auto* report says the instability was troublesome on bumpy road surfaces, while on corners taken at racing speed, the car had "a slight tendency to spin." Both characteristics imply the rear wheels were doing some adverse steering of their own, which was a fault of many early IRS systems—including those of Jaguar, Corvette and Lamborghini. It is only fair, though, to point out that Ferrari's design had teflon-coated metal rear suspension pivots, not the mushier rubber bushings present on its rivals.

Anyway, said Rosinski, "when traveling fast on the highway it is necessary to be always attentive, and absolutely avoid excessive or abrupt movements of the steering wheel. Because the suspension picks up the little undulations and changes in the pavement, and because these reactions are transmitted to the steering, one is constantly 'at work.' Due to this the GTB is slightly tiring to drive at a fast pace...."

None of this put off a large number of eager buyers, who took the GTB to their hearts and in some cases to their tracks. Quite a few of the steel-bodied cars were run in various sorts of speed tests, and the factory was soon offering an optional aluminum body. That led to production of about 14 cars strongly modified for racing. These had six-carburetor, dry-sump engines, altered chassis frames, larger fuel tanks, and aluminum bodies with prominent extractor vents behind the rear wheels. Ferrari also built up two or three out-and-out GT racers with elongated, drooping noses and small, GTO-style radiator inlets.

The earliest GTBs had an aerodynamic fault, a tendency for the front end of the body to fly at high speed. At the end of the first year of production, with approximately 250 cars already turned out, the GTB's nose was lengthened and lowered, and the radiator inlet was reduced in size—although not to the extent shown on the special GT racers. At the same time, the rear window was enlarged

177

At the beginning of 1965, the 275 GTS got revised side air-outlets (*left*) and an optional hardtop. Later in '65, the wire wheels were replaced by light alloys (*above*) and the rigid drive shaft of the GTB was adopted. The spyder in '66 got a 4-liter engine to become the 330 GTS and 4.4-liter in '68 as the 365 GTS.

for better visibility. To increase trunk volume, the original 25-gallon fuel tank was replaced by a pair of 12-gallon units housed in the rear fenders. Cargo room was further enhanced by moving the trunklid hinges to the outside. There were also numerous mechanical refinements, including the addition of valve-stem seals to reduce the exhaust smoke that had been characteristic of Ferrari V-12s from the early days.

In early 1966, a few months after these changes were made, came a design revision important enough to warrant "Series II" recognition. The revision saw the GTB's front-mount-

ed engine and rear-mounted transaxle rigidly united with a torque tube enclosing the drive shaft.

Originally, each had been independently mounted to the chassis, and the driveshaft had no universal joints. Proper alignment of the engine and transaxle with the driveshaft was a painstaking and critical procedure involving trial-and-error setups with shims, and some mechanics muffed the job. A misaligned driveshaft could set up vibrations severe enough to break something. Introducing constant-velocity joints partway through production was a partial fix, but the torque tube was a thorough cure and eliminated any possible trouble. Approximately 200 GTBs were produced in this "Series II" form.

Also in 1966, Ferrari introduced the GTB/C, a "competition" model on the Series II platform. Although it looked much like the new standard car, it varied extensively. Weight saving was

strenuously addressed, with thin-gauge aluminum bodywork, plastic side and rear windows, and lightweight metals in various parts of the chassis and running gear. Engine power was raised by means of new cams, valves, pistons, and carburetors. There was also a special crankshaft, as well as the racing-type dry-sump oiling system. Sources vary, but either 11 or 12 of these hot-rod GTBs were made during the summer of 1966. One of them had the distinction of winning the GT class at Le Mans that year, and of taking 8th place overall.

Thus came the end of the racing story of the grand old Colombo V-12, an engine that first sang out in the fervent air of Italy 20 years earlier. For even as the GTB seemed to be reaching its peak of performance, the factory was at work on a powerplant that would boost this new-technology Ferrari into an even higher orbit.

Appearing at the Paris show of

1966, the GTB/4 looked very much like the GTB Series II coupe it replaced. Apart from the longer Series II nose, however, there was an additional raised portion in the center of the hood. This very modest power bulge was entirely legitimate: It embraced a V-12 engine with four overhead camshafts.

This engine was not exactly all-new. In fact, the cylinder block was essentially that of the Colombo as modified for the Series II GTB when it adopted its torque tube. The identifying characteristic of the modified block was the removal of the four

prominent "outrigger" extensions of the casting that served as engine mounts on the original Colombo—and also on the Lampredi. The new mounting system followed modern standard practice, with a single small boss bolted to the crankcase on each side. The rear of the GTB/4 engine was carried by the torque tube that united it with the transaxle. The transaxle in turn had its own pair of mounts. But anyone looking under the hood would not likely notice the lower part of the engine. This was because of the magnificent new cylinder heads.

Ferrari's long romance with Gioacchino Colombo's single overhead-cam (sohc), rocker-type valve train had been entirely justified by the results. At the time this design was adopted, right after World War II, an engine's

(continued on page 183)

Replacing the 250 GT Lusso in 1964 was the 275 GTB (*opposite page*). For his newest gran turismo, Ferrari used some racing-inspired hardware. The engine was a competition-proven Colombo V-12 enlarged to 3.3-liters rated at 275 horsepower. It was the first touring Ferrari with an all-independent suspension and a rear-mounted gearbox.

## FERRARI CHASSIS

### All Independent, Front Engine

Despite a world-wide move to unit-body construction, Ferrari stayed with a separate frame and body when he introduced his first all-independent-suspension chassis in 1964.

The cars introduced that year were the 275 GTB, a fastback coupe, and the 275 GTS, a convertible coupe that Ferrari called a Spyder. As he had done with so many models before, Enzo showed the pair at the Paris Auto Salon in October. Pininfarina designed both body styles and built the Spyders; Scaglietta built the coupes. The real interest, however, was under the handsome coachwork.

The sohc V-12 engine was still up front, but it now displaced 3.3 liters. The clutch and flywheel were still at the back of the engine, but the 5-speed transmission was now mounted near the rear of the car, in unit with the differential. Disc brakes all around were standard.

Ferrari's first all-independent suspension used unequal-length A-arms, coil springs, and telescopic shock absorbers at all four corners. It was seen as a major step forward. Four-wheel independent suspension results in a smoother, more controllable ride, and offers improved roadholding because the wheels, with less unsprung weight, keep the tires in contact with the pavement on smooth or uneven surfaces. A car with a beam axle, by contrast, maintains poorer contact between road and rubber because a bump or dip that affects one wheel also influences the one at the other end of the axle.

By installing the transmission at the rear, Ferrari also achieved a remarkably even front/rear weight split. With the driver aboard and half a tank of fuel, weight distribution of the 275 Spyder was 48 percent front, 52 percent rear. This helped handling almost as much as the independent suspension.

A series of model changes were made in late 1966: the 275 GTS was superseded by the 330 GTS; a 330 GTC was added; and the 275 GTB received twin-cam cylinder heads and a GTB/4 tag. All retained the chassis and suspension of the previous models.

Ferraris now came equipped with Campagnolo alloy wheels, with Borrani wire wheels as an option. The Campagnolo was a dish-type wheel with 10 oblong holes for brake ventilation. It wasn't particularly handsome, but was certainly easier to maintain than a wire wheel. The 275 GTB/4 stayed in production through 1968, the 330 GTC and GTS through 1970.

In 1968, Ferrari introduced his wildest and meanest production car yet: the 365 GTB/4 "Daytona." The four-cam 4.4-liter V-12 was still up front and the five speed transmission was still at the back, in unit with the differential. The chassis and independent suspension were almost identical to the 275 and 330. Like the other coupes, the Daytona body was a Pininfarina design built by Scaglietti.

Alloy wheels for the Daytona were by Cromadora and featured a five-spoke "star" design that set the pattern for most subsequent Ferrari road wheels. In 1971, Ferrari brought out a "gentleman's cruiser" in the 365 GTC/4. It was as luxurious and refined a car as Enzo had yet built. Pininfarina designed and constructed the body, which had jump seats behind the two front seats. Ferrari never called the 365 GTC/4 a 2+2, however, because the two back seats were virtually unusable for adults.

A hefty 4000-pound curb weight was the price of the GTC/4's deluxe upholstery, audio system, heat and noise insulation, and air conditioning. Standard ZF power steering made the weight a little easier to live with.

Unlike its immediate predecessors, the

365 GTC/4 had its 5-speed transmission at the back of the engine, not near the rear of the chassis. Production of this model ran only two years, 1971-1972.

Since 1960, Ferrari had maintained a run of genuine 2+2 models concurrent with the production two-seaters. They were joined in 1967 by the 365 GT 2+2. It had a fully independent suspension, as used in the two-seaters, but it added a rear hydro-pneumatic leveling system that had been developed by Koni and Ferrari.

The 365 GT 2+2 engine had the same 4390-cc displacement as the Daytona's, but it used single-overhead camshafts. Like the GTC/4, the 365 GT 2+2's transmission was at the back of the engine. It was placed there, rather than in unit with the differential, so as not to interfere with back-seat space. Those rear seats made the 365 GT 2+2's 104.2-inch wheelbase the longest of any Ferrari of the 1960s.

The 365 GTC/4 was the last of the front-engine, two-place Ferraris, but the front-mounted four-cam V-12 continues today in the 412. The 412 began in 1972 as the 365 GT4 2+2, became the 400 GT and 400 Automatic in 1976, and then the 412 in 1985. Ferrari calls it a coupe, but Americans would more likely label it a 2-door sedan.

This sedan's 4-cam V-12 engine is that of the 365 GTC/4. A slight displacement increase, from 4390 cc to 4823 cc, merited the 400 designation. Its boost to 4932 cc made it the 412. Buyers can choose a 5-speed manual transmission or a or GM Turbo 400 3-speed automatic. Both mount at the back of the engine.

Its chassis is virtually that of the 365 GTC/4, lengthened to a 106.3-inch wheelbase. The 412 uses a steel tube frame, all-independent suspension, and 4-wheel disc brakes. Power steering and air conditioning are standard.

Though less glamorous than the two-seaters, the 412 is a magnificent Grand Touring car in the Ferrari tradition.

rpm was limited by things other than valve-train inertia. That was particularly true in an engine that had small, light valves and rockers—a by-product of having its displacement divided into so many cylinders. When Ferrari tried twin-cam heads on the supercharged Formula 1 version of the 1.5-liter Colombo, there was no meaningful

Pininfarina designed the 275 GTB and it was built by Scaglietti at Modena. After the graceful 250 GT Lusso, with its delicate, airy greenhouse, the 275 GTB (*both pages*) struck some critics as ill proportioned. They said its body was squat-looking and old fashioned. Time, however, has vindicated its lines, and the car is now considered a highly original shape that imbued the *berlinetta* with a strong character befitting its mission: carrying two people over great distances in speed, style, and safety.

improvement in power. Its replacement, the big Lampredi 4.5-liter, was able to win with the original sohc design.

As racing technology became more specialized, Ferrari did adopt double overhead-cam (dohc) designs for track use. In the early 1950s, Lampredi designed a 4-cylinder dohc powerplant that proved effective in several different displacements in F1, F2, and sports-car racing. Every F1 Ferrari from then on had dohc heads, no matter who designed it and regardless of whether it had 4, 6, 8, or 12 cylinders. When Vittorio Jano came to Ferrari in the mid-'50s, he created a third-generation racing V-12 with dohc heads, and this won numerous international sports-car events.

Still, for two decades Ferrari did not believe the necessarily heavier, bulkier, and more complex dohc concept was optimal for highway use, no matter what rival manufacturers like Aston Martin, Jaguar, and Maserati might offer. After all, only a Ferrari buyer got a V-12. In fact, the brilliantly designed and thoroughly developed sohc Colombo continued to hold its own in GT and sports-car racing right into the '60s. It last won Le Mans for Ferrari as late as 1965, in the mid-engine 250 LM.

However, as advances in metallurgy, bearings, lubrication, and even manufacturing technology improved engine durability at high rpm, it did seem more and more feasible to introduce a dohc street engine.

Ferruccio Lamborghini, that presumptuous tractor-maker-turned-exotic-car manufacturer, was getting good reviews for the quad-cam V-12 he'd sprung on a startled world in 1963. Ferrari himself was readying his son's memorial, the Dino, for production in 1967. Its little V-6 had four cams, so how could the company's flagships remain aloof from the principle?

Such was the impetus for the GTB/4. Taking full advantage of its lighter valve train, the double overhead-cam 3.3-liter engine made its peak power at 8000 rpm, a speed the old single-cam Colombo had reached only in the hands of racers willing to violate the redline. Peak horsepower was officially 300, though authority Ridgely says even the best GTB/4s actually made 260 to 265. Six carburetors were standard now. Another racing item on this street car was dry-sump lubrication, which would more positively maintain oil pressure in the

hands of owners who enjoyed strenuous maneuvering—though at oil-change time they would be pouring in 17 quarts! Yet this racing-derived engine was no intractable hot rod. Its compression ratio was still a moderate 9.2:1, and drivers found that there was even more usable mid-range torque and driving flexibility than before.

According to a full road test published in 1967 by *Car and Driver*, the GTB/4 coupe weighed 2663 pounds at the curb, a figure that rose to 2930 with driver and test equipment aboard. The weight distribution in this condition was 49 percent front/51 rear. The car accelerated from 0-to-60 mph in 6.2 seconds and to 100 in 14.5—which was precisely the quarter-mile clocking. The top speed was 166 mph, but that was an estimate. Elsewhere on the data panel is a fifth-gear maximum speed of 135 at 6500 rpm. This sounds like a real-life observation on a restricted straight-

The 275 GTB's cabin (*opposite page, top*) was comfortable for two adults, but lacked much luggage space. One road model tested turned a quarter-mile time of 13.8 seconds and had a top speed of 148 mph. Another racing version won the GT class at Le Mans in 1966.

away, although it is not referenced in the text. Another discrepancy concerns the fuel-tank capacity, which *Car and Driver* lists as 25 gallons even though the GTB/4 retained the dual 12-gallon setup. Fuel consumption ranged from 12 mpg to 15 mpg. List price was $14,680.

In the text, there was this observation about the new engine: "The noises of roller-rocker valve gear in the sohc Ferrari almost drown the exhaust note, while the 4-cam engine makes very little underhood noise, allowing the driver to savor the Ferrari exhaust note without interference."

The writer spent half his story space talking about the asymmetry of

the Scaglietti-built bodywork, a situation that had applied to every hand-made Ferrari since 1947. Once he got into the car, he discovered two annoyances: very long travel of the throttle pedal, which forced him to lift his heel from the floor to depress it fully; and brakes that wouldn't stop the car well until they had been warmed.

In fact, at the painfully slow traffic speeds necessary in the New York-Connecticut area, the Italian stallion evidently was a beast to handle. "Despite its dual-purpose nature, it's easier to drive a GTB well on a race track than it is on the street, particularly if you try to stay within the letter of the law," *Car and Driver* said. "Everything about the GTB-4 is designed to be driven hard and fast. The light fly-wheel and positive clutch don't let you make a slow shift—the car snaps at you if you mismatch the revs by even 100 rpm. You must drive this car with concentration...the kind of concentration that comes automatically with speed."

Speed was applied properly not quite a year later, when *Car and Driver* put John Fitch, one-time member of the Mercedes-Benz factory competition team, together with another GTB/4 on the Lime Rock race track. This car had a shorter rear-axle ratio, and accelerated to 60 in a sparkling 5.5 seconds. It was quicker in the quarter, too: 14.0 at 106. To get these better numbers, the engine was buzzed—at the owner's insistence—to 8500 rpm, 500 rpm past the redline.

Fitch echoed the earlier impressions, saying, "This is a car for the

business of driving fast, there's no doubt about it. You might call it pretty much a single purpose car. The steering is light, surprisingly light, and quick. You turn it less and more happens. The throttle response is superb....I'd be bored to tears driving this car at 60."

A more tolerant view was offered by *Road & Track*, which also first sampled the new dohc engine in 1967 and found its civilized nature most impressive. The test car was not the standard Berlinetta, but a special con-vertible that will be discussed below. However, the engine was the same, and in the confines of Connecticut, there was little opportunity to run the GTB/4 at the pace for which it was designed.

That didn't seem to matter to *Road & Track*. "Here's an engine that idles at 800 rpm, smoothly and quietly, and has a useful on-the-road rev range of 1500-8000 rpm. It can be lugged from 2000 rpm in 5th with a remarkable head of steam....It responds without a hitch to any throttle opening above

Jose Rosinski, a French journalist known for his high-speed driving skills, summed up the 275 GTB (*above*) as a "superlatively vigorous, very agile and quick automobile....It is a thoroughbred, with luxury devoid of excess, and a fiery temperament...." But, he added, the suspension's high-speed finickiness demanded that the driver devote constant attention to the steering wheel.

*(continued on page 190)*

Seeking an improved ride and better roadholding, Ferrari adopted the independent rear suspension used on his mid-engine race cars of the time to the 275 GTB (*both pages*). Its 5-speed gearbox was mounted in the rear for better weight distribution, another racing legacy.

2000 rpm and the plugs didn't fluff once in the pottering along we were forced to do with it...."

On the non-pottering end of the spectrum, the engine felt so smooth and eager at its 8000-rpm redline that the magazine test driver was strongly tempted to try for 9000. He didn't, but against the clock, the car reached 60 mph in 6.7 seconds, and ran the quarter-mile in 14.7 at 99. Top speed was given as 155 mph. *Road & Track* published an empty weight for the GTB/4 convertible of 2455 pounds, or 2718 as tested, distributed 49 percent front/51 rear. If those figures derived from actual weighing, not just from a brochure, they were so much lighter than the *berlinetta* weight given by *Car and Driver* that the convertible tested by *Road & Track* must have had an aluminum body.

According to Ridgley, the GTB/4 had rubber-bushed rear suspension arms instead of the GTB's teflon pivots. *Road & Track* still found the GTB/4's ride and handling better than that of the previous 275 chassis it tried. The springing was softer and more supple, and the rigidity of the engine-transaxle unit was further improved, which apparently reduced or eliminated the bump-induced instability.

In another 1967 test of a GTB/4, this one on a French Autoroute then still free of speed restrictions, professional racer Jean-Pierre Beltoise was able to cover 46 miles in under 23 minutes in Sunday traffic—including stops at toll booths. He did so "in complete safety and the greatest comfort, without having to once use the brakes hard and while carrying on a normal conversation with my passenger...." This experience, recounted originally in *l'Auto-Journal* and quoted by Prunet, gave Beltoise a firm opinion of the car. "It is, first and foremost, a serious and comfortable gran turismo, but it retains the lineage of a race car in the re-

The hood bulge identifies this car (*right*) as a 275 GTB/4. Unveiled at the Paris show in 1966, these cars retained the 3.3-liter Colombo V-12, but were treated to two camshafts per cylinder bank. Peak horsepower rose from a rated 275 at 7500 rpm to 300 at 8000 rpm. The addition of dry-sump lubrication kept the 17 quarts of oil effective in harder cornering. One GTB/4 tested weighed 2930 pounds distributed 49-percent front/51-percent rear. It ran 0-60 mph in 6.2 seconds, turned the quarter in 14.5 and had an estimated top speed of 166 mph.

sponse of the engine and the quality of the handling. The 275 GTB/4 is one of the greatest automobiles created in our times."

Unlike its immediate predecessor, the GTB/4 was not issued in any serious competition models, although some were super-tuned by the factory for competitive owners, and there were a few manufactured with aluminum bodies.

Another difference was the lack of a four-cam GTS model. At the same time the 3.3-liter sohc Colombo was retired from the 275 GTB *berlinetta*, the 275 GTS spyder was modified to take the sohc 4-liter engine from the concurrent 330 series. It was this absence of an open version of Ferrari's latest high-performance car that induced American importer Luigi Chinetti to commission a series of specially-built GTB/4s with a folding top. He called them NART Spyders, after the initials of his own North American Racing Team. One of them was in fact raced at Sebring in 1967, finishing 17th. This was the very car loaned to *Road & Track* for the test quoted above. The literature says there were never more than 10 of these spectacular NART Spyders, although a number of original coupes have been chopped by their owners in years since.

As for the GTB/4 coupe, it too had a short production life, a mere 1½ years, with a scant 280 coming off the line through early 1968. Was killing "one of the greatest automobiles created in our times" a sad and incomprehensible decision? Perhaps, but there was a still more fabulous Ferrari on the way: the Daytona.

From the cockpit of the GTB/4 (*below*) comes this account: "The noises of roller-rocker valve gear in the sohc Ferrari almost drown the exhaust note, while the 4-cam engine makes very little underhood noise, allowing the driver to savor the Ferrari exhaust note.... Everything about the GTB-4 is designed to be driven hard and fast.... You must drive this car with concentration ... the kind of concentration that comes automatically with speed."

# Chapter 13

# 365 GTB/4 Daytona: Back to Bigger Bangers

Historians have criticized Ferrari's early-1968 cancellation of the delightful 275 GTB/4. Of course, at the time the decision had to be made, Ferrari didn't enjoy the historians' hindsight. He could do only what seemed right at the time.

In fact, several forces were at work to make the sweet little quad-cam, 3.3-liter engine seem obsolete. The two strongest forces, oddly enough, came out of America.

One involved impending smog-control regulations, which would begin to take effect in 1968. These struck at the heart of everything Ferrari's name had ever meant. An engine specialist above all, Enzo could see that the mandated emission systems would strangle his highly efficient powerplants. He knew the only way to preserve Ferrari performance in his most lucrative market was to increase the physical size of his engines.

Perhaps more importantly, Ferrari had seen Ford Motor Company arise as a serious new racing challenger. In 1963, there had been a flirtation between the two firms. It had ended bitterly and Ford, the rejected suitor, was pouring millions into its effort to beat Ferrari at Le Mans and other major sport-car races. By 1965, Ford was experimenting with a 7-liter stock car thumper crammed into its high-tech, mid-engine GT40. No evolution of Ferrari's familiar little *berlinetta* was going to hold off that. Thus, by 1967, a front-line Ferrari sports racer had a 4-liter, 4-cam, 450-horsepower pure racing V-12 shoehorned into the rear

end of a road-hugging 200-mph missile. Earlier that year, a team of these 330 P4s finished 1-2-3 at Daytona to beat Ford on its home ground.

A third factor would have meant less to a man of Ferrari's self-assured temperament, but his staff must have been whispering it in his ear: Certain marques that aspired to Ferrari's standing with his patrons—Aston Martin, Maserati, Lamborghini—were offering quite advanced, double overhead-cam engines in the 4-liter class.

Obviously, it was time to strike the street market with a newer, bigger hammer.

But the GTB/4 model represented the practical limit of the performance that could be squeezed from the original Gioacchino Colombo engine. Granted, it may stretch the point to call the quad-cam, 3.3-liter 275 powerplant a direct descendant of the original single overhead-cam 1.5. So much had been changed. The factory actually had assigned the GTB/4 engine a specific type number, 226; the sohc GTB unit had been Type 168. By 1968, the 4-cam block had only two mounting points instead of four; it had larger main bearings with four stud-caps instead of two; the cam-drive chain had only two rows of rollers rather than the original three; and there were now 14 hold-down bolts for each cylinder head, not 13 as in the beginning. Of course the heads were completely different. There had also been changes in materials. Still, the basic engine block was a direct descen-

dant of the one first cast in 1946. It even had the same fundamental dimensions. The old workhorse had given astonishing service. But there was no more growth in it. A physically larger engine was at last required.

Why not simply revive the old long-block Lampredi? Probably because there was already so much engineering time invested in the Colombo, and perhaps because a 5-liter engine seemed excessive at that point. Anyway, Ferrari chose the shorter, lighter Colombo design as a point of departure.

The journey was made in two stages and actually began in 1959 with an engine given the type number 163. By increasing the deck height—the distance from the crankshaft centerline up to the top faces of the cylinder block—room was made for a longer-stroke crankshaft. The new 71-millimeter (2.80-inch) stroke was combined with a 77-mm (3.03-inch) bore, the largest considered feasible with Colombo's original bore-spacing. It gave the 400 Superamerica of 1959 a total displacement of 3967.4 cc (242 cubic inches).

The identical engine was soon installed in models of lesser pretensions, and the type number 330 was applied to these.

Ferrari phased in the next step over the first couple of years of the 1960s. Although the first-generation 4-liter worked well enough in comparatively light-duty street cars, when tried in the crucible of competition it tended to overheat. The answer was a com-

pletely new block, cast with its cylinders farther apart to allow better circulation of cooling liquid. The new bore-center spacing was up by 4 mm, to 94 mm (3.70 inches). This would have increased the engine's overall length by just about 1 inch—still 4 inches short of the Lampredi engine.

Without seeing a reference to the factory's official engine-type number—209 in this case—only a well-educated eye could tell the new engine from its immediate predecessor, the 163. Models in which the type 209 was installed were still called 330s, and had the identical cylinder dimensions of 77 mm × 71 mm.

The 330 GT 2+2 (*left*) was first shown in January 1964, to mixed reviews about its quad headlamps. The car introduced Ferrari's new 4-liter V-12, which would see extensive use in the coming years. Its more traditionally styled 330 GT 2+2 successor of '65 (*below, both pages*) had alloy, not wire, wheels and a 5-speed transmission, not a 4-speed overdrive.

This improved 4-liter quickly gained Ferrari's confidence, and was soon being used in top-rank professional racing. Its finest hour was a 1962 outright win at Le Mans, the 6th for the prancing horse. That victory was recorded by the ultimate development of the Testa Rossa series, the one-off, 360-horsepower 330 TR/LM. The following year came a very small series of four GT coupes called *tipo* 330 LMB, for Le Mans Berlinetta. They were beautiful projectiles combining the pointed nose and dramatic cooling slots of the contemporary GTO with the elegant canopy of the 250 GT Lusso, all of it wrapping the power of the previous year's Le Mans winner. One finished 5th at the race for which it was named.

On through the decade, the quasi-Colombo, sohc 4-liter engine continued to be used in both racing and touring cars. For instance, the 330 P of 1964 was a mid-engine sports-racing prototype with a claimed 370 horse-power; the concurrent 330 America and 330 GT 2+2 were 300-horse, front-engine, 4-passenger luxury models. In racing, the factory eventually turned to the dohc designs, a move that culminated in the P4 Daytona winner. For street use, however, the single-cam version remained alive, and when the 3.3-liter 275 GTS spyder was canceled, Ferrari's customers were consoled by the 1966 appearance of the 330 GTS and a companion coupe, the 330 GTC.

It was in 1965 that they saw the first example of a 365 engine. With its stroke unchanged, but its bore taken out to 81 mm (3.189 inches), the sohc engine now displaced 4390.4 cc (267.9 cubic inches). As installed in the 365 P mid-engine racer, it was said to make 380 horsepower at 7300 rpm. When put the following year into a street-going cabriolet, the 365 California, it was detuned to 320 horsepower at 6600 rpm. In 1967, the same 4.4-liter formed the basis of the 365 GT 2+2, a

graceful, glassy tourer built on a rather long, 104.3-inch wheelbase.

That was how things stood when Ferrari, deciding the time had come for a new high-performance *berlinetta*, began to lay down the fabulous Daytona.

Work actually began before the end of '66, when the Pininfarina studio was drawing concepts of a 2-seater on the chassis of the 330 GTC. From the start, the lines were unmistakably those that would appear on the Daytona, and they would turn out to be the ultimate expression of the classic Ferrari *berlinetta*.

While Lamborghini had already put the latest race-think on the road in the form of the spectacular mid-engine V-12 Miura, Ferrari's new flagship would hold fast to its heritage one more time. Defiantly so. To look at the Daytona's exaggeratedly conventional sports-car proportions—the driver nestled between the rear wheels and behind a long hood seething with power—is to hear Enzo Ferrari saying, "The horse does not push the cart, it pulls."

What a horse. Though developed from the Colombo-based sohc 365, the Daytona's dohc V-12 had the sheer presence of an all-new powerhouse. The pair of twin-cam heads and a sextet of twin-barrel Weber carburetors made a magnificent sight. The shining aluminum of the heads and crankcase; the beefy 4-bolt main bearing caps; the stupendous machining job represented by the billet-steel crankshaft; the dozen forged, polished connecting rods; the rigid dry-sump casting; the labor-costs-no-object construction philosophy apparent in every detail—this *tipo* 251 Ferrari engine was a feast for anyone with a taste for ultra high-performance technology.

It was also irresistible to anyone with a lust for power. The mighty 4.4 roared out 352 brake horsepower at 7500 rpm. The torque, spread over a very broad-shouldered rev band,

Ferrari's dramatic 330 LMB of 1963 (*both pages*) was a prototype racer that helped prove the new 4-liter in competition. Designed by the factory, the "Le Mans Berlinetta" is generally considered to have the front end of a 250 GTO and the body of a 250 GT Lusso. Its engine made 400 horsepower at 7500 rpm. In 1963, one finished 5th at the race for which it was named. This car, and its sister 250 LMB, were Ferrari's last front-engine factory prototype racers.

peaked at 315 pounds/feet at 5500. That was the street version. Before its racing career was finished, the Daytona developed as much as 450 horsepower at nearly 8500 shrieking rpm.

The 365 GTB/4 chassis continued the customary Maranello layout, with a very stout basic structure of oval-section steel tubes supporting a superstructure of round and square members. Wheelbase was the familiar 94.5 inches. As developed on the 275 and 330 chassis, there was a torque tube uniting the engine with the rear-mounted 5-speed transaxle, and all wheels were sprung on wishbone-type independent suspension.

An interesting new manufacturing technique, which had just been introduced on lesser Ferraris, was adopted for the new GTB/4: A "bathtub" of fiberglass panels was bonded to the upper side of the chassis, forming a very practical interior bodyshell. That construction continues on today's Ferraris. On the outside, steel bodywork with aluminum hood, doors, and trunklid went on most Daytonas, although a very few were paneled all in aluminum for competition.

That bodywork, of course, was stunningly beautiful. It was one of those uncanny leaps of aesthetic genius seen so often in Italian styling, and so seldom elsewhere. Somehow blending the raw-racer look of the previous competition *berlinettas* with the sweet, almost florid elegance of the 250 GT Lusso, the Daytona managed a fresh, modern statement all its own. Surely,

Ferrari's pretty 365 GTS (*both pages*) appeared in late 1968 and was gone by the middle of '69. One reason for the spyder's short life was that it was overshadowed by the Daytona. The 365 GTS was nonetheless a worthy sports car in its own right, with 320 horsepower from its 4.4-liter V-12.

any roster of the all-time great automobile bodies would be incomplete without the Ferrari 365 GTB/4 Daytona.

So far so good, but there were some Daytona downsides. First, there was a long delay before it was finally released for sale. Ferrari stopped production of the 275 GTB/4 early in 1968, but was still playing with 365

GTB/4 prototypes late that summer. The Daytona was not introduced until the Paris show in the fall, and not sold until 1969. Some observers believe this painful lag in revenue contributed to Enzo Ferrari's proposal of corporate marriage to Fiat that year.

When the new car finally did appear, many professional critics thought its front-engine layout sadly old fashioned. There were also people who didn't think much of its axe-blade front-end styling, with its four headlights shrouded in plastic.

Then there was the weight. A robust piece of work anyway, and forced to carry the millstone of the new safety and emissions rule books, the Daytona was much heavier than previous Ferrari *berlinettas*. When *Road & Track* tested one in 1970, the curb weight was a startling 3600 pounds. That rose to 3885 as tested.

**Introduced in 1967, the 365 GT 2+2 (*both pages*) set several Ferrari precedents: It was the first prancing-horse 2+2 with an all-independent suspension; it was the first Ferrari with power steering as standard equipment; and it was the first true high-performance vehicle with a self-leveling rear suspension.**

At least the avoirdupois was distributed 50-50. Once on the road, the car's performance proved amazingly athletic. The sprint to 60 mph took a mere 5.9 seconds, the standing quarter-mile only 13.8, with a terminal speed of 107.5 mph.

*Road & Track* pointed the Daytona down a straightaway and saw an indicated 180 mph at a flat-out 7000 rpm, though top speed later was calculated at a true 173. Aboard the car on that occasion was Ferrari authority Dean Batchelor, who took a photo of the instruments at the moment of truth. "The car was smooth as glass at that speed," he remembers. "It was easy." He also says he'll never forget the in-

*(continued on page 203)*

Defiantly upholding Ferrari's front-drive tradition in a world filling quickly with mid-engine exotics, the 365 GTB/4 Daytona (*both pages*) burst upon the motoring public at the Paris Salon of 1968. The car's exaggeratedly conventional sports-car proportions—a long hood sheltering a big V-12 (*above*) and a short rear deck—shouted Enzo's homily that "The horse does not push the cart, it pulls."

credible feeling of ongoing acceleration at very high velocities. As the clutch bit for the shift into fifth gear at 148 mph, he remembers being slammed back in his seat almost as though it were second gear.

The factory's own top-speed claim was 174. In Ferrari's past, that figure would have been one to take salted. But there is ample evidence from other sources to corroborate that such a heady velocity was routine for the 365 GTB/4. No question about it: The Daytona was a rocket.

But unfortunately it was also a rocket *sled*. Very quickly the word went around among Ferraristi weaned on the light and lithe coupes of the '60s that the one for the '70s felt like a truck. Where the 275 had impressed everyone with its light steering, at least at low speeds, the 365's struck everyone as being heavy. So did the throttle and clutch pedals, though by unpleasant contrast, the brakes were over-assisted. The brakes themselves would sometimes fade in hard stops from high speed, a shortfall blamed on the Daytona's weight.

Fashionable as the Daytona coupe was in the late '60s (*right*), Pininfarina created a positively haute car simply by slicing off its roof. The 365 GTS/4 (*above and opposite page*) lost none of the *berlinetta*'s stunning impact while acquiring a character all its own. The Daytona spyder retained the GTB/4's dimensions and running gear, but came standard with Borrani wire wheels instead of the coupe's trademark star-pattern Cromodora alloys (the Borrani wires subsequently became a GTB/4 option). The spyder was unveiled in September 1969, at the Frankfurt Salon.

Cockpit ergonomics did nothing to dispel this impression of excess mass, for as some testers complained, the seat was indeed set rather low in relation to the steering wheel and pedals. Also, the upturn of the engine cowl that shielded the wipers blocked the driver's view of the opposite fender. Some made a point of noting that the one-piece seats afforded no possible adjustment of seatback angle. The human species is, however, endowed with the ability to adjust to any new condition. A few miles, a few judicious stabs at the throttle, and the critics started finding things to like about the Daytona.

Effortless acceleration, for instance. Comparing the Daytona's 4.4 with the 275 GTB/4's 3.3 in a 1973 article for Britain's *Motor*, Roger Bell said, "Certainly it is much easier to jump into and drive. There's much more punch and you really feel that you can avoid any crisis merely by leaning on the right-hand pedal and disappearing into the middle distance." He came away from the test wishing he could own the older 275 GTB/4, but had to admit that the bigger, newer model was "an extraordinarily fast car and on the correct roads is great fun to drive."

In their book, *Daytona*, Pat Braden and Gerald Roush make a good point in response to those who call the big car truckish: "The Daytona really only begins to come into its own at about 70 mph, and hits stride above 140 mph. At speeds below 80 mph the car is a bit bumpy, but the suspension be-

gins to work smoothly as speed builds, and steering becomes appropriate. Owners who complain of the heavy steering should remember their baby was designed for precise control at 174 mph. Parking lots were low on the priority list."

Writing for *Motor* in 1969, Paul Frere, the Belgian journalist and race driver—a one-time Le Mans winner for Ferrari—pried a couple of the then-new Daytonas away from the factory for a "very full day" of romping in the Italian countryside. First things first: he timed a mean maximum speed of 176 mph.

That was "the fastest I have ever done with a normal road car," he stated succinctly. He did it on a normal, everyday Autostrada carrying mid-day summer traffic. Bar the odd Fiat veering into his path "when we were approaching at a relative speed of 120 mph," it was an incident-free exercise. Indeed, the big, chisel-nosed Ferrari was impressively stable: "Never was there any suggestion of the front end getting light or the car starting to wander."

Up in the mountains behind Maranello, on the sinuous roads of the Futa and Raticosa passes along the old Mille Miglia route, Frere discovered that, "On its big, fat tyres, the Ferrari could

*(continued on page 209)*

The two 365 GTB/4 oddities on this page are prototypes of American-specification cars. Their uninviting headlamp arrangements are in response to U.S. regulations prohibiting the European version's clear headlight covers. Ferrari's solution—pop-up headlamps for the U.S. market—preserved the Daytona's smooth prow. Ferrari's range of 4.4-liter 4-cam cars included the 365 GTC 2+2 (*opposite page, top*), which was offered from 1971 to '73. Sidedraft mounting of its six twin-throat carburetors made possible the 365 GTC 2+2's low hoodline. Vignale used a 365 GTC for the basis of this 1969 station-wagon exercise (*opposite page, bottom*).

really be flung around the corners, quite irrespective of the state of the none-to-well-maintained surface. It certainly did not feel very big and its agility belied its weight....

"The general cornering attitude is that of a slightly understeering car, with a small tendency to tuck into the bend as the throttle is closed, which is exactly what I like. There is practically no trace of roll and the moderately light steering (which by the way has quite inadequate lock) is very precise

Ferrari's luxury offering for 1966 was the 365 California (*top, both pages*). This 365 GTC Speciale (*opposite page, bottom*) is a one-off built for a member of the Dutch royal family. The handsome 365 GT4 2+2 (*left*) of 1972 was a built on a stretched 365 GTC/4 chassis.

while retaining that slightly dead feel which has for long been characteristic of Ferraris." By "inadequate lock," Frere meant the Daytona had a large turning circle; *Road & Track* measured it at 39.0 feet.

In summary, the Belgian said, "there is little to remind the driver how fast the Ferrari eats up the miles; even noise remains quite reasonable though the 365 GTB-4 is not by any means a silent car and the radio provided in the second car was useless when you reached the 100 to 120 m.p.h. bracket. If you go faster, it's the engine that makes the music, the finest music of all to the ears of the enthusiast and a music he can enjoy in the comfort of a well-sprung car, fitted with such amenities as electric window lifters, air conditioning (that could be improved) and a really capacious luggage locker—a Grand Touring car par excellence."

A lot of people must have agreed, for Ferrari built and sold between 1350 and 1400 Daytonas through 1973, including a little more than 100 original convertibles and 15 competition versions.

And, as Fiat had purchased 40 percent of Ferrari in 1969 and was now running the production side of the factory, this sales performance somewhat vindicated changes instituted by the new parent company. For instance, in the glorious, but sometimes chaotic old days, Maranello had been a circus, with dozens of automotive acts going on at once and special cars being turned out at anyone's request. Fiat's more traditional management imposed order. The precision with which the factory now quoted Ferrari horsepower was a sign of that. So was the improved accuracy of its top-speed claims.

Another sign was that the Daytona underwent fewer revisions and was issued in fewer permutations than so many previous models. There was not even any major difference in the cars made for the U.S. market; more accurately, developments made to meet American laws usually were built into Daytonas sold everywhere.

Whatever else it may have been in its own right as a supercar, the mighty 365 GTB/4 Daytona marked the beginning of Ferrari's maturity as an automaker.

Happily, maturity did not bring with it a turn away from racing. Though the 15 specially built competition Daytonas were not for use by the factory, they were designed and crafted by the factory to be campaigned by factory *concessionaires*—distributors. The modifications were standard practice. Weight was reduced by means of aluminum bodies on most cars, stripping out all excess equipment, even fitting fiberglass doors, hoods, and trunklids. Safety equipment, including roll bars and later roll cages, was installed, and the suspensions beefed up. Engines were put through a hop-up routine.

*Road & Track* tested one of these in 1974. It seems to have been one with a steel body, though it weighed 400 pounds less than the standard Daytona the magazine had tested in '70. Curb weight of the competition car was 3190 pounds; its test weight was 3380. Apparently the excess poundage had been taken off the rear, because the distribution was now 51/49. Stated horsepower at 8300 rpm was 402, which was still nearly 50 short of the ultimate version of the racing Daytona.

The street-stock Daytona *Road & Track* had tested was also faster in some measurements of acceleration. The track version's top speed was up a little, to 183 mph, but mainly because of taller gearing given by taller rear tires. The test was conducted in good conditions, but apparently the competition car was tired and had to be babied. A test of a fresher racing Daytona, one that had run at Le Mans in '72, was carried out by *Autocar* in August 1978. That car ran 0-60 mph in 5.0 seconds and turned a 12.8 quarter-mile at 112 mph.

Nonetheless, the record shows a competition Daytona in race-ready form was plenty fast and was durable enough to win its class in races held throughout the decade. In 1972, one of these super-supercars finished 1st in class at Le Mans and Watkins Glen and won the Tour de France outright. The competition model won its class at Le Mans in '73 and '74. Among several other important placings, the Daytona picked up class laurels at Daytona in '73 and '75, and finally, at a ripe old age for a race car, in '79—when it came home second overall.

Racing-modified Daytonas were known as big, brutal machines that relied on power for their speed. As expressed eloquently in a story in *Cavallino* magazine, "A Daytona at full clip was a sight to behold, mean looking and muscled, weaving dramatically on its overworked suspension, shaking and darting under heavy braking in a corner; literally pushing air and dust aside, leaving a wake and making its own weather; loud as hell and scattering birds and what all to the four winds.

"The gentlemen drivers loved it, since it inspired all those emotions that move men to attempt heroic, although essentially irrational, deeds. It required of you strength, courage, and endurance, yet was strong and forgiving; there was no embarrassment in racing it, it was a worthy contender, and more often than not, it brought you home a winner."

In short, the last front-engine Ferraris were true descendants of their stupendously powerful ancestors of the '50s. And they were compelling sights for any decade.

This is a genuine Daytona Spyder (*above*), but the car inspired many aftermarket coupe conversions. Nothing could imitate the Daytona's 4-cam V-12 (*opposite page*).

# FERRARI ENGINES

## 4-Cam V-12s (275, 365, 400 & 412)

Ferrari's early fame was largely due to the Colombo-designed single-overhead-cam V-12, but double-overhead camshafts were in use at Ferrari as far back as 1949. Some of these dohc engines were Lampredi-designed fours or sixes, and some were V-6s and V-8s. The V-8s were developed from the Jano-designed Lancia Grand Prix car, which Ferrari took over in 1955. This was the car Juan Manuel Fangio drove to his fourth World Championship, in 1956.

Some of these dohc engines were also V-12s: the 1949 125 F-1, for example; the 166 Formula 2; the 290 Sport; the 315 Sport; the 335 Sport; and the 412 MI. These competition engines are not as well known as the engines that were installed in road machines to be sold to the public. Hence, the Ferrari mystique, at least for the first 20 years, was predominantly based on the engine in Ferraris generally sold to non-racers: the sohc Colombo V-12.

The first road car to come from Ferrari with all independent suspension, the 275 GTB (*berlinetta*) and 275 GTS (*spyder*), was introduced at the Paris Auto Salon in October 1964. It had a Colombo-type V-12 up front, three downdraft Weber carburetors, and torque-tube drive to the rear transaxle.

The 275 GTB/4 made its debut at the Paris Salon two years later. The car looked similar to the previous model, but had a slight hood bulge to clear the air cleaner for the six Weber downdraft carburetors. This was the first customer road Ferrari to have double-overhead camshafts. The basic chassis layout and drivetrain of the 275 GTB were continued.

These four-cam V-12 engines were modified versions of the original Colombo-designed single-cam V-12 that had been in production at Ferrari since 1947. The major difference, aside from the dohc cylinder heads, was a redesign of the cylinder block. This was necessary because the transmission had been relocated at the rear axle. Clutch and bell housing were still at the back of the engine, however.

These 275 dohc engines were little more than 275 sohc engine blocks with new cylinder heads. Both powerplants had the same 77 mm × 58.8 mm bore and stroke, resulting in a 3286-cc (200.5 cubic-inch) displacement.

The sohc GTB engine had been rated at 280 horsepower at 7600 rpm. With four cams it came up to 300 horsepower at 8000. The compression ratio was 9.2:1 on both engines, and they both had six twin-

choke downdraft Weber carburetors.

In 1968, two years after the 275 GTB/4 introduction, Ferrari again stunned the Paris Salon with a new car that boasted a bigger engine in a bigger chassis, more power, and more speed. This was the four-cam 365 GTB/4, which became known as the "Daytona."

Although the 365's Pininfarina body was dramatically different from the 275's, the two cars' chassis were very much alike. The engines, still a Colombo derivation, were also similar, though the 365's block size was increased with added distance between cylinder bores, to accommodate a larger displacement.

Bore and stroke of the 365 were 81 mm × 71 mm, which gave a displacement of 4390 cc (268 cubic inches). With an 8.8:1 compression ratio and still with six twin-choke downdraft Webers, horsepower was 352 at 7500 rpm. Like the 275 GTB, but unlike the 275 GTB/4, a competition version of the Daytona was built. The racer had 405 horsepower and a lighter body.

Both the 275 and 365 dohc V-12s had camshafts operating directly on the valves through cups and spacers, and all these engines had two valves per cylinder. Also, both engines' carburetors, set in a row down the center of the Vee, fed into individual intake ports on the inside of the heads.

In March 1971, a new Ferrari "deluxe tourer" was unveiled at the Geneva show. This was the 365 GTC/4, which was one of the largest and heaviest Ferraris to date. It was a true touring car for the rich owner

who had no aspirations for competition on or off the track.

The engine it used was basically the same as the Daytona powerplant: same bore, stroke, and displacement, but with less horsepower, only 320 at 6200.

This was the first Ferrari designed for the U.S. market after emissions controls became a way of automotive life in America. To leave the center of the Vee open for emissions equipment, the manifolding for the six side-draft Weber twin-choke carburetors was incorporated into the exhaust cam covers. (This also helped reduce hood height to accommodate Pininfarina's body design.) Thus, instead of feeding the intake valves from the side of the head, the mixture came from the top of the head. This made the engine substantially lower, but a lot wider, and it is one of the most expensive of Ferrari motors to work on because of this carburetion arrangement.

This engine also is used in the 365 GT4 2+2 and the 400 GT. It's also in the 400 Automatic with a Weber-carbureted 4832 cc and 340 horsepower at 6500 rpm. And it's in the newer 412 with Bosch K-Jetronic injection, good for 340 horsepower at 6000 rpm.

As the 1980s drew to a close, the 412 was the only Ferrari in production with a V-12 engine and was the only one being built with the engine in front. As perhaps the last in a long series of front-engine Ferraris, it also is the last to use a derivative of an engine first penned by Gioacchino Colombo in 1946. His is an enduring design that has served for more than 40 years.

# Chapter 14:

# 250 LM: Enzo Puts the Cart Before the Horse

To understand the turn his high performance road cars took after the mighty Daytona of 1968, it's helpful to go back to Enzo Ferrari's creative inspiration, the race track. The 365 GTB/4, magnificent as it was, represented Maranello's last expression of the traditional *gran turismo*. A new day had dawned even before the Daytona bowed. As early as 1960, Ferrari himself was on the road to the modern, mid-engine era.

Experiments began that year with a Formula 1 Ferrari that placed its V-6 engine behind the driver. Enzo had relented after witnessing the layout's success in the hands of the Cooper team and then at Lotus. Those Britishers proved that a mid-engine F1 car could be made smaller and lighter than the traditional front-engine racers, that it offered nimbler handling, and that it could get its horsepower to the road with less wheelspin.

Ferrari learned quickly. His American driver, Phil Hill, won the 1961 World Championship in a mid-engine single-seater. Soon there were mid-engine Ferrari sports-racers, and the 1963 Le Mans race was won by one with a 3-liter Colombo V-12 nestled between its rear wheels. That car was called the 250 P. The "P" stood for *prototipo*, and for once the designation turned out to mean something: The open-topped 250 P Le Mans winner was the direct predecessor of the 250 Le Mans Berlinetta of 1964.

The progression was spurred partly by Ford. Enzo had recently flirted with

the Detroit giant, then refused to sell it a share in his company. Ford set out to assuage the wound. Working with Lola, another British constructor, the American automaker had designed a very advanced mid-engine car to meet the contemporary racing rules for both Prototype and GT cars. Ford's GT40 was certainly going to be much faster than the suddenly old-fashioned, front-engine GTO, and would be a formidable challenger in the top Prototype class. Ferrari dared not slip behind in the technology race; the stakes were victory in the world's most prestigious sports-car event, the 24 Hours of Le Mans.

This was a golden moment in automotive history. Enjoying what seemed like bottomless resources, Ford assembled a powerful team of some of racing's best talent and applied the latest scientific thinking against Ferrari's decades of hard-won experience. Best of all, this titanic struggle was being played out in a regulatory climate that, for the last time, required true dual-purpose cars. The Ford GT40 and the Ferrari 250 LM were racers first and foremost, but they had to be built with cockpit and ground clearance dimensions that made them suitable for transporting two occupants on the public highway.

This didn't necessarily make the 250 LM a good road car, however. As with the GTO before it, driving the raw, raucous LM anywhere away from a race track was an escapade. Nor did the LM design lead directly to

a proper highway vehicle; none of Ferrari's subsequent mid-engine production cars would have a V-12 engine.

But the LM has significance. For one thing, it demonstrated that Ferrari had his finger on the pulse of performance. Many ardent Ferraristi surely believed it was only a matter of time before this technology trickled down to their hands. For another, the 250 LM was an aesthetically appealing design. Finally, though its victory was a fluke, it was the last Ferrari to win Le Mans while Enzo lived.

Structurally, the 250 LM owed nothing to previous Ferrari GT design. As in the 250 P, its chassis was a multi-tube space frame; nothing remained of the old chassis style with its two large oval members. Like its racing prototype, the LM's suspension was independent at all four corners by means of wishbones and coil springs. The aluminum body was virtually a reproduction of a 250 P roadster onto which designer Pininfarina had grafted the '64 GTO's "tunnel-roof" hardtop.

Both the '63 250 P Le Mans winner and the LM used the sohc Colombo V-12. In the first LM built, it was the familiar 2.953-liter (180-cubic-inch)

Ferrari's first mid-engine grand-touring car was the 250 LM (*right*). Enzo relaxed his front-engine obsession after single-seat racers proved that Ferraris could win with an engine behind the driver. Introduced in November 1962, the 2-seat 250 LM was ostensibly a dual-purpose road-and-racing car, though the FIA was reluctant to sanction it as such. In practice, the car was unsuited for street use.

displacement. Every 250 LM thereafter had the displacement taken out to the same 3286 cc used on the contemporary 275 GTB. The LM had a hotter state of tune, though, and put out 320 horsepower at 7500 rpm to the 275's 300 horsepower at 8000. The LM engine drove through a 5-speed, nonsynchromesh gearbox. Claimed dry weight was 1874 pounds and the factory said the car was capable of 183 mph, though it didn't come with a speedometer.

The LM introduced Ferrari buyers to an ergonomic failing common in large, mid-engine cars. The LM's engine alone was a long 37 inches in length, and following typical racing practice, both it and the clutch were situated ahead of the differential. This positioning of the long V-12 and its clutch assembly in Ferrari's short, 94.5-inch wheelbase made the 250 LM a doubtful proposition as a road car. The driver and passenger were forced to sit so far forward that their legs had to angle sharply between the front wheels and toward the center of the car. Pedal offset is a vice found in many mid-engine cars, from the Ford GT40 of the '60s to the Lamborghini Countach of today. But in few was it so severe as in the LM. This was a particular bother to the driver. All but two LMs were made with right-hand drive, and the driver's right leg, which had to work the accelerator and brake pedal, was the most crooked.

Ferrari's new "GT" had another volumetric shortfall typical of the breed: lack of luggage capacity. Once places have been found for transaxles, exhaust pipes, fuel tanks, dry-sump oil tanks, radiators, batteries, and spare wheels in a mid-engine car, there's precious little room left to carry a bag. Certainly there's no space

The 250 LM (*both pages*) was the last Ferrari to win Le Mans during Enzo's lifetime, when Jochen Rindt and Masten Gregory placed first overall in a stunning 1965 upset. Pininfarina designed the aluminum body over a multi-tube space frame. Only the first 250 LM used a 3-liter V-12; subsequent 250 LMs used a 3.3-liter, though homologation politics forced Ferrari to retain the 250 LM nomenclature.

behind the seats. And like that of its Ford rival, the Ferrari's cockpit could become an oven from hot water and oil running past the passengers to and from the front-mounted radiators. In fact, some of the 250 LM's actual frame tubing was used as conduits.

Still, even if it wasn't a grand tourer suited to comfortable long-distance journeys, the LM was at least the most up-to-the-minute sports car for quick Sunday drives. It had all the power of the hottest GTO, with the traction, braking power, road holding, and handling sophistication of an F1 car. It also looked stunningly exotic in the early 1960s.

Only two LMs were finished by the factory for street use. One was a show car designed by Pininfarina for the 1965 Geneva Motor Show. In addition to bumpers and electric window lifts, it featured auxiliary gull-wing panels in the roof to improve access. It also had a huge plastic rear window that greatly improved the car's lines, though it was probably less practical than the stubby roof.

Several owners of LM racers did use their cars on the road, at least occasionally." In his book, *Ferrari 250LM*, Marcel Massini mentions an American owner who once drove his car "from New Orleans to Indianapolis, his wife keeping the luggage on her lap." That droll remark paints a picture, but the enthusiast literature contains few substantial driving impressions of the 250 LM.

One exception is David E. Davis' 1965 account in *Car and Driver*. "It's really remarkable how comfortable it is," Davis said. "It rides better than the 2+2! If it wasn't for all the exhaust noise and the banging and crashing in the suspension, it could be a touring car."

He continued, "The reclining seat position is really very nice. Once you learn to throw the shift lever fast enough, it's very nice too, with minimum graunching. The pedals are offset rather sharply toward the center of the car, which takes some getting used to, but you get used to it. The pedal travel is almost directly horizontal, so that you have to sort of point your toe like a ballet dancer to get the full travel, then you catch the heel of your loafer on the floor when you let

the clutch out, and that doesn't make for the world's smoothest shifts.

"The steering is super-accurate and right-now quick. The brakes require all the strength you can muster, but they stop the thing like it ran into something. There's a dead-pedal to the left of the clutch that would make a fine footrest in a race, but tends to be where the passenger's feet are, when you have a passenger." Fresh-air vents brought some relief to the hot cockpit, Davis said, but they also spewed road dirt. He also noted that the passenger's knees had a tendency to jam against the fuse panel on the dashboard. Visibility forward was "fantastic," to the rear it was "pretty good."

Michael Bowler of *Motor* sampled a 250 LM on the roads of England in 1971. He, too, found the mid-engine design a novel driving experience. "As the front falls away so sharply you just can't see anything solid in front of the screen—you drive along feeling as

though your legs are dangling over the edge of a cliff and conscious that behind there is a great mass of Ferrari which might catch up your toes at any provocation." But the car proved very stable. As had Davis, Bowler commented on how angled one's legs were, but added that "the actual placing of the controls was much better than with the front-engine cars." Unfortunately, no performance data were taken during either of these tests.

The 250 LM's historic record is more complete. The first one appeared at the Paris show in October 1963. That very car was raced the following year in America, but with no success, and was soon damaged in a fire at Sebring. It remained the only 250 LM ever fitted with an actual "250" engine, which, under Ferrari's system of multiplying displacement, meant a 3-liter. All its successors had the 3.3-liter version of the sohc power-

plant. And although many outsiders began calling it the "275 LM," Ferrari never officially changed the nomenclature. Enzo's reluctance stems from his struggle to get the car homologated in the GT category.

In 1962, the FIA had bought Ferrari's argument that the GTO was merely a version of the existing 250 GT SWB. International racing's governing body agreed to homologate the GTO even though far fewer than the required 100 examples were ever produced. Cobra manufacturer Carroll Shelby and other Ferrari competitors in the GT class protested bitterly, but to no avail. This time, however, when

**In a huff over the FIA's delay in homologating the 250 LM as a *gran turismo*, Ferrari painted his Formula 1 cars in the American colors of white and blue (*below*), ran them under the North American Racing Team, and won the '64 World Championship. The 330 P2 (*opposite page*), a racing cousin to the 250 LM, used a V-12 of nearly 4-liters to the 250 LM's 3.3.**

Ferrari's application for the LM couldn't be supported by mass production, the FIA turned down its homologation for the GT class.

The FIA didn't announce its decision until late in the summer of '64. Enraged, Ferrari officially withdrew from competition for the rest of the year. Sort of. Painted in the American colors of white and blue, his Formula 1 cars continued to run under the guise of Luigi Chinetti's North American Racing Team. They won the World Championship.

Meanwhile, the 3.3-liter 250 LMs raced as Prototypes for 1964 and again in '65. They did well in national and local events, but in full international contests they were outclassed by their more advanced, purpose-built siblings, the 275 P and by the still-bigger-engined 330 P, as well as by Ford's gradually improving GT40. In June 1965, however, occurred one of those amazing upsets that so enliven all sports: An LM entered by Chinetti's NART won Le Mans.

Faced with overwhelmingly faster opposition, NART drivers Jochen Rindt and Masten Gregory figured they had no chance at an overall victory. Rindt, in particular, wanted to get it over with; the rising Grand Prix star felt he had better things to do than pass hour after hour trundling a boring loop of flat French roads in a heavy old coupe. So Rindt and Gregory set out to drive the wheels off their LM. They failed. All the faster cars dropped out instead, and at 4 o'clock on Sunday afternoon the NART 250 LM howled across the finish line first overall. A sister LM was second. It was Ferrari's 6th straight Le Mans victory, its 9th in all—and the last to date.

The LM continued to race in 1966, when it was finally accorded GT competition status because the FIA production requirement dropped to 50. Only 32 LMs were in fact built, so Enzo may have gotten the last laugh. But it was too late for homologation to matter anyway.

Ferrari paved the way for the *berlinetta* 250 LM of '64 with the 250 P (*left*). The first 250 P prototype was tested in 1962 by John Surtees at Monza, where he proceeded to break the lap record. Fitted later with the "basket-handle" roll bar seen here, the 250 P made its race debut at Sebring in March 1963, where it won the 12-hour race. Later that year, a 250 P scored Ferrari's 4th consecutive Le Mans win.

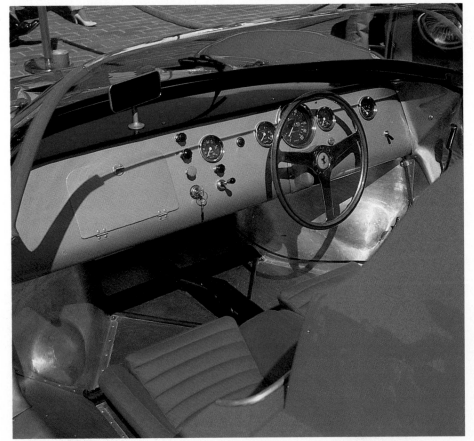

The pace of racing development was extremely rapid. Great strides were being made in engines, tires, and aerodynamics, and the LM's 1963 design was soon hopelessly obsolete. In fact, none of Ferrari's later Prototypes, not even the mighty P4 of 1967, could consistently hold off massively financed and soundly engineered Ford. The American juggernaut racked up four straight Le Mans victories, 1966, '67, '68, and '69. Ferrari never got back on form in France.

Evolutionary dead end it may be, but the 250 LM represents an important Ferrari landmark. It stands undiminished as a driving instrument and as an objet d'art. And it remains the most modern and sophisticated roadworthy vehicle to carry the magnificent and historic Colombo V-12.

The 250 P (*both pages*), was powered by a nearly standard 3-liter Testa Rossa engine situated midships. It rode on a slightly lengthened chassis from the Dino V-6 and V-8 mid-engine racing cars. The 250 P was one Ferrari that lived up to the truest meaning of its "prototype" tag because it spawned a production car of very similar design.

# Chapter 15:

# The Dinos: Prancing Ponies

Some enthusiasts of the prancing horse harbor a strong prejudice that the only true Ferrari has a large, powerful engine with 12 cylinders. Anything less is simply not a Ferrari. There is no fault in this conceit. Much of the Ferrari mystique is, after all, based on emotion. It's worth noting, however, that Enzo Ferrari didn't always sanctify the 12-cylinder sentiment.

He was adamant that his original 1947 car have a twelve. But as early as 1951, Ferrari allowed his second engine man, Aurelio Lampredi, to start work on a family of 4-cylinder, twin-cam racing designs. As 2-liters, these carried Alberto Ascari to the World Championship in 1952 and '53, and also formed the basis for the 500 Mondial line of competition roadsters and GT coupes. Later they were developed into the first Testa Rossa, a highly successful and beautiful sports-racer particularly well received in America.

Ferrari carried on in 1954 with a 2.5-liter four in Formula 1, and also put fours as large as 3.5-liters into the Monza series of sports-racers. He built inline sixes, too, adding a pair of cylinders to the basic Monza design to make an engine of 4.4-liters for a 1955 sports-racer called the 121 LM.

An adventure with V-8s began that same year, when erstwhile rival Lancia dropped out of racing and handed Ferrari its entire F1 program. Modified and developed, the Lancia-derived Ferrari V-8 took Juan Manuel Fangio to the world title in 1956. In later years, Ferrari put all-new V-8s into mid-engine F1 and sports-racing cars.

Then there was the V-6 configuration espoused by Enzo's first son, Alfredino. The first of these ran only a few months after the young man's tragically early death in 1956. The engines carried Alfredino's nickname, Dino, though Vittorio Jano did the actual design work. The Dino V-6 in 2.4-liter form took Britisher Mike Hawthorn to the 1958 World Championship. Three years later a 1.5-liter development helped American Phil Hill to the same honor. There were also some V-6s of various sizes in the front ends of F2 and sports-racing cars during the late 1950s, while in 1961, Ferrari's first mid-engine sports-racing cars had 2.4-liter Dino power.

There is also the 2.5-liter, twin-cylinder F1 engine Ferrari built in 1955, though he never raced it. Four years later he collaborated with the Gilera motorcycle company to make drawings of an air-cooled, inline-8 for the upcoming 1.5-liter F1.

So it's clear the V-12 mystique didn't blind Enzo to the virtues of other engine configurations. Nor was he necessarily mad for power. Remember, as an automaker Enzo had started out with an engine of 1.5 liters producing, in street-going form, barely over 70 horsepower. As that original Colombo V-12 grew to twice the displacement and more than four times the power, it must have seemed more and more commercially sensible to produce a less intimidating model.

The "baby Ferrari" that appeared in 1959 was the first tangible form of an idea The Boss apparently had nursed for some time. The car used a Fiat 1100 chassis dressed in a rather awkward Pininfarina coupe body. Never anything more than a prototype, it was used extensively for testing and as Enzo Ferrari's personal wheels. Power was provided by Ferrari's first really small engine, an 849.5-cc (51.8-cubic-inch) unit designated the 854, for its 850 cc and four cylinders. It was very much like one-third of a Colombo, with a single overhead-camshaft operating inclined valves in a hemihead. Its bore and stroke of 65 mm × 64 mm, though, indicates there were few, if any, V-12 parts in it. At its best, the 850 was said to produce 86 horsepower at 7000 rpm.

One day during this period, Innes Ireland, then a racing driver and later a journalist, went with the Old Man for a memorable ride recounted years later in *Road & Track*. "Out of the factory we turned left and soon were winding our way up into the mountains, through cobblestoned streets. It was here I came to know he retained his great flair as a racing driver, his braking points and gear changes precise and crisp, the little car on the limits of engine revs in every gear, the limits of adhesion on every corner. On our return the village streets were lined with locals, all clapping their hands and cheering...."

The factory never called this prototype by anything other than its engine-type number, although the press quickly came up with two names. One, logically enough, was "Ferrarina." The other was "Tommygun." It seems the 854's grille was decorated with a likeness of the famous weapon, though it's not clear which came first, name or insignia. Perhaps the rapid-fire exhaust note of the tiny four is explanation enough. Or maybe it was the way Ingegnere Ferrari shot up local traffic.

Tommy the toy Testa Rossa never went into production. A completely revised successor was unveiled at the Turin show in November of 1961. This one wasn't called a Ferrari either, appearing only under the name "Mille," for "thousand," in reference to its swept volume. With a "square" bore and stroke of 69 mm × 69 mm (2.717 inches) the inline-4 actually displaced 1032 cc (62.98 cubic inches). It had the sohc-head design and was rated at 100 horsepower at 7200 rpm. This engine was put into a chassis built for the purpose and given a pretty body by the coachbuilder Bertone.

Ferrari apparently never planned to manufacture the baby car himself. The project was handed over to ASA, a Milan firm formed to do the project. ASA evidently had more ambition than ability. Called the ASA 1000 GT, the appealing little car never really got off the ground, and the venture died in 1967 after only about 100 were built.

How disappointed Enzo was at the failure of the Mille cannot now be gauged, but it didn't kill his taste for a smaller Ferrari. The next time, however, he would enlist the aid of a larger, much more solid firm: Fiat. He would also make it more recognizably a *cavallino* by building it around the V-6 named in memory of his son. And he would base it initially on a Ferrari racing car.

Pininfarina's stand at the 1965 Paris auto show displayed a mockup of a mid-engine coupe called the Dino 206 GT Speciale. Built on the chassis of the Dino 206 S competition sports car, the styling exercise was impractically low-slung for an everyday automobile. But it showed most of the design elements that would go into mass production three years later. After a succession of further prototypes, the definitive Dino street car appeared at the Turin show in November 1967, and in customers' hands in 1968.

The Dino in its original 2-liter form (*right, top and bottom*) was first delivered to customers in 1969. Called the Dino 206 GT, the coupe carried no Ferrari identification. Fiat built the transverse-mounted engine, which Ferrari then massaged to extract about 180 horsepower at 8000 rpm. Ferrari constructed the chassis and Scaglietti assembled the aluminum body to Pininfarina's design. The 206 GT was retired in late '69 after about 150 were made.

Note that this was the same year the big, 4.4-liter Daytona went on sale. Many found it curious that Ferrari's flagship GT retained a front-engine design, while the firm's truly modern, mid-engine car wasn't even labeled a Ferrari. Indeed, Ferrari's name appeared nowhere on the car. Neither did that of Fiat, the company that actually built its engine. It was known simply as a Dino.

The most important mechanical point about the little coupe was that it had its midships engine mounted as a "sidewinder." In the prototypes, the engine had been situated in the conventional racing position: longitudinally, ahead of the transaxle. But in the production model, the V-6 was turned 90 degrees and mounted transversely, so that its crankshaft lay across the car, its clutch-end to the

left. A train of gears took the power down to the 5-speed transmission, which was located in a sort of extended engine-sump casting under the crankcase. The differential grew out of this casting toward the rear. Care had been taken to seal the crankcase from the transaxle housing so that proper gear lube could be used and so that a limited-slip differential could be fitted.

Transverse packaging was not new. Lamborghini's mighty Miura had been introduced with it in 1966. And counting both front- and rear-engine designs, there had been several sidewinders back through history. In fact, Ferrari's 1959 air-cooled straight-8 F1 concept was to be mounted transversely.

Following the Dino, of course, numerous other sports cars would favor

the mid-engine configuration for its ability to arrange bulky elements compactly. Sure enough, at 89.8 inches, the wheelbase of the production Dino was 2.4 inches shorter than that of the racer-based Speciale show car. Even with the extra space afforded by the transverse positioning, however, the Dino's pedal cluster was somewhat offset toward the center of the car.

The first Dino's type number was 206 GT, denoting six cylinders and two liters of displacement. The exact capacity was 1986.6 cc (121.2 cubic inches), from its bore and stroke of 86 mm × 57 mm (3.386 × 2.244 inches). Following Ferrari practice, the entire engine block was cast in aluminum, but the angle between the cylinder banks of the V-6 was 65 degrees, rather than the traditional 60 degrees.

224

Each head housed two overhead camshafts, all four driven by chains. A trio of Webers gave each cylinder its own carburetor barrel. The compression ratio was 9.0:1 and rated horsepower was 180 at 8000 rpm. Torque was 137 pounds/feet at 6500. The 206 GT's suspension was fully independent and each wheel had a disc brake. This was the first Ferrari with rack-and-pinion steering. Its chassis was a steel construction blending tubing with sheet-metal. Bodywork on the 206 GT was aluminum.

In the summer of 1968, while the Dino was still under development, Enzo Ferrari gave journalist Paul Frere a quick demonstration ride in one. Writing about it for the British weekly *Motor*, Frere—once a member of Ferrari's racing team—felt compelled to report on his host's driving.

"It is 10 years since I was last driven by the boss himself, who is now 70, but I must say, the precision, authority and speed with which this racing driver of 45 years ago handles his car are still really impressive. . . ."

As for the car, it was "a revelation: with its light weight (less than a ton), low centre of gravity and very low polar moment, it corners as flat as a kipper, seems perfectly neutral and incredibly agile. Even in this light car, it is evident that the engine does not produce a lot of power below 5,000 r.p.m., but with the (Ferrari-designed and made) five-speed gear-box, it is very easy to keep the revs above this, when the engine really comes into life, right up to the 8,000 r.p.m. limit. The noise level is quite acceptable, about the same as a Porsche 911, and the marvellous handling has not been

achieved at the cost of comfort. As a result of the low drag, Ferrari says all three cars made were timed at between 143 and 146 m.p.h."

Those "three cars" were prototypes and considerably lighter than the final version would be. About six months after his first ride, Frere got his hands on a production Dino, took it to a scale, and found the weight to be 2514 pounds. He also took it to the Auto-

Pininfarina's stand at the 1965 Paris auto show displayed a mockup of a mid-engine coupe called the Dino 206 GT Speciale (*both pages*). It was built on the chassis of the Dino 206 S competition sports car; its "engine" was devoid of internal parts. The styling exercise was impractical for an everyday automobile. But it showed most of the design elements that would characterize the production Dino and, in fact, an entire generation of Ferrari sports cars.

strada, where he timed a top speed of 140 mph. Zero-60 took 7.5 seconds, and the quarter-mile consumed 15.5 at just a touch over 90 mph. "Of production 2-liter cars, only the Porsche 911S can just match these figures..." Frere said in *Motor*. The Dino he drove had already run a gauntlet of other testers. A fresh, standard 206 GT could sprint to 100 km/h (62 mph) in 7.2 seconds and would top out at 142 mph, according to *The Ferrari Legend: The Road Cars*, by Antoine Prunet.

Nothing about the 206 GT's handling disappointed Frere. "In fact, crisp, beautifully balanced handling and quite exceptional road holding are the Dino's major virtues....Stability at speed is wonderful and the car behaved beautifully in my favourite 125 m.p.h. + S-bend of the Autostrada where it drifted through needing practically no correction at all...but when it eventually goes, it goes quickly because of the very low polar moment of inertia so correction must be immediate and accurate."

That behavior seems to have been characteristic of close-coupled mid-engine cars of the day, which offered many of the handling advantages of contemporary racing cars, but also much of their unforgiving nature.

As a sports-driving instrument, Frere said in his book, "The Dino has about everything you could wish for in the circumstances: enormous cornering power, perfect balance which keeps the car in an almost perfectly neutral attitude whatever you do with the accelerator (as long as you don't provoke a power slide), and enough power to push you around into the following straight." He also noted the exceptional traction from a standing start conferred by the rearward weight bias and the limited-slip.

Frere's criticism includes the carburetion, which had a tendency to starve the engine in sharp corners, and the steering feel, which, despite the rack

and pinion, felt "dead" and suffered an erratically stiff movement. He also singled out noise from the engine housed so close behind his ears. But all in all, he regretted having to give the 206 back to its owner.

The Dino had a limited life span in its original 2-liter form. As with so many Ferraris, the first model was rather quickly replaced with a substantially altered successor. Production of the 206 ended late in 1969 after somewhere between 100 and 180 cars, with 150 authoritatively considered to be about the right number.

Succeeding the 206 GT was the 246 GT, but there was more to this altera-tion than simply increasing the engine size by 20 percent. Although the transaxle case remained aluminum, Fiat was now making the block in cast iron. And while the body looked almost identical, the wheelbase was increased by 2.3 inches, to 92.1, and the main panels were now steel. Obviously, the revised car was heavier—Prunet's book puts the increase at 331 pounds (150 kg). But the 246 also had more power. The new cylinder dimensions of 92.5 mm × 60 mm (3.642 × 2.362 inches) gave a displacement of 2419.2 cc (147.6 cubic inches). Horsepower increased to 195 at 7600 rpm, torque was up to 165 at 5500.

Succeeding the 206 GT at the end of 1969 was the 246 GT (*both pages*). Its engine was increased to 2.4-liters, gaining 15 horsepower and more torque, and the wheelbase was up by 2.3 inches. One test measured 0-60 mph in 7.1 seconds and a top speed of 148 mph. The car was considered extraordinarily balanced, though its engine was starved of fuel in hard cornering.

227

In contrast to the short-lived 2-liter, the 2.4 had a long production run that lasted into 1974 and amounted to more than 3000 cars. During that time there were several detail changes, such as 5-bolt wheels replacing the single-center-nut originals. In 1972, the hard-roofed GT was joined by a GTS, which was a Spyder that featured a Porsche-type removable Targa roof panel. Unfortunately, the Targa design dictated that the coupe's functional rear-quarter windows be replaced with opaque sail panels.

A Dino 246 GT featured in a 1971 *Motor* road test weighed 2610 pounds with only a couple of gallons of fuel

aboard. The ballast was distributed 43 percent front/57 rear. Test weight rose to 3035, but the car nevertheless accelerated to 60 in 7.1 seconds and ran the quarter-mile in 15.4. No trap speed was given, but it would have been in the low 90s because the 0-90 time was 14.2 seconds and the 0-100 clocking was 17.6. Top speed was 148. This performance was fully on a par with some of the 12-cylinder Ferraris that so impressed the testers of the 1950s.

The Dino 246 was an appealing sports car that garnered much attention in the enthusiast press. *Motor* used such words as "perfection," "superb,"

Joining the 246 GT coupe in 1972 was the 246 GTS (*both pages*). The two were mechanically identical except for the GTS's targa-roof, which in Ferrari's eyes, qualified the car as a spyder. These baby Ferraris were retired in 1974 without ever gaining a Ferrari badge or prancing horse. Production totaled about 2800 GT coupes and 1200 GTSs.

and "excellent." The car "cannot be faulted in any area of importance," particularly in the area of handling, the journal enthused. The Dino offers "forgiving and controllable behavior when its limit of adhesion is finally exceeded, an important advance for a mid-engine vehicle which has revived our wavering faith in the concept for roadgoing cars."

Perhaps it was the longer wheelbase of the 246, or maybe something had been done to refine suspension behavior since Frere drove the 206, but the new Dino had no cornering flaws that *Motor* staffers could detect. "Even the Dino must run out of grip eventually—what happens when it does?" the magazine wondered. "For the practised anticipation and lightning responses of the professional racing driver, mid-engine cars may be fine, but with their centrally located masses they do tend to spin rapidly when all is finally lost, an unsatisfactory characteristic for the more ordinary mortals likely to drive Dinos on the road...." But *Motor* maintained that the little mid-engine Ferrari was an exception. Even when deliberately broken loose, it remained "gentle and controllable."

Other areas also were improved, for the magazine described "superbly precise, direct steering which gives good feel with little kickback and is one of the joys of the car." Most *Motor* drivers said the engine was still a little noisy on long trips and some found the seat design uncomfortable. The carburetor cutout problem was still there, too. But the engine itself, the gearbox, brakes, and controls, the ride, aerodynamics, visibility, and looks—everything that mattered in a tool created for the joy of driving—was "perfection" and contributed to "the feeling of unity with the machine that the Dino imparts."

Pity the V-12 chauvinist who refused to drive this gem because it wasn't a real Ferrari.

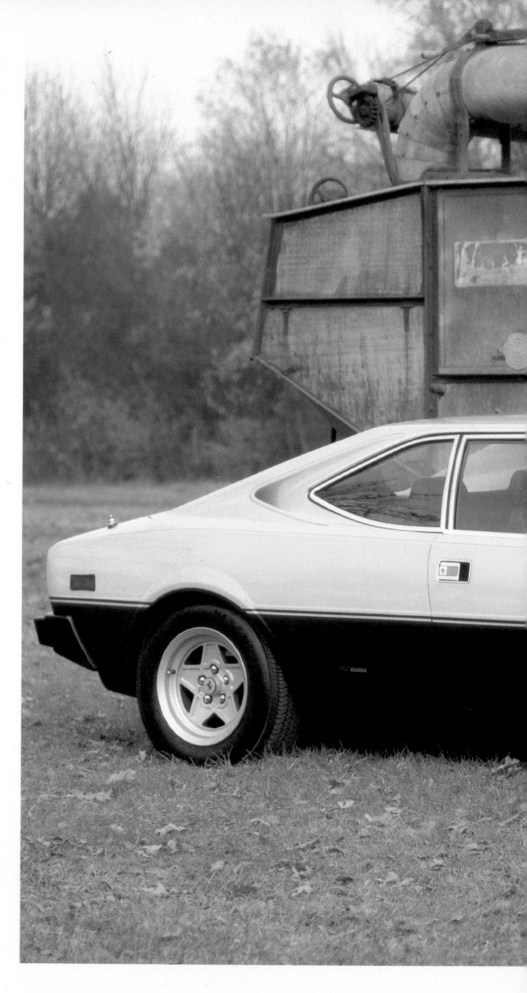

The Dino 308 GT4 (*right*) was unveiled at the 1973 Paris Salon. It was Ferrari's first mid-engine 4-seater and the first Ferrari to have a transverse-mounted V-8. This 2+2 also was the first production Ferrari in 20 years with a body designed by a coachbuilder other than Pininfarina. Bertone did the 308 GT4's steel body, apparently using a design derived from a rejected Lamborghini styling prototype.

Happy Dino days lingered into 1974; then, disaster. For a reason still unfathomable—but one with all the earmarks of a committee verdict—Ferrari replaced a universally loved sports coupe with a widely scorned 2+2, the Dino 308 GT4.

Introduced at the end of 1973, the GT4 must have seemed like a good idea at the time to somebody—somebody at Fiat, most likely. Turin's giant had been running little Maranello's production-car side since 1969. And Enzo's interest in road vehicles, never that intense anyway, had been declining as their relevance to his beloved racing machines faded. If anyone actually asked his opinion, Enzo may well have agreed that, sure, a new Dino with four seats sounded okay if it would broaden the customer base.

The 308 GT4 chassis was evolved from that of the V-6 Dinos, but its wheelbase was stretched to 100.4 inches to accommodate the small rear seats. Track dimensions were wider, too, and *Motor* said unladen weight was up to 2800 pounds.

To cloak the new platform, Ferrari turned away from Pininfarina and to

Bertone, a *carrozzeria* then more commonly identified with Lamborghini. Bertone had been working on Lamborghini's rival Urraco, another 2+2 with a midships V-8. The design house literally gave Ferrari the back seat on this one, using for the 308 GT4 steel bodywork derived from a rejected Lamborghini styling prototype. Bertone had penned some voluptuous cars—the stunning Miura, the gracefully rounded final Urraco—but the angular 308 GT4 was one of the most severe Ferraris ever.

At least there was nothing wrong with the engine. As its new-style designation implies, the 308 powerplant was a 3-liter of eight cylinders. In some respects it was two-thirds of the contemporary 365 V-12, sharing the identical bore and stroke of 81 mm × 71 mm, or 3.189 × 2.795 inches. It displaced 2926.9 cc, or 178.6 cubic inches, and the eight cylinders were arranged in a 90-degree Vee. Block material was once again aluminum. The four overhead cams, driven this time by toothed rubber belts, operated two valves per cylinder. Again there were enough twin-throat Webers to

provide a carburetor barrel to each cylinder. As with the Dino V-6, the Dino V-8 was mounted transversely with a 5-speed transaxle below and behind.

A spread of horsepower figures has been issued for this first 3-liter V-8, from 205 at 6600 rpm to 255 at 7700. Compression ratios range from 8.1 to 8.8:1. This confusion may well reflect the increasingly stringent U.S. emissions regulations, which in the early '70s were forcing production of different models for different markets. If it can be taken at face value, one published torque figure is 210 pounds/feet at 5000 rpm.

Once again *Motor* produced a comprehensive evaluation and found things to like about the GT4. Its performance was excellent: 0-60 in 6.4 seconds, the quarter-mile in 14.7, and a 152-mph top speed. This obviously was a full-power, European-spec engine. *Motor* judged the handling very good, stable, and without any surprises, "though perhaps lacking the precision and agility of the 246's...." Thanks mainly to the belt camshaft drive, the 308 GT4's engine mechani-

Enzo finally granted the Dino official prancing-horse status in 1976 by affixing the Ferrari name and insignia to the 308 GT4 (*both pages*). The car's twin-cam engine (*left*) furnished fine acceleration. Despite lack of rear-seat room (*opposite page*), subpar steering and shifting action, inadequate climate-control system, and a poor finish, the 2+2 sold 3500 over seven years.

cal noise was subdued enough for occupants to enjoy its sweet exhaust note.

*Motor*'s list of negatives was longer. It included "very poor fuel consumption; 'dead' steering, indifferent gearchange, poor [steering] lock; inefficient heating and non-existent face-level ventilation; poor finish." The rear seats were a painful joke for anyone taller than a small child, though this criticism could be applied to most 2+2s, including the Lamborghini Urraco.

Despite lukewarm press reviews, the wedge-shaped GT4 sold a bit better than had the late, lamented 246. Dealers moved nearly 3500 copies over its seven-year life span. Late in 1976, the car began appearing with Ferrari badges, which replaced the original Dino emblems everywhere but on the tail. But not even this official recognition could sway enthusiasts who had been pining for another "real" Dino. Their wish was granted in 1975, with the 308 GTB.

It's likely the 2-seat GTB had been planned all along and was merely late coming out. No one has ever fully justified the gap between the last of the 246s, in mid-1974, and the availability of the 308, late in 1975. Whatever the reason, the car seemed worth the wait.

Wheelbase was back down to a nimble 92.1 inches and the GTB weighed about 200 pounds less than the longer GT4. The engine had dry-sump lubrication (except the U.S. model) and a less-restrictive exhaust system. Its body, developed in a wind tunnel by

Ferrari's true Dino successor was the 308 GTB (*both pages*), presented late in 1975. With its 2-seat configuration, sensuous lines, mid-engine form, and use of V-8 engines, this car set the tone for Ferrari's "volume" offerings for the balance of the '70s, all of the '80s, and into the '90s. Its 250-horsepower engine was identical to the GT4's except for the use of dry-sump lubrication on non-U.S. models. All early 308 GTBs had bodies of fiberglass.

Pininfarina for low drag and high stability, was made of lightweight fiberglass. And it came with the Ferrari
badging from the start.

Paul Frere wrung out an early production example on Ferrari's Fiorano
test track and in the hills above Maranello in late 1975. He told *Motor* read-
ers that "Dino 246 fans—of which
there are many—now have a worthy
successor to their favourite car, as the
308 GTB is even faster, quieter and
more comfortable." Acceleration to 60
mph took 6.4 seconds, the quarter-
mile passed in 14.6, and top speed was
153.5 mph. Even more impressive was
the smooth, fuss-free nature of the
performance, Frere said. "There is no

dramatic unleashing of power as the
engine comes 'on the cam,' just a
smooth flow from 3000 rpm to the
7700 rpm red line."

An experienced tester, he found the
handling strongly biased toward understeer, though there was enough
torque in the lower gears to bring the
tail out in sharper turns. Stability on
140-mph bends and at top speed was
outstanding. The suspension travel
was greater than in the old Dino,
which meant improved comfort and
roadholding on bad pavement. Bumps
did kick back through the wheel, but
this time Frere didn't complain about
the steering feel. He also noted with
approval that this was "one of the first

Ferraris to have a reasonable turning
circle." Braking power and fade resis-
tance in the mountains were excellent.

Frere expressed displeasure with
the GTB's instrumentation, finding
the dials hard to read at a glance and

*(continued on page 240)*

To beat the Italian tax on engines over 2-
liters, Ferrari provided his home market
with the 208 GTB Turbo (*above*) powered by
a turbocharged 1991-cc V-8 of 220
horsepower. Both it and its V-8 sibling
(*opposite page*) were considered faster, quieter,
and more comfortable than their V-6 Dino
predecessor. A '75 308 GTB was timed at 6.4
seconds 0-60 mph; 14.6 in the quarter-mile.
Top speed was 153 mph.

In 1980, Ferrari took the 308 GTB engine and chassis, stretched the wheelbase to 104.3 inches, added a rear seat, commissioned a new Pininfarina body, and produced the Mondial 8. Given the 3.2-liter V-8 from the 328 GTB, it became the 3.2 Mondial (*this page, top*). A cabriolet version was introduced in '83 (*this page, bottom, and opposite page*).

some gauges that seemed misplaced. He also criticized the clutch linkage, which incorporated an over-center spring that sometimes refused to let the clutch reengage properly. "But these few, easily remedied shortcomings can hardly detract from the fascination of the most charming car yet to come from Ferrari."

Ferraristi seemed to agree, and the 2-seater V-8 proved very popular. With several model variations and periodic mechanical evolutions, it was the car that carried the prancing horse into the modern era.

For the Italian market only, where there is a major tax break for engines below 2000 cc, Ferrari extended to the

GTB an option available on the 2+2 and offered a 208 engine. This was accomplished by reducing the bore to 66.8 mm, which brought the capacity to 1991 cc. Horsepower dropped substantially, to 170, so in 1983, Ferrari applied a turbocharger. The 208 Turbo was rated at 220 horsepower at 7000 rpm.

Smog regulations, meanwhile, had cut into the prowess of the 3-liter engine. From an original high of around 250 horsepower at 7700 rpm, output fell to 214 horsepower in Europe and to 205 in the U.S., both at a mere 6600 rpm. Fuel injection generally advances performance, but Ferrari adopted it in 1980 simply to help reduce emissions.

The 308s so equipped can be identified by the "i," for "injection," at the end of their model designations.

Fighting back further, Ferrari drew on racing know-how and developed new cylinder heads with four valves per combustion chamber. These *quattrovalvole* heads were put into production in 1982, and bumped horse-

The Mondial (*above*) is Ferrari's mid-engine 2+2 follow-up to the 308 GT4. Its Pininfarina designed-body is more organic in shape than its sharply creased Bertone predecessor and is a pleasing solution to the challenges presented by a mid-engine, 4-seat design. It's no high-performance sports car, but has been well received by its public and some insist it's the sweetest Ferrari of all to drive.

The 328 GTS (*opposite page*) and GTB (*this page*) were evolutions of the 308 GTB/GTS. Introduced in 1986, their V-8s had increased displacement, fuel injection, and the 4-valve heads introduced to the 308 engine in 1982. It had 13 percent more horsepower and 13 percent more torque than the fuel-injected 308 GTBi. The grille was also revised.

power to 240 at 7000 rpm.

For 1985, the car was rechristened the 328. Its V-8 was bored and stroked to 83 mm × 73.6 mm (3.268 × 2.898 inches) to raise displacement to 3185.7 cc (291.6 cubic inches). Horsepower was now 270 at 7000, torque was 224 pounds/feet at 5500.

Ferrari took a cue from the evolution of the 246 Dino and introduced a Targa-topped 308 GTS in 1977. Fiberglass was dropped that year as a body material in favor of steel, though the fiberglass interior "tub" remained, as on the Daytona. With the 3.2 engine came a bodywork update most noticeable in the grille area.

While all this attention was being paid to the 2-seater, Ferrari-Fiat decided that a new 2+2 was needed and the Mondial was introduced in 1980.

A Pininfarina design built on a 104.3-inch wheelbase—even longer than that of the GT4—this was no high-performance sports car. But it was well received by its public and there are those who insist it's the sweetest Ferrari of all to drive. There was soon a cabriolet version, and the Mondial was kept mechanically abreast with the V-8's periodic improvements.

The car that carried Ferrari's hard-core sports-car standard through most of the '80s, though, was the 2-seater. A good example was the American-specification 328 GTS evaluated by *Car and Driver* in its May 1986 issue.

The Ferrari's full-tank weight was 3090 pounds, distributed 41.7/58.3. Net horsepower was 260 at 7000 rpm; torque was 213 pounds/feet at 5500. The car got to 60 in 5.6 seconds, finished the quarter-mile in 14.2 at 97, and topped out at 153. Sixteen mpg was observed. List price was $64,393.

*Car and Driver*'s harshest criticism concerned the Targa body's lack of structural rigidity on bumpy roads. The next most serious flaw was tricky handling at the limits of tire adhesion. As Tony Assenza put it, "your workload increases geometrically with road speed. In fast transitions, you're al-

A 328 GTS (*above*) was evaluated by *Car and Driver* in its May 1986 issue. The American-specification Ferrari's full-tank weight was 3090 pounds, distributed 41.7-percent front/58.3-percent rear. Horsepower was 260 at 7000 rpm; torque was 213 pounds/feet at 5500. The car ran 0-60 mph in 5.6 seconds, the quarter-mile in 14.2 at 97 mph, and topped out at 153. List price was $64,393.

ways aware that the majority of the car's mass is back there over the rear wheels and that it takes that mass a certain amount of time to settle down during quick right-left-right combinations. You really become aware of the mass if you decide to cancel some of the inherent understeer with lift-throttle oversteer. Lifting off for too long will produce more oversteer than you want, and the result is guaranteed

to light up every neuron in your brain. It takes a brave and judicious right foot to get the balance just right."

On the other hand, Assenza said, the 328 "has one of the world's best V-8s, inspired looks, a fine suspension design, and a lock on about two-thirds of the world's automotive magic." Once warmed to operating temperature, the gearbox made it "one of the handful of cars in the world that you

shift even when you don't really need to. You find yourself going down through the gears for every stop sign and traffic light just to hear the motor sing and feel the gears notch into place."

*Car and Driver* editor Don Sherman submitted that "Not long ago, Ferraris were fine, expensive toys that most folks could stand to drive only once or twice a week. The factory has now

taken steps to change that dismal state of affairs, making the 328GTS a worthwhile daily-transportation tool. The seats are comfortable; the heating-and-ventilation system works; the exhaust note is mellow and nice." Ferrari reliability, he contended, had reached the point that buyers and dealers had become "total strangers."

Technical editor Csaba Csere endorsed the staff's generally favorable

impression. "The revamped engine is powerful and willing throughout its rpm range, transforming the GTS into one of the quickest cars on the market . . . the GTS deserves to wear its prancing horse as proudly as the best of the twelve-cylinder cars."

Enzo Ferrari probably read that; he had everything written about him and his cars translated so he could. It must have made him smile.

Though Ferrari calls it a spyder, the 328 GTS (*above*) really has a targa-type roof with a removable center panel that stores behind the front seats. Some testers have found the targa body to lack structural rigidity on bumpy roads and its rearward weight bias to prompt tricky handling in very fast maneuvers. But its V-8 engine, suspension, and gear box, its looks, sounds, and feel make it a worthy heir of Ferrari's best 12-cylinder cars.

## FERRARI ENGINES

### The Dino V-6

Ferrari's V-6 engine configuration goes back to 1956, when his engineers developed a concept by Vittorio Jano, who designed the V-6 engine for Lancia's Aurelia.

Maranello's first V-6 was originally created for Formula 2 racing. It was a 65-degree Vee with chain-driven double overhead camshafts, twin-magneto ignition, and dry-sump lubrication. This basic design was developed into two sub-series, each with different bore centers. The smaller block was available in a 1.5-liter displacement, for Formula 2 racing, and in a larger block of 2.4, 2.8, and 2.96 liters.

A Ferrari 120-degree Dino V-6 was built exclusively for Grand Prix racing. It was designed by Carlo Chitit and used everything from the 65-degree engine except the cylinder block itself.

A 60-degree Dino V-6 with single ignition was introduced in 1957. It was used in Sports Racers for sale to customers. Basically half a production V-12, it had a chain-driven single-overhead camshaft.

A third Dino V-6 was designed by Ingegnere Franco Rocchi. This engine was to be produced by Fiat in at least 500 production cars to qualify it as a stock-block for Formula 2 racing in 1967. The Rocchi engine was a double overhead-camshaft 65-degree V-6 like the first Dino. It powered a trio of cars: the Dino 206 SP Sports Prototype racer; the Fiat Dino GT, a front-engined, rear-drive sports model in both roadster and coupe body styles; and the Dino 206/246 GTs, where it was mounted transversely behind the driver.

The Dino engine series inaugurated a new Ferrari identification system in which the first two digits represented the engine displacement and the third the number of cylinders. Thus, a Dino 206 was a 2.0-liter, 6-cylinder car, and a 246 was a 2.4-liter 6-

cylinder car. This replaced a more confusing nomenclature based on the displacement in cubic centimeters of one cylinder. Under that arrangement, the 166 was a 2-liter car, the 212 was a 2.3-liter, and the 250 was a 3-liter. No longer would Ferrari followers be puzzled by a system in which a 250 Testa Rossa was a V-12 with 3-liters displacement, but a 500 Testa Rossa was a 4-cylinder with 2-liters.

The Rocchi-designed, third-series Dino engine had a lot in common with the original Dino V-6. One difference, however, was that the original was of aluminum alloy with steel press-fit cylinder liners, while the third-series design had a cast-iron block and aluminum heads.

Rocchi retained the 65-degree angle between cylinder banks. This allowed space to accommodate the three twin-choke Weber 40 DCNF/7 carburetors and their attendant manifolding. With a 2418-cc displacement and a 9.0:1 compression ratio, the V-6 put out 195 horsepower at 7600 rpm and 165 pounds/feet of torque at 5500. By the time the 246 reached American shores, horsepower was down to 175 and performance was hampered significantly. The power-robbing culprits were U.S. emissions requirements, principally an air pump to blow air into the exhaust headers.

Tests in European and American automotive magazines produced the following results:

| | 206 (Euro.) | 246 (Euro.) | 246 (U.S.) |
|---|---|---|---|
| 0-50 | 5.6 sec | 5.5 sec | 6.2 sec |
| 0-60 | 7.5 | 7.1 | 7.9 |
| 0-70 | 9.8 | 9.2 | 10.1 |
| 0-80 | 12.2 | 11.4 | 13.1 |
| 0-90 | 15.3 | 14.5 | 15.9* |
| 0-100 | 19.2 | 17.6 | 21.5 |
| 0-120 | 30.6 | 28.5 | |
| Top Speed | 140 | 148 | 141 |
| Horse-power/ rpm | 180/ 8000 | 195/ 7600 | 175/ 7000 |
| Torque/ rpm | 138/ 6500 | 165/ 5500 | 160/ 5500 (est.) |

*Standing-start ¼-mile at 87 mph.

The main reason for building the production engine in 2.4-liters displacement was to be just under the maximum for European taxable horsepower limits. Over that size, the licensing tax would be prohibitive to all but the most affluent potential buyers.

Because the engine was mounted transversely, drive off the "rear" end of the crankshaft was transferred via three helical spur gears down to a five-speed transmission, which had its housing cast integrally with the alloy sump. Transmission and differential oil were carried in the same reservoir, but kept separate from engine oil.

These 246 Dino engines would pull from about 1800 rpm with judicious throttle application. They worked really well if kept above 3500 rpm and would run freely right up to the 7800-rpm redline. Unfortunately, the use of a cast-iron

block and the addition of U.S.-mandated emission and safety equipment added several hundred pounds to the car—again it could ill afford after losing 20 horsepower to antismog hardware.

Still, the flexibility of its engine made the 246 Dino easy and pleasant to drive. And the owner could brag that his engine was a development of the V-6 that powered Ferrari Grand Prix cars from 1957-1960, including the one in which Mike Hawthorn won the 1958 World Drivers Championship.

The Dino 246 engine (*both pages*) had a cast-iron block and aluminum cylinder heads. The 5-speed transmission's housing was cast integrally with the alloy sump, but its oil was kept separate from engine oil. This road-going V-6 traces its lineage to racing versions, including those that took Ferraris to Formula 1 World Championships in the '50s and '60s.

# FERRARI ENGINES

## The Dino V-8

Ferrari's name never graced the Dino 246. The Dino was simply a Dino, not a Ferrari. During its eight-year production run (1967-1974) it was another make of car as far as Enzo Ferrari was concerned.

Even the 308 GT4, which had a V-8 instead of a V-6, was called a Dino when it was introduced in 1973. The badge embargo ended in 1975, with the 308 GTB. That car was a Ferrari Dino, complete with the prancing-horse insignia on the nose, horn button, and road-wheel hubs. On the rear deck was the name "Ferrari."

The V-8 that was the basis for that car remains in use today and will likely have applications well into the future. It has undergone several changes during its life, however. As initially designed, the 90-degree V-8 had a 2926-cc displacement, four twin-choke Weber 40 DCNF carburetors, and two Marelli distributors. Its twin overhead camshafts were driven by toothed belts, an innovation that had been introduced by Ferrari in the 365 Berlinetta Boxer. Compression was 8.8:1 and horsepower was rated at 205 at 6600 rpm.

Like the V-6, the V-8 was transversely mounted behind the driver and power was directed to the 5-speed transmission by three spur gears at the "back" of the engine. The car in which this V-8 was installed was a Bertone-bodied 2+2, which was to last only through 1979.

The "real" Ferrari production model of the 1980s, the 308 GTB, came on the scene in 1975. It used the same V-8 engine, but a different body, a Pininfarina-designed, Scaglietti-built 2-seater. It's seen nearly 15 years of continuous production in several variations.

The 308's Franco Rocchi-designed four-cam V-8 remained virtually unchanged until 1981, when it received Bosch K-Jetronic fuel injection. In 1982, it was fitted with new heads that used four valves per cylinder and the engine and the car were retabbed the "Quattrovalvole." Displacement and compression ratio were unchanged, but horsepower went to 230 at 6800 rpm.

All 308 engines had their bore increased by 2 millimeters and their stroke by 2.6 in 1985. That brought displacement up to 3185 cc and with it a new designation: 328 GTB for the *berlinetta*, or 328 GTS for the targa-top "spyder." Horsepower increased to 260 at 7000 rpm, torque to 215 pounds/feet at 5500. Bosch K-Jetronic injection was retained, but the ignition was changed from Digiplex to Multiplex, which Ferrari said was more versatile and could control more functions.

The Mondial, a new four-passenger, mid-engine Ferrari, replaced the GT4 in 1980. It shared the 308 GTB's engine treated to the same mechanical changes over the years. These changes saw carburetors replaced by fuel injection, 4-valve heads added, and displacement increased. But none of these gave the 308/328 engine design the kind of boost it got—literally and figuratively—in 1984. That's when the V-8 was turbocharged and adapted to the new GTO. Using the basic 308 engine, the displacement was *reduced* to 2855 cc by having one millimeter less bore (81 mm × 80 mm) than the 308; the stroke remained at 71 mm. But twin IHI turbochargers blowing through an intercooler into a Weber-Marelli injection system raised

horsepower to 400 at 7000 rpm.

Installing the twin-turbo system on the transverse-mounted engine would have created too many production and servicing problems. So the V-8 had to be mounted longitudinally. This necessitated a stretch in the wheelbase, from 92.2 inches to 96.5.

The engine underwent other changes to suit the GTO's role as both a street car and a competition car. Retained were the nickel-treated aluminum cylinder liners, but fitted were new pistons cooled by an oil spray from below. The crankshaft was redesigned in anticipation of more load from turbocharger pressure on pistons, rods, and crank.

The GTO's compression ratio was only 7.6:1, but when the engine was producing

maximum power at full boost, the internal pressures were enormous. In racing tune, the engine would likely put out 500-plus horsepower, compared to about 400 for the street version.

This engine was also used in the 40th anniversary Ferrari, the F40. For this car, however, the dohc V-8's bore was increased to 82 mm, from the GTO's 81, and the stroke decreased to 69.5 mm, from the GTO's 71. This gave a displacement of 2963 cc. Boost pressure from the twin turbos, which are slightly larger than those on the GTO, was set at 1.1 *bar* maximum, versus the GTO's 0.80. The result is 478 horsepower at 7000 rpm and 425 pounds/feet of torque at 4000.

The F40 will haul its 2425-pound curb weight from a standing start to 100 mph in 12 seconds and touch 201 mph in fifth gear, according to published road tests. The GTO has been lauded for race-car performance and touring-car comfort.

Some who worship the sound and soul of a Ferrari V-12 are disappointed in the V-8-engine models. Realistically, though, Ferrari has achieved performance from its V-8 engines that make a twelve unnecessary. The compact dimensions and lighter weight of the V-8 translate into smaller and lighter cars, qualities that enhance the vehicle's agility and responsiveness.

The Dino V-8 has served Ferrari well, and it appears that this configuration will continue as the Ferrari engine of choice for years to come.

The 328 GTB (*above*) is powered by the ultimate rendition of Ferrari's naturally aspirated V-8. Its 3185-cc engine is rated at 260 horsepower at 7000 rpm and provides the basis for the 400-horsepower, twin-turbo 2855-cc V-8 used in the GTO and for the 478-horsepower turbocharged 2936-cc V-8 powering the F40. From the carbureted 308 GTB of 1975 to today's computer-assisted fuel-injected F40, Ferrari has shown that the V-8 has an important role as the cars from Maranello seek the leading edge of performance in a changing world.

# FERRARI CHASSIS

## The V-6 Dinos

The 1969 introduction of the 246 Dino marked several Ferrari milestones: It was the company's first car with unit body/frame construction; it was the first mid-engine Ferrari design offered to the public; and it was the first car produced by the Maranello concern since the 1939 model 815 that didn't carry the Ferrari name.

Another waypost of sorts was the engine. Though designed by Ferrari, it was built by Fiat, which had just purchased 40 percent of Enzo's company.

The 246's basic layout had been around Ferrari since 1965, when Pininfarina showed a Dino 206 S Speciale at the Paris Auto Salon. That car was a styling exercise on a Ferrari racing chassis, however, and the engine was a hollow shell built only for show.

A working prototype, the Dino Berlinetta GT, was displayed at Turin in '66. This was not to be the production version of the car, though it had a running engine mounted longitudinally. Another year passed, and at the '67 Turin show the *real* car debuted: the 206 Dino GT. It still had the familiar 2-liter, double overhead-cam V-6, but this time the engine was placed transversely behind the passenger compartment and ahead of the rear axle.

This 2-liter engine was built by Fiat and installed in the Ferrari-designed chassis. The Pininfarina-penned body was constructed at Scaglietti after the chassis was received from Ferrari and the engine from Fiat.

A 246 version (2.4-liters, 6 cylinders) was announced early in 1969, but didn't go into production until late in the year. These cars were destined for export, while the 206 was for the European market.

The thought behind the 206/246 was to compete with the Porsche 911. At the same time, it was to give Ferrari an "entry-level" car to be sold along with the Daytona, which went for just under $20,000 at the time. But at $14,500, the 246 Dino was considerably more expensive than the 911, and hardly entry level for most buyers.

With approximately 175 horsepower at 7000 rpm, and with a curb weight of 2770 pounds, the 246 was a more-than-adequate performer, though not a full-fledged a neck snapper in acceleration. Top speed was approximately 140 mph, which certainly put it in the Porsche performance bracket.

More importantly, the 246 was a demon on twisty, curving roads. Credit the 92.1-inch wheelbase and race-car weight distribution. With the driver aboard, 41 percent of its ballast was on the front tires, 59 per-

cent was on the rear. Equipped with a 5-speed manual transmission and ventilated disc brakes, the 246 was a delight to drive, if a bit noisy inside.

The unit chassis was solid and stiff, allowing the 4-wheel independent suspension to do its work. Typical of modern Ferrari design, unequal-length A-arms, coil springs and tubular shock absorbers were at all four corners, and an anti-roll bar was fitted at each end. Steering was by rack and pinion.

The alloy wheels were by Cromadora. At first, they were center-lock, knock-off types with three-eared hubs, but in 1970, they were replaced by five-lug, bolt-on wheels of basically the same design.

A GTS version was introduced in 1972. Though called the Grand Touring Spyder, it wasn't a convertible. Rather, its targa-type roof had a removable panel over the passengers.

The Dino's interior was adequate for an average-size person, a bit tight for those over 6 feet. The instrument panel looked like the Ferrari Daytona's, but the gauges themselves were different. Outward visibility was pretty good—excellent for this

The mid-engine Dino 246 GTS (*above*) had unit body/frame construction, an all-independent suspension, and a 41-percent front/59-percent rear weight distribution. With its high-revving V-6, it was a delight to drive on twisty roads.

type of car—but engine noise could make a long trip tiring.

A 6.7-cubic foot luggage compartment was provided just behind the rear axle. Little cargo could be carried in the front compartment, which was virtually filled with spare tire and a tool kit.

Production continued through 1974, when the V-6 was phased out to make way for the upcoming V-8 Dino. The car was never called anything but a Dino during the 246 production, and most Ferrari enthusiasts refused to consider the model a real Ferrari.

It was, however, designed at Ferrari, the majority of the mechanical bits, even the later engines, were built at Ferrari, and the cars were sold and serviced by Ferrari dealers. Moreover, their current values as "collector cars" suggests that they are now quite accepted as Ferraris.

# FERRARI CHASSIS

## The V-8 Dinos

Ferrari demonstrated its design flexibility at the 1973 Paris Salon when it ushered in the 308 GT4. This was Enzo's first mid-engine 2+2, and for it, he returned to separate frame-and-body construction instead of simply picking up the 246's unit body/frame.

In another first, Carrozzeria Bertone designed and built the four-place steel body. No house other than Pininfarina had ever created a production Ferrari. Wedgy and somewhat sharp-edged, the Bertone design was mounted on a steel-tube frame. Suspension was still all-independent with unequal-length A-arms, coil springs, tubular shock absorbers, and anti-roll bars at each end.

Like the 206/246, the 308 GT4 was still called a Dino; Ferrari's name appeared nowhere on the car. However, many 246s and 308s that came to the U.S. have had Ferrari badges attached by owners, but none are original or authentic.

"A Ferrari has twelve cylinders," Enzo Ferrari is said to have remarked, and some insist this the reason he never called the 246 or 308 GT4 a Ferrari. That argument is undermined by the non-12-cylinder competition cars built by the company—V-6s, inline fours and sixes, V-8s, and flat-8s—all entered as Ferraris.

Further rebuke came in October 1975, when the 308 GTB appeared at the Paris Salon carrying the designation "Ferrari 308 GTB." It was still a Dino, but a Ferrari Dino.

This replacement for the 246 was again a Pininfarina design built by Scaglietti. Its construction, however, was separate frame and body like the 308 GT4, rather than the steel unit body/frame of the 246. A major break with either predecessor was the use of fiberglass for the GTB's body panels. Enzo employed this material for the shells of quite a few of his mid-engine competition cars, but the 308 GTB was the first production Ferrari fashioned of fiberglass.

Some of Ferrari's more influential buyers are said to have reacted adversely to the use of fiberglass on the new mid-engine 2-seater. There's no firm evidence that Ferrari bowed to such criticism, but steel body panels did replace the 308 GTB's fiberglass ones before the year was up.

Regardless, the body material was of minor value insofar as strength or rigidity was concerned. All the chassis loads were carried by the steel-tube frame. Its rigid and strong scuttle hoop formed a combination bulkhead and support for doors, windshield and posts, pedal assembly, and steering column.

The 308 GTB wheelbase was 92.1 inches, compared to the 100.4 inches of the 308 GT4, which needed the extra length to accommodate the rear seat. Otherwise,

the chassis details were almost identical. Short and long A-arms, coil springs, and tubular shock absorbers were used at all four corners. Anti-roll bars at each end had become standard, as had disc brakes and a 5-speed transmission.

While the 308 GTB replaced the 2-seat 246 Dino, a new four-place model was conceived to replace the 308 GT4. This was the Mondial. Pininfarina once again handled body design and the lines it conceived were far more handsome than those Bertone drew for the 308 GT4. The Mondial also was a larger car than its immediate predecessor. It had almost four additional inches of wheelbase (104.2, up from 100.4), which made it far more comfortable and practical than the GT4.

The Mondial made its first public appearance in March 1980 at the Geneva auto show. With minor mechanical and visual changes, it was still in production nine years later. Available in both closed and convertible form, the Mondial in '89 was the world's only mid-engine, four-passenger production car.

It shares its chassis design, suspension, engine, and transmission with the contemporary 308 GTB and GTS models. Me-

**This cut-away view of Ferrari's 3.2 Mondial (*below*) shows how Maranello met the challenge of packaging four seats in a mid-engine design.**

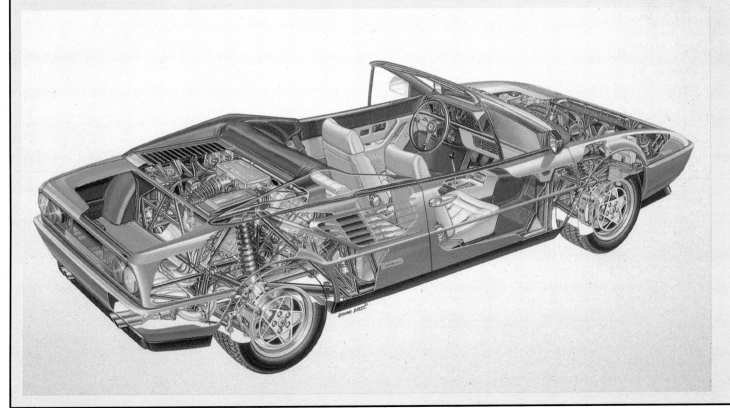

chanical alterations made through the years to one were made to all. One major change was the 1985 increase in displacement that turned the 308 engine to a 328 (3.2 liters, eight cylinders).

The evolution was to continue at the 1989 Geneva show with the introduction of the Mondial 8 T. Distinguished externally from its predecessor primarily by fog lamps, the 8 T was to feature the first use of Ferrari's new 3.4-liter, 32-valve V-8. This replacement for the 328 engine has new castings for the block, heads, and crankcase. It will be mounted about six inches lower than the 328, which puts the Mondial's center of gravity closer to the pavement and allows Ferrari to recalibrate the suspension to improve handling. This engine also will be used in the replacement for the 328 GTB/GTS, the new Ferrari 348, which is set to debut at the 1989 Frankfurt Motor Show.

Mid-engine cars do offer advantages in acceleration because their weight is on the driving wheels. And they enjoy outstanding braking because the forward shift of weight loads all wheels equally. The downside, however, is that the mid-engine configuration makes it difficult to create much space for passengers or cargo. It is a credit to Ferrari and Pininfarina that the Mondial is as good as it is in this regard.

The prancing-horse stable holds more exotic offerings, but the Ferrari Dino 3-series is still the basic Ferrari of the 1980s—and very likely for at least the first part of the 1990s. Longtime Ferrari enthusiasts found reasons to be derisive of the V-6 and then the V-8. But the Dino Ferrari's good looks, excellent handling, and general demeanor have won many of them over. It's still not a twelve, but it *is* a Ferrari.

The 308 GT4 (*above*) was spawned during the early 1970s, at a time when Enzo Ferrari's attention was focused away from his road cars and toward his racing efforts. Hence, some observers see it as the ill-conceived product of meddling by Ferrari's parent company, Fiat. It proved to be an important car, however, by validating the concept of a mid-engine 2+2 and also by selling well.

# Chapter 16:

# Boxer and Testarossa:
# The New Shape of Ferrari Power

Ferrari began racing a new 1.5-liter 12-cylinder competition engine late in the 1964 Formula 1 season. It had two banks of six cylinders positioned horizontally, parallel to the road, opposing one another from opposite sides of the crankshaft. Often called "flat" engines, such powerplants also are nicknamed "boxers," for the image of the pistons "punching" at their opposite numbers.

Flat engines were nothing new in 1964. Porsche, Volkswagen, and others had been making horizontally opposed auto engines for decades, and it was a common configuration in both motorcycling and aviation. Just before World War II, in fact, Enzo Ferrari's alma mater, Alfa Romeo, had built a flat-12 racing engine. An advantage common to all boxers is the lowest center of gravity possible for an engine; disadvantages include the greatest possible width.

Ferrari's first boxer had only one full racing season before the 1.5-liter formula was terminated at the end of 1965. Enzo went back to a V-12 for the first year of the new 3-liter F1.

But Maranello didn't bury the boxer concept. Its champion, engineer Mauro Forghieri, revived the layout in 3-liter form during 1969, and it reentered F1 in 1970. This time it was decidedly successful. The flat-12 was the mainstay of the Ferrari F1 team for the entire decade, the power behind three world driving championships and four world manufacturers' titles. It also won sports-car races.

It's not difficult to understand how

those at Ferrari now came to think of the boxer as the "true" prancing-horse twelve. It took no great leap of faith to include one in the specification of the mid-engine GT that would replace the Daytona.

Other cylinder and packaging configurations for this new Ferrari flagship were not dismissed out of hand, however. One thought must have been to develop the old mid-engine 250 LM of 1964. That GT carried its 3.3-liter V-12 in the conventional racing position: longitudinally mounted ahead of the differential and clutch. The configuration consumed a lot of space, however, and unless the wheelbase was made unreasonably long, it created a rather cramped cockpit. The problem would have been worse with the Daytona's bigger 4.4-liter V-12.

A 1966 Pininfarina-penned Ferrari show car, the 365 P Berlinetta, addressed the problem of distorted foot space in a mid-engine coupe. The 365 P placed the driver in the middle of the car, with a passenger seat on each side. To most observers this was too radical a solution.

A better idea might have been to modify the V-6 Dino platform to accept a twelve. A transversely mounted V-12 with 60-degree cylinder banks gave a comparatively short power package. But perhaps it was out of the question to appear to clone Lamborghini's hot new Miura, which debuted in 1966 with a sidewinder V-12. Lamborghini was returning to a longitudinal layout for the Countach it would unveil in 1971. But this new

supercar would mount its engine facing rearward, with the clutch and transmission situated toward the front. That enabled designers to move the Countach's long V-12 close to its differential, thus shortening the needed wheelbase. Ferrari's development team is likely to have known about the new Lamborghini, and again would not have wanted to seem to be copying it.

Besides, the boxer design itself offered a way to shorten the engine-package length. Because the weight of the cylinders and heads were at the same level as the crankshaft, the entire engine could be mounted *above* the transaxle without raising the engine's center of gravity unmanageably high. After all, the Dino's engine was over the transmission, and everybody loved that car's handling. Plus, the shift linkage could be very simple, with a straight shot from gear lever to transmission. This wasn't possible in Lamborghini's Miura, where the transaxle was behind the engine.

As it jelled, the unnamed new Ferrari used a longitudinally mounted flat 12 with its clutch toward the car's tail. A train of three gears at the extreme rear transferred power diagonally down to the transaxle, which occupied some of the space that would be known as the sump in a conventional engine.

To save space, the gear cluster was offset to the left of the engine centerline, and the uppermost shaft was slightly outboard of the lower one. This allowed the crankshaft to ride as

low as possible. A deep, narrow chamber running alongside to the right of the gear cluster constituted the actual engine sump; the dry-sump system of the Daytona was not adopted.

Engineers put the 5-speed gearset forward of the differential, so the halfshafts emerged approximately under the second pair of cylinders, counting from the back. That meant the engine's center of gravity was slightly ahead of the wheels, legitimizing the car's mid-engine label.

The new car's 98.4-inch wheelbase

Rolling off the Maranello line in 1984, this 512 Berlinetta Boxer (*opposite page*) traces its roots to such concept cars as the 365 P (*this page*), a 1966 Pininfarina mid-engine exercise that placed the driver's seat in the middle.

was nearly four inches longer than the front-engine Daytona's, but it was precisely the same as the production Miura's. Since the Lamborghini's front wheelwells didn't intrude on cabin space, however, its pedals could be sited straight ahead of the driver's seat. The Ferrari buyer was asked to accept some offset.

Another Ferrari sacrifice was luggage space. The only compartment dedicated to this necessary ingredient of a genuine Grand Tourer was a shallow bay in the front, already half-filled with the half-sized spare tire. A small shelf behind the seats, over the engine, provided space for oddments, but the short-tail styling left no room for a rear trunk.

This daughter-of-Daytona was 171.1 inches long, 70.9 inches wide, and 44.1 inches tall. That's about 2.5 inches shorter than its front-engine predecessor, 1.5 inches wider, and a very noticeable five inches lower. It ran on the same wheels and tires.

A genuine weight never has been pinned down, but the mid-engine car probably was in the region of 3200-3400 pounds, empty. That would have

been some 200 pounds lighter than the Daytona. Weight distribution was about 43-percent front/57-percent rear.

The mid-engine car's structural design was derived from that of Ferrari's Dino. The stout-looking chassis frame was of welded steel tubing, most of it square-section, reinforced with welded-in sheetmetal. Suspension was by means of wishbone-type links at all four corners, with dual springs/shocks at each rear wheel. Steering was rack-and-pinion. The radiator was at the front. Two fuel tanks, one on each side of the engine behind the doors, carried a total of 31.7 U.S. gallons.

Ferrari's now-typical inner bodywork lining of fiberglass was used, as were fiberglass inner fender liners. The lower exterior bodywork, including the bumpers, was also of fiberglass and was usually painted black. The rest of the outer paneling was a mix of steel and aluminum.

This new Ferrari appeared as a concept car at the Turin show in the autumn of 1971. It had an engine of 4.4-liters, just like the Daytona, and was

called the 365 GT4/Berlinetta Boxer. By the time production began in 1973, the car was universally known as simply, "The Boxer."

The car's flat-12 used the Daytona V-12's pistons and connecting rods, but the boxer's bore centers were up one millimeter, to 95. Both had double-overhead camshafts, but refinements—including belt-drive for the cams—made the flat engine more efficient than its Vee-configured predecessor, despite meeting more restrictive pollution controls.

According to Mel Nichols, who interviewed the project engineers for his book, *Ferrari Berlinetta Boxer*, the development motor produced 380 horsepower at 7000 rpm, nearly 30 more horsepower than the same-sized V-12, and at 500 rpm less. The engineers said the prototype reached 302 kilometers per hour, or 188 mph—some 15 mph better than the Daytona. For production, horsepower was backed off to 360 at 7000 and speed dropped to 181. Torque in the production 4.4-liter engine was 311 pounds/feet at 4500 rpm, just about the same as the Daytona, but peaking

1000 rpm lower, said the Ferrari men.

Road tester Nichols was rapturous about the 365 Boxer, particularly its engine. The joy began the instant it fired with a "fierce, stunning bark like that of a Formula One engine except that the beat that followed was steady and free of the popping and spluttering of the race-car engine. Nor was the noise quite so savagely loud. But, by God, it had an awesome wail, deep and unmistakably the end product of enormous strength. Even those used to the marvellous sounds of multi-cylinder Modenese engines tended to sit and listen to it for a few minutes, marvelling...."

As promised by the sound, "...acceleration was just one long, superlative, staggering thrust forward, so incredibly fast and so undramatic too." In

Pininfarina's P6 of 1968 (*opposite page*) was another rung in the development of a mid-engine Ferrari coupe. The 512 S racer of '69 (*this page*) contested the Manufacturers Championship with a 48-valve V-12.

fifth gear, at 30 mph or at 150, plant the throttle pedal and the feeling was the same, "...a great, solid, incredible surging forwards, tremendously powerful but silky smooth too, and accompanied by a glorious, unique noise."

Its fabulous engine was the dominant element of the 365 BB experience. If the car wasn't quite as exciting in most other respects, that was deliberate.

The rival Countach compromised all else for performance. Ferruccio Lamborghini created a single-minded driving machine that was enormously satisfying when given its head on fast, open roads, but excruciatingly unsatisfactory in any other circumstance. By contrast, Enzo Ferrari was determined to keep the Boxer buyer's goodwill in everyday traffic. There may have been little space for luggage, but

the Boxer's cockpit was roomy and visibility was good. The controls were easy to work, the ride comfortable. And the handling was carefully tuned for forgiveness. The car understeered enough to balance the great power and to warn clearly about the approaching cornering limit, a limit at which the Boxer could be tricky.

"Despite the smooth and light steering," Nichols cautioned, "it was never possible to forget that the Boxer was a big and heavy two-seater, and ... there were times when it seemed as if the weight would take over and wrest control from you." Another problem, noted by Nichols and others, was a slightly wayward feeling at high speeds, as though the nose were developing aerodynamic lift. The engineers later admitted to Nichols that in fact it was lifting, by about one inch at top speed.

Nichols' advice was to accept the 365 GT4/BB as "a fleet-footed grand touring car for two people rather than the ultimate, steel-honed sports car." Keep the car within itself, he said, and any drive was a joy. "...[Y]ou would arrive at a destination hundreds of miles away feeling fresh and happy, aware that you had travelled fast and in great safety and with enormous enjoyment."

Paul Frere, writing this time in *Sportmoteur* and quoted in the Antoine Prunet book, *The Ferrari Legend: The Road Cars*, was similarly positive: "The session on the Fiorano circuit was a true pleasure, the available power always being sufficient to exit the corners with a great deal of acceleration, after breaking the rear wheels loose in a well-controlled slide...."

Frere judged the steering a definite improvement over the nose-heavy

Daytona: quicker, lighter, more precise. "On the comfort level as well," he added, "the BB illustrated the progress made in later years by the fastest vehicles: a lower center of gravity, a better distribution of weight, and a modern suspension all permitting the adoption of relatively soft springing without harming the handling on the good surfaces while assuring not only adequate comfort but also better road holding on the mediocre roads."

While there was a new sense of composure, the Boxer wasn't without its compromises. Some who sampled it wrote of overweight steering and a too-heavy clutch. The gearshift took learning because Ferrari's rigid gate constrained the lever. Others said the engine's mechanical noise grew wearing on long trips, while radiator water pipes running along the center of the floor transmitted excessive heat to the cockpit. Luggage capacity was desperately short for everyone.

"Boxers are fantastic cars to drive, with little raison d'etre other than the sheer pleasure of driving the ultimate sporting GT car," explained Dean Batchelor in his book, *Illustrated Ferrari Buyer's Guide*. "In other words, you'll get tremendous enjoyment from driving a boxer, but don't plan a trip great-

Considered one of Pininfarina's best concept designs of the late 1960s, the 512 S (*both pages*) was built on a 512 S racing chassis. Unlike the earlier engine-less P6, the 512 S show car had a running V-12.

er than a few hundred miles if it is necessary to take anything with you other than a travelling companion. And that should be someone who enjoys the car as much as you do."

Some of the Boxer's shortcomings were exaggerated by American highway conditions, which are so very different from those in Europe. Ferraris have always been European cars first and foremost. Indeed, Ferrari never saw any sense in "federalizing" the Boxer, that is, modifying it to meet

U.S. noise, emissions, and safety standards. Still, quite a few were brought into America independently and subjected to varying amounts of modification. That's why only road tests carried out in Europe on standard cars have historical meaning.

The German magazine *Auto, Motor und Sport* ran the Boxer against several of its rivals in comparison trials. Recapped in Prunet's book, they show that the 365 Boxer was fast, but not blindingly so. It matched a Porsche

930 Turbo's 25.2 seconds in the standing-start kilometer, but neither car could equal the Countach's 24.3 (as Prunet says a Daytona could). The Boxer in this test might have been slightly off-song because its top speed was only 174, four mph back of the Countach. This was still much faster than the Porsche, which topped out at 155 mph.

*Motor* published acceleration times for another Boxer of 6.5 seconds 0-60 mph and of 13.5 0-100 mph. The best

acceleration figures mentioned by Nichols were those he achieved: 0-60 mph in 5.3 seconds; 0-100 in 11.3. He didn't claim to have seen 180 mph himself, but believed it possible. Furthermore, he's convinced this 4.4-liter model was both quicker and faster than its successor, the 5-liter 512 Berlinetta Boxer.

The 512 BB debuted in 1977, taking the place of the 365 GT4/BB after fewer than 400 were built. Its larger engine was Ferrari's response to in-

creasingly severe exhaust-emissions and noise-suppression standards instituted by European governments.

To preserve performance, the bore was increased from 81 mm to 82 mm (3.228 inches), and the stroke from 71 mm to 78 mm (3.071 inches). That brought displacement up to 4943.03 cc (301.6 cubic inches). With a boost in compression ratio from 8.8 to 9.2:1, torque jumped from 311 pounds/feet to 331. Peak-horsepower rpm, however, dropped from 7000 to 6200. This

Ferrari's first production mid-engine 12-cylinder car was the 365 GT/4 Berlinetta Boxer (*both pages*). Also called "The Boxer," it had a 4.4-liter flat-12 rated at 360 horsepower and a body of steel, aluminum and fiberglass. It debuted 1971; production began in '73.

was due to the longer stroke, and probably to the added smog and noise controls.

Nichols' *Ferrari Berlinetta Boxer* lists the 5-liter's maximum horsepower at 340, down from the production 4.4's 360. The factory brochure said the 512 BB had 360 horsepower and, typically, other data have been published elsewhere.

There were some improvements to offset the loss in horsepower. In partial compensation for the lower rev limit, the overall gear ratio was changed from 3.46 to 3.2:1. And the 512 engine's torque curve was not only taller, it was broader, for more low-end response. To handle the greater torque, the clutch—which some owners had found to be a weak point—was changed from a single- to

a double-plate design; that made the pedal movement both shorter and lighter. Friction was also reduced in the gearshift mechanism to ease the action. And the engine got a dry-sump lubrication system to ensure a steady supply of oil under hard maneuvering.

Ferrari refined other aspects of the car as well. Occupant comfort was enhanced by improved seats and by air conditioning that was now standard instead of optional. Handling was improved by an increase in rear-wheel and tire size, from 215-section tires on 7.5-inch-wide rims to 225 on 9-inch rims. This change required widening the body by more than one inch, to 72 inches. A chin spoiler was added to tame the aerodynamic lift and NACA ducts on the lower-body sides now cooled the rear brakes. There were

numerous other exterior detail alterations, some simply for styling, some for better engine-compartment ventilation, and some as a result of development in Pininfarina's wind tunnel.

With less power, taller gearing, and perhaps with greater weight as well (again, hard numbers are sketchy), it wasn't a surprise to find the new Boxer slightly slower than the old.

A good example of the 5-liter model might reach 176 mph, according to one of its designers, though some magazines said the 512 could be edged out at the top end by the Daytona. In a 1978 512 test quoted by Godfrey Eaton in his *The Complete Ferrari*, Britain's *Autocar* magazine saw 0-60 mph in 6.2 seconds and the quarter-mile in

*(continued on page 269)*

Ferrari succeeded the 365 GT/4 BB with the 512 BB (*both pages*) in 1977. Its flat-12 (*right*) was larger to compensate for new government regulations that burdened it with power-sapping emissions and noise hardware. It was more refined but a bit slower than the 365 GT/4 BB.

The factory never raced the Boxer, but privateers did. This is the North American Racing Team's 512 BB (*above*) fitted with an extended tail for improved aerodynamics.

13.6 at 100 mph. The test 512 weighed 3854 pounds, by the way. Slightly slower than its supercar cousins, maybe, but the new mid-engine Ferrari was a subtly improved vehicle.

"The 512," Mel Nichols wrote, "emerged immediately as an even more sophisticated car, even easier to drive, even more appealing, even more impressive. This was a Boxer with more charm as well as more fight, more poise as well as more spirit." The beefier engine gave the car more "aplomb" in traffic, he said, and "just sent you gliding along even more effortlessly than before." The wider rear tires were apparently augmented by associated suspension changes. Tight-road handling was improved,

the rear end had better grip in corners, and there was less body squat and wheelspin on acceleration. Nichols reported that the non-lift nose made the Boxer "steadier and more purposeful" at high speeds, and "therefore that little bit more relaxing and reassuring for the driver."

The last significant modifications to the Boxer occurred during 1981, when tighter European emissions standards retired the magnificent quartet of three-throat Webers in favor of fuel injection. A switch to the designation 512i signified the change. The factory said horsepower was now 340 at 6000 rpm and that torque was 333 pounds/feet at 4200. The car also got slight revisions in bodywork

The factory never contemplated a racing version of any Boxer, but that didn't dampen the competitive fires of several Ferrari distributors. Luigi Chinetti and his North American Racing Team acted first, running a highly modified 365 in several endurance races during 1975 and in later years. Some of Chinetti's European counterparts followed up by talking the factory into helping them with even more radical 512s. Visually and viscerally these enormously long and very wide cars were quite impressive, and they gained a cult status among en-

The 512 BB's cabin (*opposite page, top*) was a setting for speed. Its body opened clamshell-like for access to engine and cargo (*above*).

thusiasts. Nothing like real success ever came the way of the racing Boxers, however. The gap between track and road now was simply too great. Still, the Boxer embodied Ferrari's vision of a streetgoing supercar

and so he felt no need to change focus when it came time to replace the car with a new model.

The successor was introduced in 1984. It was an outgrowth of Boxer technology, then 13 years old, but was

significantly different in many details. Though it was conceived, designed, and developed strictly for everyday highway use, Ferrari bestowed upon it one of the grandest names from Maranello's glorious racing past—albeit

shortened to one word: Testarossa.

For those who came upon a Testarossa for the first time, the overriding impression was one of enormous width. Part of the effect was the no-apologies Pininfarina shape, but the body did indeed measure 77.8 inches across. That was nearly six inches broader than the wide-rear-track 512 BB, and up by nearly seven on the contemporary Corvette. Compared to the Boxer, the Testarossa's 100.4-inch

The striking Testarossa (*above*) assumed the mantle of Ferrari's flagship in 1984. Its cockpit is larger and more comfortable than the Boxer's and its luggage capacity is greater.

wheelbase was two inches longer and its 176.6-inch body was longer by five. It was also slightly taller, 44.5 inches to 44.1. By contrast, Lamborghini's Countach was only 163 inches long and 42.1 inches high on a wheelbase of 96.5 inches. And the Countach took up even more road width, its giant flares projecting to 78.7 inches.

Not that Ferrari was concerned with Lamborghini. The Testarossa had its own agenda. It was very much a sports car in the satiny, civilized mold of the Boxer, its every refinement directed toward pleasurable everyday driving. The added body length, for instance, increased the size of the cockpit, particularly the storage area behind the seats. Volume of the front luggage bay was also greatly expanded. And where the Boxer's cabin suffered the heat of coolant passing between the mid-mounted engine and front-mounted radiator, the Testarossa's flat-12 was served by a pair of radiators installed aft of the passenger compartment, in the flanks just ahead of the rear wheels.

Because the engine was substantially more powerful than the Boxer's, cooling proved critical. The size and shape of the Testarossa's large radiator inlets also had a great bearing on aerodynamics, and proper ducting demanded many wind-tunnel hours. So

did the location of the radiator-air outlets, which used extractors built into the sail panels on either side of the engine bay behind the cockpit.

Although the basic horizontally opposed design was carried over and the bore/stroke remained the same, there were many detail changes, and the Testarossa's powerplant was actually lighter than the Boxer's by some 44 pounds. The biggest performance gain came from all-new cylinder heads, which incorporated modern 4-valve technology. Painted crimson, they gave currency to the literal meaning of *testa rossa*: red head. With the compression ratio still 9.2:1, factory-rated horsepower was now 390 at 6800 rpm, and torque went up to 362 pounds/feet at 4500. To handle this output, the twin-plate clutch was larger, and the rear tires were increased to 255-section on 10-inch rims.

Once again Paul Frere was one of the early journalists to get his hands on a new Ferrari, and he sent his impressions to *Road & Track* early in 1985. "What an engine the Testarossa has, complete with the best Ferrari music," Frere wrote. "Power is there in plenty, right up to the 7000-rpm limit. . . . For all its futuristic looks, the Testarossa is a civilized and practical car. There is a well about 10 in. deep behind the

seats where I had no problem stowing my small bag and coat, while the front locker will also take some luggage. The steering column is adjustable for height, the seats are electrically adjustable for height, reach and backrest angle, and the air conditioning is standard and very easy to adjust." He was not overly conscious of the car's width from the driver's seat, and he noted that vision to the rear and sides was "quite good."

On the negative side, Frere found that the very wide door sills collected mud in wet weather, which "guaranteed" one's pants would be soiled. The windshield wipers didn't clear enough of the glass, and Enzo's new road missile was cursed with "grossly inadequate headlights." But performance was still the Testarossa's reason-for-being, and this one proved Ferraris were still exhilarating.

Frere took his Testarossa on the local Autostrada. "All other cars seemed to be left standing and when the very dense traffic was momentarily clear, I would shift down to 4th or 3rd and the speedometer needle

*Testarossa's huge side vents (both pages) feed air to its radiators. Their "cheese-slicer" grilles help the car meet European laws limiting the size of bodyside openings.*

would soar to the equivalent of 150 or even 155 mph...."

On the Fiorano test track, in wet conditions, Frere found the big, heavy new *cavallino* frisky as a colt. "Obviously, with so much power at the tip of your foot, it is never difficult to induce wheelspin coming out of a bend in 2nd gear (which is good for about 85 mph at 7000 rpm). The grip provided by the huge Michelin TRX tires is remarkable, and the limited-slip differential helps prevent premature wheelspin. The very accurate and fairly quick rack-and-pinion steering is excellent."

While deliberately booting the car into lurid powerslides for the benefit of his photographer, Frere discovered

"...the Testarossa's handling reminds one much more of a full-blood racing car than a road car, both for its agility, no doubt due to its low polar moment of inertia, and to the lack of any rubbery feel in the suspension."

Later that year, *Car and Driver* put a new Testarossa through its paces in America just before the car was privately federalized. Even though this was a Euro-spec engine with no U.S. emissions controls, the data panel accompanying the report gave lower engine output numbers than released earlier by the factory: 370 horsepower at 6300, and 348 pounds/feet of torque at 4500. Another discrepancy from earlier information concerned

the tires, which were now 240-section at the front, 280 at the rear. Weight with 30.4 gallons of fuel, but no occupants, was 3643 pounds, distributed 41.4-percent front/58.6-percent rear.

*Car and Driver*'s Testarossa sprang to 60 mph in 5 seconds, passed 100 in 11.2, and ripped off the quarter-mile in 13.1 at 107-mph. The testers saw a top speed of 181 and observed fuel economy of 11 mpg.

The slippery leather seats were too wide to lock slim-hipped editor Larry Griffin in place in turns and thus inhibited truly spirited cornering. The gated shifter was revealed as "a

*(continued on page 277)*

A Testarossa (*both pages*) stays well-mannered even at speeds approaching its 181 mph top end. With crimson-painted cylinder heads (*right*), it is literally a *testa rossa*: red head. Fuel filler cap (*above*) is accessible via hinged front and rear body sections (*top*).

276

grating anachronism" when quick gear changes were attempted. "Luckily," Griffin said, "the gearing is so well spaced and the engine is so strong that shifting can be viewed as entertainment rather than necessity."

Compared to the Boxer, the Testarossa cornered with less understeer, and was also "...less likely to initiate unstable cyclings between the initial understeer and the lurking final oversteer." The steering seemed slow and heavy at city speeds, "...but it's spot on in the open territory where the Testarossa frees up and flies," Griffin wrote. "At 181 mph the Testarossa is still in its element: a little busy and quite noisy, but squirming from cheek to cheek no more than a well-mannered nine-year-old on an uncushioned pew."

An American-spec car was put through its paces in Italy by *Road &*

*Track* in 1985. With the compression ratio down to 8.7:1, SAE net horsepower was given as 380 at 5750 rpm and torque as 354 pounds/feet at 4500. Curb weight was 3660 pounds; the as-tested weight of 3945, with driver seated, was distributed 40-percent front/60-percent rear. Zero-to-60 mph passed in 5.3 seconds, 100 was reached in 12.2, and the quarter-mile expired in 13.6 at 105. Estimates by the magazine put top speed at 178 at 6800 rpm and fuel consumption at 12 mpg. Port-of-entry price was $87,000.

"The Testarossa's ride and handling reflect its development in northern Italy, a place where roads vary from quite good to downright nasty," wrote *Road and Track*'s Dennis Simanaitis. "The suspension communicates these changing surfaces very well; even a slight kickback in the steering—very much a Ferrari characteristic—carries

useful information content. And this is combined with an absolutely astounding solidity of chassis and bodywork. I got the distinct impression that at least a couple of Targa Florios are built into this Ferrari."

Ferrari proved you can put some racetrack in the Testarossa without putting the Testarossa on a racetrack. But what about the honor of that hallowed name, which, after all, was made famous in competition? Here, the last word belongs to Paul Frere, co-winner of Le Mans in 1960 in a V-12 Testa Rossa. Twenty-five years later, Frere felt Ferrari's flat-12 flagship required no apologies. "Surely," he declared, "the Testarossa deserves its glorious name...."

With a beam of 77.8 inches, the Testarossa (*opposite page*) is one of the world's widest cars. Lined up at the factory (*above*).

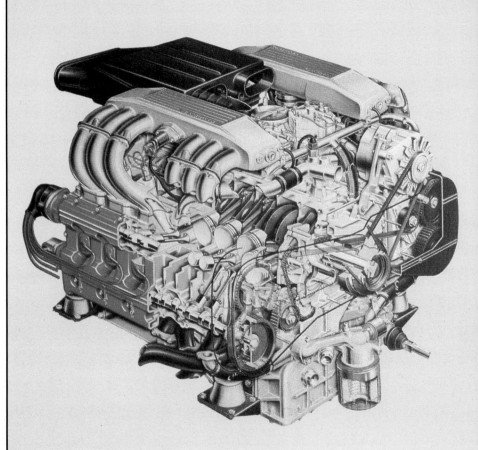

## FERRARI ENGINES

### The Boxer 12s

The Germans coined the term "boxer" to describe the engines in their Volkswagens and Porsches. It refers to a "flat" configuration in which the pistons' reciprocating movement is toward and away from each other.

Ferrari's first flat engine was built in 1964. It was a 12-cylinder, 1.5-liter Formula 1 motor with an 11:1 compression ratio, Lucas·fuel injection, and 210 horsepower at 11,000 rpm.

Several other competition Ferraris, both Sports and Grand Prix cars, were built with boxer engines. The first customer road Ferrari with this type of engine was shown at the Turin show in October 1971. It went into production in 1973 as the 365 GT4 BB. The 365 referred to the engine displacement—365 cc × 12 = 4380 cc. The rest of the name stood for Grand Touring, four-cam Berlinetta Boxer. With its 4.4-liter motor mounted behind the driver and ahead of the rear axle, the 365 GT4 BB was the first mid-engine production car to

carry the Ferrari name. (The Dino 246 was in production first but wasn't called a Ferrari.)

The 365 GT4 BB's double-overhead camshafts were driven by a toothed belt, also a first for Ferrari. Four triple-throat Weber downdraft carburetors fed into 12 intake ports, which were located on the upper side of the engine; the exhaust ports were on the lower side. The rods, pistons, and valve gear were interchangeable with the 365 GTC/4 V-12.

The boxer flat-12 and the 365 GTC/4 V-12 had identical displacements and compression ratios, yet the boxer put out 24 more horsepower, 344 at 7000 rpm, compared to 320 at 6200 rpm. The boxer produced eight fewer horsepower, however, than the V-12 in the 365 GTB/4 Daytona, a front-engine car. There's an explanation for the difference.

Assuming that valve timing and lift are similar for the three engines, we can look to the location of the ports. The design used for the boxer and GTB/4 puts the intake and exhaust ports on opposite sides of the cylinder. This seems to provide a better flow of fuel and air than does the 365 GTC/4 system, in which the intake is on

the top of the cylinder and the exhaust on the side.

Production of the 365 GT4 BB continued through the first part of 1976. In the fall of '76, a 512 BB was announced as a replacement for the 365. Ferrari had once again gone to the Dino system of number designation. With the first digit denoting displacement and the second and third indicating number of cylinders, the 512 BB was identified as having 5-liters and 12 cylinders. BB again stood for Berlinetta Boxer.

Bore and stroke were boosted to 82 mm and 78 mm, and displacement increased to 4942 cc (302.0 cubic inches). With a 9.2:1 compression ratio and a quartet of Weber triple-choke downdraft carburetors, horsepower was up to 360 at 6200 rpm. The power increase was just over five percent, but increased torque, in both numbers and spread, made the 512 a much more flexible car to drive on the road, particularly around town.

The 512's replacement, the Testarossa, went into production as a 1985 model. It had been shown at the Paris Auto Salon in 1984, where it inaugurated Ferrari's treatment of Testarossa as one word, as op-

posed to a two-word usage when the originals were racing in the late 1950s.

Ferrari exported 365 Boxers to America, and a few 512s came to the states through the grey market. The Testarossa was designed for the American market. Even with U.S.-mandated emissions equipment, its flat 12 put out 380 horsepower at 5750 rpm This figure was obtained by a combination of 4-valve-per-cylinder heads, Bosch K-Jetronic fuel injection, and Marelli's new Multiplex ignition.

The 365, 512, and Testarossa all share the basic engine designed by long-time Ferrari engineer Mauro Forghieri. Other than minor changes in dimension, mounting points, and exhaust systems, it remained unchanged in all three cars.

The advantages in retaining the flat-12 included a center of gravity much lower than that possible with a V-type engine or a vertical inline design. One downside of a boxer design, however, is that it requires a wider track to accommodate the engine, its accessories, and necessary plumbing.

Simply reaching its service points is also a major handicap. Ferrari and Pininfarina, the firm responsible for the body design and construction, tackled this last problem head on. They hinged nearly the entire aft half of the body at the rear, allowing it to open, clam-shell-like, to provide access to the engine and its associated parts.

A major change in component layout for the Testarossa was the use of two radiators. One was mounted on either side of the body, just behind the cockpit. Air intakes extended forward to almost the front of the doors. This wasn't done because of engine-cooling problems. Instead, it was the result of complaints from 512 customers. In those cars, pipes running between the front-mounted radiators and alongside the passenger compartment to the mid-mounted engine transmitted too much heat to the cockpit.

Power from the Testarossa engine goes through a twin-disc clutch, as on the 512. The newer car's 362 pounds/feet of torque at 4500 rpm, however, requires a 9.5-inch

diameter clutch, one inch larger than the 512's.

The 12-cylinder boxer engine has proven to be a reasonable way to go for these super high-performance road Ferraris. It was equally good in Grand Prix cars until racing-federation rules, the competition, and aerodynamic considerations forced changes in the Grand Prix chassis. A low, flat engine, it turns out, is a detriment to underbody airflow. So Grand Prix Ferraris went back to the V-type engine, which had only the narrow sump sticking below the main bodywork, leaving room for air passage on either side of the sump and between the wheels.

The term "boxer" refers to the way in which the pistons move in opposition to one another in an engine with a "flat" configuration. Ferrari's Testarossa engine (*opposite page*) is a fine example. The 12-cylinder is mounted longitudinally amidships in the 2-seat coupe (*above*). This layout affords the car a low center of gravity that helps improve handling.

## FERRARI CHASSIS

### The 12-Cylinder Boxers

Pure competition Ferraris had used mid-mounted engines exclusively since 1961. And Enzo first employed a flat, or boxer, 12-cylinder in his 1964 Formula 1 car. But he waited until 1971 to build a street Ferrari with anything but a conventionally configured engine mounted in front.

The ground breaking *cavallino* was the 365 GT4 BB, for 365 Grand Touring 4-cam Berlinetta Boxer. A replacement for the Daytona, it was unveiled at the Turin auto show. Its 4.4-liter flat 12 was mounted behind the driver and ahead of the rear axle. This was the same placement used by the Dino, starting in 1965, but that car wasn't called a Ferrari until its 1975 incarnation.

The 365 GT4 BB's frame was assembled of round and oval steel tubing. It was called a "truss type" frame to describe the way it combined the best features of the traditional ladder-type and the more complicated space frame. When the model went into production, in late 1972, square- and rectangular-section tubing was employed because it was easier to fabricate than the round and oval pieces.

Steel stampings were used for the inner structure and some outer pieces of the Pininfarina-designed, Scaglietti-built body. The doors, belly pan, and nose and tail sections were aluminum. The lower body sections front and rear were fiberglass.

With five inches less overall height than the Daytona, the Boxer looked a lot longer, but it was in fact 2.5 inches shorter and 1.6 inches wider than the front-engine classic. These first type 365 Boxers were available in several colors, but the lower body panel was always in matte black, a division that probably emphasized the longer look.

The all-independent suspension was similar to the Daytona's, though the two were not interchangeable. Unequal-length A-arms and coil springs were used front and rear in the Boxer, as were anti-roll bars. One tubular shock absorber was mounted at each front wheel; two tubular shocks were used at each rear wheel.

Long pieces of tubing transferred coolant between the front-mounted radiator and the engine. The spare tire was carried in the front compartment, using up most of what minimal luggage space was available. Boxer drivers traveled light.

The Boxer looked like a fastback from the side, thanks to rear body quarter panels that swept back alongside the engine lid. But these buttresses hid a vertical rear window located just behind the seats and ahead of the engine-hood opening.

A 365 Boxer was an exciting and spectacular-looking Grand Touring car, if not a very practical one. With 344 horsepower at 7200 rpm, top speed was around 175 mph. And fast drivers appreciated the strong, well-balance, 4-wheel ventilated disc brakes.

In late 1976, the Boxer got an increase in engine size to 4942 cc and was rebadged the 512. Horsepower was up to 360 at 6200 rpm. The chassis and exterior design were virtually identical to the 365, though the 512's rear body was a barely noticeable 1.5 inches longer. Small additions distinguishing the 512 were a chin spoiler, a NACA air intake on the side panel just before the rear wheelwells, and four taillights instead of six.

Ferrari targeted the European market with his 365 and 512 Boxers. But at the 1984 Paris show, he drew back the curtain on a successor aimed at America. This was the Testarossa. Put into production in '85, the Testarossa chassis was almost identical to that of the 512 on which it was based. It was slightly larger, however. The Testarossa's 100.4-inch wheelbase was longer by two inches, its front track was widened by 0.7 of an inch, to 59.8, and its rear track was expanded by 4 inches, to 65.4. Despite the Testarossa's apparent bulk—it's body is 77.5 inches wide—the car weighs 40 pounds less than a 512 Boxer.

Sweeping changes were made to the body shape. Its design was determined with the help of Pininfarina's full-size wind tunnel. Some of the changes suited aerodynamic considerations; some also accommodated the new radiator placement.

Owners of the 365 and 512 Boxers had complained of excessive cockpit heat from coolant being routed forward to the radiator from the mid-mounted engine. As a result, Ferrari called on Grand Prix car design experience and relocated the radiators (two now instead of one) to the sides of the car just forward of the rear wheels.

Wind tunnel tests indicated that the air intakes should start well forward on the car's flanks, so they begin in the leading section of each door. Working under European laws that limit the size of body-side openings, Pininfarina came up with "cheese-slicer" grillework applied boldly to the Testarossa's lengthy ducts.

Enthusiasts at first were cool to the Testarossa's size and styling. Time has vindicated Pininfarina's vision, however, and the Testarossa has assumed its place among classic Ferrari designs. As for those cheese-slicer air intakes, they're now among the most copied features in the automotive world.

**Testarossa used its space efficiently (*above*) and kept radiator heat away from the cabin.**

# Chapter 17:

# F40: Enzo Ferrari's Ultimate Fantasy

**H**ad he been an ordinary man, Enzo Ferrari would've retired sometime during the 1960s. Had his first son lived to assume control, Enzo might have at least withdrawn to the background. But even after Ferrari sold a share of his company to Fiat in 1969, when he was 71 years old, no thought of a quiet life seems to have crossed his mind.

He did let go of the production-car side of his business, content in the role of an honored consultant to the Fiat bureaucracy. Of his first love, his racing team, Enzo remained firmly the boss and kept on working as hard as ever. Obviously, to the Old Man this was no work at all.

Ferrari intensified his concentration during the 1970s on Formula 1, which was growing ever more technically complex and expensive. His last factory-operated sports-racers to contest Le Mans and similar events ran in 1973. After that, Maranello only occasionally assisted its distributors and good customers with projects such as the racing Boxers. In 1983, it did develop a turbocharged racing V-8 engine for Lancia, which itself was now Fiat-owned. But none of these efforts compared with Ferrari's Grand Prix pursuits.

In 1984, though, the company became interested in producing competition-oriented 2-seaters again. The impetus was a new category called Group B, which racing's governing body, the International Automobile Federation (FIA), had invented in hopes of attracting participation by just such firms as Ferrari. Group B was founded on the concept of one basic car that could contest both track races and long-distance road rallies. The design would have to pack outstanding performance and handling with such features as an interior suitable for two, good ground clearance, and highway-legal lighting. In other words, just the sort of genuine GT for which Ferrari had become famous in years past.

The beauty of the FIA's new scheme was that manufacturers had to produce 200 examples of their Group B car to qualify it for homologation. Obviously, finding buyers for that many cars would be possible only if the Group B entry could genuinely be used on the street.

Ferrari was game, and revived for its Group B car a glorious old name, GTO. Outwardly, this new Gran Turismo Omologato appeared to be built out of the popular 308 GTB, but it was really almost entirely new. Its heart was a small quad-cam, 32-valve V-8 like the 308's, but the GTO's was turbocharged. It also was turned from a transverse to a longitudinal position in the chassis. This was done partly to allow more room for turbocharger hardware, and partly because Ferrari wanted to use a conventional, rear-mounted transaxle. This gearbox, manufactured by the German firm, ZF, was stronger than the 308's in-the-sump transaxle, and it also allowed the quick ratio swapping necessary to set up a car for modern racing. A side benefit of moving the gears out from under the engine was that the V-8 could be mounted lower, dropping the car's center of gravity. The new GTO powertrain configuration required the wheelbase to be lengthened by 4.4 inches over the 308's, to 96.5.

The car was officially known as the 288 Gran Turismo Omologato because its new V-8 displaced 2855 cc (174.2 cubic inches). With a bore and stroke of 80 mm × 71 mm (3.150 × 2.795 inches), the engine was similar to, but a little larger than the one built the year before for Lancia. Its displacement was chosen because of the turbocharging, for when multiplied by an FIA equivalency factor of 1.4, the engine would just qualify for the 4-liter class at a virtual 3997 cc.

In the old days, a genuine 4-liter Ferrari engine would have been expected to generate a little under 400 horsepower. Indeed, the 2.86-liter GTO had an official SAE rating of 394 horsepower at 7000 rpm. The standard torque was 366 pounds/feet at 3800 rpm. Of course, a turbocharged engine's power output can, within limits, be dialed-in to suit the needs of the moment, and the GTO in racing trim would be expected to make something over 600 horsepower.

As a streetgoing car, the GTO had a compression ratio of 7.6:1 and a maximum boost pressure of 11.6-pounds-per-square inch over atmospheric (1.8 bar). The boost was generated by a

pair of small IHI turbos made in Japan, with the incoming charge cooled by two German-made air-to-air Behr intercoolers. Turbo lag was minimized by the small size of the blowers and further controlled by a throttle-linked bypass valve that kept the intake flow circulating when the accelerator was released. Fuel delivery and ignition were coupled and managed by a single, sophisticated computerized system devised by Weber and Magneti-Marelli from their F1 experience with Ferrari.

In addition to its advanced engine technology, the GTO employed such modern structural materials as aluminum honeycomb and carbon, Kevlar, and Nomex composites. These materials, along with fiberglass, were used in the new bodywork, which was detailed in Pininfarina's wind tunnel.

While the GTO's exterior panels resembled those of the 308 GTB's, they were much wider than the 308's because they had to cover fatter tires.

The GTO's chassis was a multitube space frame. Its suspension, though similar to the 308's, was tuned for the much wider, lower-profile Goodyear rubber, which was mounted on three-element, center-nut Speedline racing wheels. These wheels were 16 inches in diameter, but the front rims were eight inches wide, and the rears were 10. The suspension incorporated height adjustment, so the car could be set for street or track running.

*Car and Driver*'s Don Sherman got an early look at the GTO in the summer of 1984, when only two running prototypes existed. He wasn't allowed to drive, but was chauffeured around

the Fiorano track by Ferrari's test driver, Dario Benuzzi.

"On the roll, every dynamic sensation from the GTO is Ferrari 308 to the fourth or fifth power," Sherman wrote. "Of course it's faster, with a power-to-weight ratio that's neatly *doubled* (assuming the factory's curb-weight and horsepower figures are honest!). Of course it corners with leechlike adhesion, thanks to all the

*(continued on page 285)*

In 1984, Ferrari revived a hallowed old name for his new homologated road/racing car: GTO (*both pages*). Developing themes set forth with the 308 GTB a decade earlier, Pininfarina clothed the new steed in fluid lines that suggested the muscle beneath. Its V-8 carried two turbochargers and was rated at 394 horsepower at 7000 rpm. In racing trim, it could be expected to produce about 600 horsepower.

world's tread width. And of course it will smoke the back tires and cock its tail smartly sideways in the lower gears."

Sherman continued, "The steering ratio seemed a bit slow—as does the 308's—but the handling appeared to be a delightful blend of power-off understeer and power-on oversteer. Through several of the slower bends, the leather-wrapped steering wheel was more a hand rest than a guidance control, as Benuzzi selected his drift angles by dipping generously into the long-travel throttle. The fat boots in back howled in protest....

"Although there was nothing real-world about the thrill ride, we took note of a few practical concerns anyway. Throttle response is virtually non-existent at low speeds—we're talking seconds—but nearly instantaneous once the turbine wheels have spooled up. And the turbochargers make terrific rotary mufflers: there isn't a shred of ripping canvas to be heard in the back bay, merely the hushed sounds of air and fuel turning into horsepower as if by nuclear fission.

"The GTO is not what you would call quiet, but instead of the din of a poorly engineered exhaust system, the newest Ferrari's sound track is all earth, wind and fire: tire tread noise, high-speed air over the side windows, and the crackle of an engine under pressure."

Sherman was right to question the factory's weight and power figures. A year later, in its first full GTO road test, *Car and Driver* discovered a production example had a curb weight of 2880 pounds, 330 pounds over what Sherman had been led to expect. Additionally, the engine was developing only 8.5 psi of boost pressure, 3.1 psi below specification. And on a level stretch of straight road in California's High Desert, the GTO couldn't reach beyond 175 mph, 15 under Ferrari's claim.

On the other hand, this production engine proved much easier to drive

Designed to compete as a sports-racer, the GTO (*both pages*) needed a cabin suited for two, as well as instrumentation, lighting, ground clearance, mirrors, and windshield wipers that would make it legal for use on the public roads. Unfortunately, the international racing series in which it was to run, Group B, was dissolved before the Ferrari could turn a wheel in anger.

than the prototype observed in Italy. "The throttle response is linear and eager off the boost," Sherman said. "This little Ferrari feels as if it would be perfectly comfortable delivering kids to school or picking up the shirts at the laundry, at least until you drop your right foot. Then a 747 rolls up

The GTO (*opposite page*) retained the 308/328's steel-tube frame, but added four inches for a wheelbase of 96.5 inches. Its all-independent suspension is similar to that of the F40's (*this page*), though the F40 uses Koni adjustable tube shocks and has a system for raising and lower its chassis ride height.

from the rear and leans against the bumper...."

Wide-open throttle "catapulted" the GTO to 60 mph in 5.0 seconds and through the quarter-mile in 13.1 at 112 mph. These times, good as they were, didn't really tell the story, cautioned the tester. Sherman had to cope with wheelspin off the line, and had to waste time with a gear shift just before reaching 60 mph and again at 93, "...so the test-track figures are less impressive than the jet thrust in the small of your back whenever the boost is up."

Keeping up the boost required fre-

quent use of the shift lever. The action seemed heavy at first, and tricky because of the typical Ferrari gate, but soon became second nature, Sherman said.

The handling was even better than he'd anticipated. "Factory drivers had previously demonstrated the GTO's ravenous hunger for power oversteer at Fiorano, but this in no way prepared us for limit cornering with our own hands on the wheel. Testing on our standard 300-foot asphalt skidpad, we found that the GTO's handling is delightfully near neutral. A twitch of either the wheel or the

## FERRARI CHASSIS

### GTO & F 40

Ferrari in 1984 introduced its first GTO since the 1962-64 original. The newest bearer of this proud standard in many ways looked like a 308/328 with a few slight modifications. These included large, "flag-shaped" mirrors that sprouted from the front of each door, three slanted louvers that sliced the body behind the rear wheels, and four driving lights that graced the outer ends of the grille. A quick glance also revealed that the GTO's front and rear spoilers were larger than those of the 308/328.

Underneath, the steel-tube frame was identical to the 308/328, except for the added length. The GTO also retained the familiar all-independent suspension with unequal-length A-arms, coil springs, tube shocks, anti-roll bars, and vented disc brakes. But the casual eye wasn't likely to notice a wheelbase increase of four inches, from 92.5 to 96.5. This was made necessary by the longitudinal installation of the V-8 engine, rather than the transverse mounting used in the 308/328.

Nor would it be immediately apparent that the body material had changed. Where the 308/328's body was steel, the GTO's was fiberglass. The GTO's hood, however, was made of Kevlar, and the roof was a blend of Kevlar and carbon fiber. The firewall was a sandwich of aluminum honeycomb, Kevlar, and Nomex.

Also not obvious at a quick glance was the increase in width over the 308/328. Front track was up 3.3 inches, from 58.1 inches to 61.4, and rear track was up 3.8 inches, from 57.5 inches to 61.5. Instead of simply adding fender flares over the wheel arches, the entire fender was puffed out, for a broad-shouldered look.

The GTO's interior is as luxurious as could be hoped for in a car of this type. It

has leather upholstery, carpeted floors, a deluxe audio system, and air conditioning.

The original premise of the new GTO was to build an FISA Group B competition car, which was one of the main reasons for the high-tech lightweight body materials. To qualify under Group B regulations, the FISA required a production run of at least 200 cars. Ferrari did indeed build 200, though none was for export to America and no planned certification of the GTO for the U.S. As could be expected, a few nonetheless found their way to the States.

Ferrari's use of space-age composites in the GTO's body helped pave the way for the F40. Bowing in 1987, the car was named to commemorate Ferrari's 40th year as a manufacturer. This bespoilered brut of a *berlinetta* made no pretext at being a road car. Created for the racer, it was devoid of luxury items and carried minimal insulation.

Starting out with a welded-up steel tube frame, with attaching points for suspen-

sion and engine, the chassis forsook the usual steel box-sections, favoring instead cross members and improved structural rigidity. Kevlar and carbon-composite moldings were bonded to the steel frame with structural adhesives. In addition to providing the required strength and stiffness, these composites were lighter than the steel they replaced and, in many cases, stronger. One penalty is that current technology does not allow for mass production of these materials. But Ferrari engineers say chassis weight was reduced 20 percent though the use of these composites and this method of construction. Chassis strength was increased three-fold, they say.

Wheelbase of the F40 is the same as the GTO's, 96.5 inches. At 62.8 inches in front and 63.4 at the rear, the F40's track is wider, however. Its overall body length of 174.4 inches falls between that of the GTO and Testarossa.

Suspension is pretty much as seen on the 328 and GTO, with short and long A-arms, coil springs, Koni adjustable tube shocks all around, and the required anti-roll bars at each end. Chassis ride height is adjustable: fairly high for in-town or slow driving; lowered automatically at high speed.

The F40's basic body shape is very much GTO, though the F40 sports a rear wing and a more aggressively shaped chin. It also has more air intakes, which, along with every other aspect of the body, were designed in the wind tunnel.

The result is a car that is not as pretty as a 328 or GTO. Its purpose, however, is not to look pretty, but to be the fastest car on the road and to be able to perform with safety at its claimed maximum of 201 mph.

This is the last Ferrari introduced before Enzo's death. He had said his desire was to create the "best Ferrari ever." Respected critics who have driven the car in its element say that, in all-around performance, Enzo's goal was achieved.

throttle can overcook one end or the other briefly, but when left to its own devices, this car will centrifuge its driver all day long at 0.88 g. The four fat tires hang on for dear life, the wheel effort is light, and the steering ratio is speedy enough to keep up with the predictable chassis. If there is such a thing as handling perfection, it comes as standard equipment with the GTO."

This car's optional equipment consisted of air conditioning and power windows for a 1985 U.S. sticker of $125,000. At that, it was underpriced, for the limited number of GTOs immediately began trading hands at substantially elevated figures.

Sadly, Ferrari's original intent with the GTO was shot down when Group B was canceled after some of the rally events resulted in fatal accidents. How much of the blame belonged to the cars themselves is uncertain, but the FIA was obviously sensitive to public outcry about the wooly machines, which had been dubbed, "Killer Bees." Ferrari halted work on its GTO Evoluzione, an "evolutionary" pure-race version of the car. Along with similarly adventurous cars from Audi, Ford, Peugeot, Porsche, and others, it now had nowhere to run.

The spirit that made Ferraris more than mere cars was unthwarted, however. To commemorate the 40th anniversary of the firm, Enzo's engineers set about creating the ultimate Ferrari: the F40. It was at once a return to roots and a leap toward the future. Though derived from the high-tech GTO, the F40 was even more advanced.

Out of the expertise Ferrari gained with lightweight composites in F1 came an enormously strong, feathery-light chassis of molded carbon-fiber and Kevlar panels bonded to large-diameter steel tubing. This produced a structure that was said to be three times as stiff and 20 percent lighter than conventional construction. The body was made of similar aerospace plastics.

The body of the GTO (*right*) employed such modern structural materials as aluminum honeycomb and carbon, Kevlar, and Nomex composites. These materials, along with fiberglass, were shaped in Pininfarina's wind tunnel. While the GTO's exterior panels resembled those of the 308/328's, they were much wider to cover fatter tires. The "flag" mirrors are a stylish concession to function.

The F40's suspension was further revised to exploit Pirelli's new P Zeros, ultra-high-performance tires with a section width of 245 mm at the front and 335 mm at the rear. These huge tires were mounted on multi-piece wheels 10 inches wide in the front and 13 inches wide in the rear. All the wheels were 17 inches in diameter to make room for giant, 13-inch-diameter brake rotors. Ferrari

did not fit an anti-lock system to this car, relying instead on the driver's ability to decelerate under control.

All that strength, tread, and stopping power was made necessary by the F40's engine. The new V-8 was similar to that of the GTO, but with 81 cc more displacement and 4.4 psi more boost, it produced 77 more horsepower. Substantially more over-square than its predecessor, the F40

powerplant measured 82 mm × 69.5 mm (3.228 × 2.736 inches) to displace 2936.2 cc (179.2 cubic inches). If multiplied by 1.4, the new engine was a 4.1-liter in the FIA's eyes, but that didn't matter any more. Compression ratio was up to 7.8:1, and boost pressure to 16 psi (just over 2 bar). Ferrari quoted the maximum horsepower as 471 at 7000 and the torque as 426 pounds/feet at 4000 rpm. The F40's tachom-

eter redline was the only thing about the engine that was lower than the GTO's: 7750 versus 7800.

The F40 retained the 96.5-inch wheelbase of the GTO, but at 174.4 inches, it was 5.5 inches longer, and at 78 inches, it was wider. The F40 and Testarossa were nearly equal in length and stood an identical 44.5 inches tall. But the semi-racer F40 weighed half-a-ton less, an estimated 2650 pounds

with its two rubber-cell fuel tanks full.

The F40's nose swept down to a wind-piercing prow of dramatic simplicity. The completely new, wider rear bodywork mounted a bold airfoil set much higher than would be allowed in any FIA racing category. Under the F40's tail were a pair of air extractor ducts resembling those used on racing machines to generate ground-effects downforce. The body

The GTO (*above*) was officially known as the 288 Gran Turismo Omologato because its turbocharged V-8 displaced 2855 cc. Under the FIA equivalency factor, it would have qualified for the Group B 4-liter class at 3997 cc. Its two turbos were made in Japan; its air-to-air intercoolers were of German manufacture.

was hinged to provide access to the engine compartment and the tiny front boot.

Visually, the cockpit structure resembled the GTO's, though the new car's side windows were not roll-up glass, but a two-piece, sliding plastic pane like those of so many historic GT racers. Sloping aft of the roof was more plastic in a huge, louvered piece over the engine. The same glass rear cockpit window used on the 308, 328, and GTO was retained inside to insulate the F40's cabin from the engine.

Where the Boxer and Testarossa had been relatively civilized supercars, the F40 made few concessions to comfort in the traditional sense. There were no interior door handles, for instance, only primitive pull cords. The outside mirrors were not adjustable from inside the car. Air conditioning was standard, but only in so much as it was a functional item that would help

keep the driver alert and undistracted. Pure function also was evident in the drilled, bare-metal pedals, slightly offset from straight ahead of the driver's seat. There was no carpeting; the dashboard was covered in grey cloth. Much of the switchgear was drawn from the Fiat/Lancia parts bin. A production run of 700-800 F40s over a 24-month period ending sometime in 1990 was planned. Some 160-200 were to be sent to the U.S.

Enzo Ferrari himself unveiled the F40 at a moving ceremony in Maranello's civic center on July 21, 1987. *Road & Track*'s Dennis Simanaitis described the occasion this way: The hall "was filled to overflowing, not to say overheating, with a goodly number of the world's automotive press. In glaring focus at its center was a form draped in Ferrari red, the cloth obviously masking a steeply raked windshield and high rear spoiler, but not

much more was terribly obvious. Ferrari staff people milled around; for some reason or other, it wasn't quite time to begin.

"But then a commotion at the side entrance made it all clear; Enzo Ferrari, the Old Man, a patriarch evidently loved and respected, moved to his central position at the speakers' table amid applause from journalists and company people alike. His walk was stately, slow and not entirely firm, but when he spoke, his voice betrayed none of the frailty that you would expect of 89 years.

"'Little more than a year ago,' he

The F40 under construction at Maranello (*both pages*) calls upon the accumulated knowledge of Ferrari engine artisans and the skills and imagination of its chassis mavens. Their powers are then combined with the expertise Ferrari gained with lightweight composites in Formula 1 racing. The results, even on the assembly line, are breathtaking.

said through an English interpreter, 'I expressed my wish to the engineers. Build a car to be the best in the world. And now the car is here.'

"With that, the red covering was swept aside to reveal another red shape beneath. Applause erupted and, for a time, no words were spoken. Photographers swarmed around the starkly lit car. How can they shoot in this light, I wondered.

"'*Bello, molto bello*,' I heard a voice say softly. And then I realized that Signor Ferrari's microphone had been inadvertently left on."

The last car of Enzo Ferrari's life was not only "beautiful, very beautiful," it was fast, very fast. In the hands of factory test drivers, it reportedly accelerated from a standstill to 60 mph in 3.5 seconds. It passed 124 mph—200 km/h—in 12 seconds and covered the standing kilometer in 21.0 seconds, accelerating hard through 168 mph as it did. It didn't stop gaining speed until 201 mph. The price was set at $260,000 American.

It was nearly a year before the press was invited back to actually drive the F40. They did so at Fiorano, one by one, standing in line. They found it worth the wait.

"I was amazed by what a friend this marvelously potent F40 could be," *Road & Track*'s Simanaitis wrote. No matter what he tried, "The car did nothing silly, even when encountering the dreaded marbles; it just drifted outward." He discovered that "the F40 was prepared to meet me halfway. Its controls communicated in loud clear voices. Its steering told me all I needed to know about grip, with just enough kickback to warn of a deteriorated surface....Its brakes hauled the car down embarrassingly quickly. More than once, I found myself puttering through a corner because I got onto the binders way too soon. Throughout, I was agog at how benign the car felt as I probed my limits."

Simanaitis found he could "enter a sweeper too quickly for my own senses, turn in and scrub off speed. Or

(continued on page 297)

The F40 (*both pages*) was built upon an enormously strong, feathery-light chassis of molded carbon-fiber and Kevlar panels bonded to large-diameter steel tubing. The body was made of similar aerospace plastics. The F40's suspension was further revised to exploit Pirelli's P Zero ultra-high-performance tires.

I could muster up a bit more confidence, let the car work a little harder—and find its limits were still beyond mine." He calculated a reading of 0.95 *g* around the Fiorano skidpad.

The tester judged the engine's manners about as perfect as those of its suspension. The F40 was "remarkably docile when driven gently. No sputters, no lack of low-end torque.... Ease up to around 4000 in a GTO, then tip into the throttle. You can sense the GTO first coil itself up, then explode. By contrast, do the same routine with the F40 and it simply *goes. And now!*"

Given his shot, *Car and Driver*'s William Jeanes described the experience as "unforgettable." It started while he waited on line, absorbing the mood of the hour. "From 30 degrees above the horizon the sun spreads a bright but hazy glow over the Italian landscape," Jeanes began his report. "Beneath the luminescent clouds, curving through a field of scrubby green grass splashed here and there with crimson poppies and dotted with the yellow and white of daisies, twists the Pista di Fiorano, three kilometers of macadam over which Ferrari puts its prancing horsepower to the test.

"Beside the Fiorano track, crouched on a rectangle made of deep-red concrete, sits the latest legend-to-be, a Ferrari-red F40. Men move about it slowly, as if awed by its presence.

"On the Fiorano grounds, within sight of the tiny pit area where the F40 waits, is No. 5 Via Agazzotti—a white, two-story house with red shutters and pale-green blinds that is technically in the village of Spezzano. Here, from time to time, Enzo Ferrari, now 90, still takes lunch and a nap. From the house, *Il Commendatore* can look across the track to the Ferrari Formula 1 section, separated by a few blocks from the auto factory. There, where the race cars are built, one can find Enzo Ferrari's office. And his heart."

Jeanes settled into the nest of black carbon fiber and thin red upholstery.

Strategically placed ducts (*left*) feed air to the F40's radiators and brakes, while gill-like vents (*top*) remove air from its engine bay/rear fender housing. Its tires, wider in the rear than in the front, mount 17-inch diameter wheels, large enough for giant, 13-inch-diameter brake rotors. Ferrari did not fit an anti-lock system, relying instead on the driver's ability to decelerate under control.

He turned the ignition key, thumbed the starter button, "and, for an instant, the metallic whine of the starter motor tears a strip from the fabric of Fiorano's silence. Then the engine fires, without so much as a stutter. The F40 emits a growl, then a louder growl—the snarl of a German shepherd before it lunges."

The *Car and Driver* editor believed he knew what was in store, but he found something different. "The average or even above-average driver, if placed in a racing car, will experience a shortness of breath akin to panic. There you are, all of a sudden, at the wheel of something that has only one purpose: to go like the hounds of hell....What comes very quickly as you drive the F40 at Fiorano is the realization that you are going to have to try very hard to hurt yourself. Exiting a corner in low gear, you simply press the throttle until the rear wheels hand you a note that says, 'Say, we're about to break loose from the pavement back here and we thought you might like to know about it'....Unless you perform a monumentally stupid act, hard driving in the F40 is just as exhilarating as you think it should be."

Like his colleague, Jeanes found the F40 clutch heavy and the shifting action stiff. The huge, powerful brakes were surprisingly light even though there was no servo assist, and the non-power steering was easy to turn despite the muscular front tires. But there was a lot of noise in the cockpit, not very much ventilation, and the car seemed very wide for something theoretically capable of handling city traffic. But none of these faults could alloy the joy of driving it, he said.

"Although you will likely find yourself perspiring with mental and physical effort, listening to yourself blip the throttle during repeated downshifts is a thrill that no self-respecting human should be denied. And if you are selfish enough to require more emotional reward, you have the knowledge that you are one of perhaps two or three dozen people who will ever drive the F40 at speed on Ferrari's own test track within earshot of *Il Commendatore* himself."

In a Spartan cockpit devoid of all amenities save air conditioning (*right*), there was little to distract the driver aiming for 200 mph. Its shape, its 471 horsepower, and its cabin were all proof that Ferrari's F40 (*this page,top and opposite page*) was tilted toward performance.

Driving the F40 anywhere was an indelible experience. Journalist Roger Bell took one out of London, through the English countryside, and back one weekend for Britain's *Car* magazine. "By a huge margin," he wrote, "it is the most exciting, exhilarating car I have driven in 35 years." Cradled in its seat after 600 miles, Bell had these thoughts:

"I switched it off and pondered in the dark. What a magnificently absurd machine. It had thrilled and enthralled, worried and frightened like no other car in my experience. In the wrong hands, it would be lethal. Even in the rights ones, it needs huge respect and understanding. As practical transport, it is seriously flawed by excessive (and unpleasant) noise, poor visibility and minimal luggage accommodation. As raw entertainment it is the world's greatest sports car. Isn't that what Ferrari set out to make?

"Bullseye."

It's significant that Enzo's aim wasn't to out-high-tech the other premier sports car of the day, the smooth, controllable 4-wheel drive Porsche 959. No, Enzo probably knew the F40 would be his last Ferrari, and he wanted to take the glove off the fist. It's both touching and fitting that this was the kind of untamed street racer that made Ferrari's name in the first place. In its simplicity and power, the F40 took Enzo home.

In the wrong hands it could be lethal. In the right ones, a tool of unprecedented automotive excitement. Built to commemorate Ferrari's 40th year as an automaker, the F40 (*below*) returned Enzo to his street-racer roots. It was no high-tech tour de force. Rather, it was simply the best sports car in the world.

# Postscript:

# Ferrari
# After Ferrari

When an automobile factory is so strongly a product of one man's will as was Enzo Ferrari's, there's no realistic possibility of it continuing unchanged after his death. They may have respect for the founder's spirit, but those who finally inherit the firm will react according to their own nature as new circumstances arise.

In the case of FERRARI Societa per Azioni Esercizio Fabbriche Automobili e Corse, however, chances are good

The F40 (*above*), the last Ferrari introduced during Enzo's lifetime, recalls Ferrari's past with its raucous, racer-for-the-road manner, but also harkens to its future though the use of space-age materials.

301

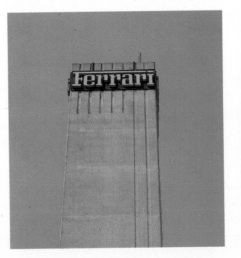

that things will go on in familiar ways, at least for a while.

For one thing, Ingegnere Ferrari transferred effective management control of the production-car portion of his company to Fiat some 19 years before his death. If the Ferraris produced since 1969 were not Fiats, neither were they quite Ferraris in the original sense. Fiat brought a cold rationality to the product planning and manufacturing process that had been missing in the tempestuous, sometimes chaotic old days. So in one sense, the future of Ferrari was established long ago.

Another force for stability is the stature of the name Ferrari, especially

in Italy, where it's an institution, an actual national treasure. Ferraristi can expect Fiat to treat the name with reverence. Those working on new models will feel the Old Man looking over their shoulders for some time to come. Their market and their country will countenance no less.

As for Enzo's personal fiefdom, the racing side, it will certainly miss the force of his personality. His power to mold drivers and engineers to his vision was unprecedented. Yet, he had been slowing in recent years, tiring. No longer was he quite the *Eminence Grise* of international racing politics, pulling strings behind the scenes.

Plus, his colleagues took pains to plan for a future that would not be dominated by Enzo Ferrari. While the loss of a great team's founder may be keenly felt, numerous examples in racing history show that the survivors usually have enough talent, experience, and motivation to carry on with great purpose.

In the case of Ferrari, the Formula 1 effort was buoyed by a victory at their home Grand Prix at Monza, Italy, just two weeks after Enzo's death. The team had been floundering for several seasons, and success had become rare.

The Monza triumph was a source of renewed confidence.

That will come in handy. No matter what commercial justifications may be presented for auto racing, the sport rests solely on a foundation of enthusiasm, not profit. Racing was the grand passion of Enzo Ferrari's life, and even he was frequently on the brink of giving it up. It's widely believed he supported his racing team out of his own pocket. Fiat, which now owns 90 percent of the firm, racing side and all, will one day find itself forced to decide, coldly and rationally, whether to continue racing. Various Ferrari rivals, notably Porsche, have faced such a decision and have decided it is in their best interests to stay in racing. Others have not. Would Ferrari road cars made by a Ferrari that no longer races still be Ferraris?

One positive sign has been Fiat's use of the Maranello establishment to develop advanced technology for the racetrack and the highway. Automotive advances in the past half-decade encompass aerodynamics, construction materials, drive systems, electronics, engine management, and suspension dynamics. Ferrari has been aggressive in exploring these new fields and the performance enhancements they offer. On the track, for example, Ferrari has successfully employed an innovative "semi-automatic" transmission controlled by switches mounted ahead of the steering wheel. It allows the driver to shift without taking his hands from the wheel. On the road, Ferrari's Type 408, an advanced-concepts vehicle, has demonstrated the possibilities of bonded-chassis construction, among other intriguing ideas.

Whether these technologies will see a Ferrari production line is not as important to the company's future as is the fact that its new owner is using Ferrari to pursue them vigorously.

The Ferrari factory, which once turned out raw *barchetta* sports cars (*top*), has been under Fiat's control since 1969. The giant corporation has shown sensitivity to the meaning of Ferrari, however, and it's within reason to expect more cars as significant and as true to the Ferrari colors as the F40 (*opposite page, top*).

Nevertheless, no Ferrari enthusiast can hide from the reality that an era has closed. That's one reason many older Ferraris have so astonishingly appreciated in value. Those built during Enzo's lifetime, particularly during the years he had full and sole control of his factory, will always have the golden aura of personally signed masterworks. No matter how exciting the prancing horses of the future may be, no matter how fast they may cover ground, none can have quite the same spring in their step.

Their master is gone.

Enzo Ferrari (*above*) was at ease among mechanics and kings. Here, he strolls with a stern-faced Don Vincenzo Florio (*right*), the powerful Sicilian who created the famous Targa Florio long distance road race.

## 166 Inter

| | |
|---|---|
| years | 1948-50 |
| number built | 37 |

**engine**

| | |
|---|---|
| configuration/placement | V-12 (60 degree)/front |
| bore, mm/in. | 60/2.36 |
| stroke, mm/in. | 58.8/2.31 |
| displacement, cc/ci | 1995/121.5 |
| valve operation | sohc |
| ignition | single distributor |
| spark plugs per cylinder | 1 |
| compression ratio | 8.0:1 |
| carburetion | 1 Weber 32 DCF |
| bhp | 110 at 6000 rpm |

**drivetrain**

| | |
|---|---|
| clutch | single dry plate |
| transmission | 5-speed w/reverse, in unit with engine; non-synchromesh |

**chassis**

| | |
|---|---|
| wheelbase, mm/in. | 2200/86.6 |
| track, front, mm/in. | 1270/50.0 |
| track, rear, mm/in. | 1250/49.2 |
| suspension, front | independent; double wishbone, transverse leaf spring |
| suspension, rear | live axle; semi-elliptic leaf springs, trailing arms |
| brakes | hydraulic; aluminum drums, iron liners |
| wheels | Borrani wire; center lock, knockoff |

**performance (approx.)**

| | |
|---|---|
| top speed, mph | 120 |
| 0-100 mph | 27 seconds |

---

## 212 Export

| | |
|---|---|
| years | 1950-53 |
| number built | including the Inter model: 110 |

**engine**

| | |
|---|---|
| configuration/placement | V-12 (60 degree)/front |
| bore, mm/in. | 68/2.68 |
| stroke, mm/in. | 58.8/2.31 |
| displacement, cc/ci | 2562/156.3 |
| valve operation | sohc |
| ignition | 2 Marelli distributors |
| spark plugs per cylinder | 1 |
| compression ratio | 8.0:1 |
| carburetion | 3 Weber 36 DCF |
| bhp | 150 at 6500 rpm |

**drivetrain**

| | |
|---|---|
| clutch | single dry plate |
| transmission | 5-speed w/reverse; non-synchromesh, in unit with engine |

**chassis**

| | |
|---|---|
| wheelbase, mm/in. | 2250/88.6 |
| track, front, mm/in. | 1270/50.0 |
| track, rear, mm/in. | 1250/49.2 |
| suspension, front | independent; double wishbone, transverse leaf spring |
| suspension, rear | live axle; semi-elliptic leaf springs, trailing arms |
| brakes | hydraulic; aluminum drums, iron liners |
| wheels | Borrani wire, center lock, knockoff |

**performance (approx.)**

| | |
|---|---|
| top speed, mph | 140 |
| 0-100 mph | 18.1 seconds |

# 250 MM

| | |
|---|---|
| years | 1952-53 |
| number built | 31 |
| **engine** | |
| configuration/placement | V-12 (60 degree)/front |
| bore, mm/in. | 73/2.87 |
| stroke, mm/in. | 58.8/2.31 |
| displacement, cc/ci | 2953/180.2 |
| valve operation | sohc |
| ignition | 2 Marelli distributors |
| spark plugs per cylinder | 1 |
| compression ratio | 9.0:1 |
| carburetion | 3 Weber 40 1F4C or 36DCF/3 |
| bhp | 240 at 7200 |
| **drivetrain** | |
| clutch | multiple disc |
| transmission | 4-speed w/reverse; all synchromesh, in unit with engine |
| **chassis** | |
| wheelbase, mm/in. | 2400/94.5 |
| track, front, mm/in. | 1300/51.2 |
| track, rear, mm/in. | 1320/52.0 |
| suspension, front | independent; double wishbone, transverse leaf spring |
| suspension, rear | live axle; semi-elliptic leaf springs, trailing arms |
| brakes | hydraulic; aluminum drums, iron liners |
| wheels | Borrani wire, center lock, knockoff |
| **performance (approx.)** | |
| top speed, mph | 158 |
| 0-100 mph | 17 seconds |

# 375 MM

| | |
|---|---|
| years | 1953-54 |
| number built | not more than 18 |
| **engine** | |
| configuration/placement | V-12 (60 degree)/front |
| bore, mm/in. | 80/3.20 ] works cars        84/3.36 ] customer cars |
| stroke, mm/in. | 74.5/2.98                     68/2.72 |
| displacement, cc/ci | 4494/274.1               4522/275.8 |
| valve operation | sohc |
| ignition | 2 Marelli magnetos |
| spark plugs per cylinder | 1 |
| compression ratio | 9.0:1 |
| carburetion | 3 Weber 1F/4C or 42 DCZ |
| bhp | 320 at 7000 rpm (works cars) |
| | 340 at 7000 rpm (customer cars) |
| **drivetrain** | |
| clutch | multiple disc |
| transmission | 4-speed w/reverse, all synchromesh |
| **chassis** | |
| wheelbase, mm/in. | 2600/104.0 |
| track, front, mm/in. | 1325/53.0 |
| track, rear, mm/in. | 1320/52.8 |
| suspension, front | independent; double wishbone, transverse leaf spring |
| suspension, rear | live axle, semi-elliptic leaf springs, trailing arms |
| brakes | hydraulic; aluminum drums, iron liners |
| wheels | Borrani wire; center lock, knockoff |
| **performance (approx.)** | |
| top speed, mph | 180 plus (depending on rear axle ratio) |
| 0-100 mph | 11.5 seconds |

<table>
<tr><td align="right">years</td><td>1954</td><td></td></tr>
<tr><td align="right">number built</td><td>29</td><td></td></tr>
</table>

# 750 Monza

| | |
|---|---|
| **engine** | |
| configuration/placement | inline 4/front |
| bore, mm/in. | 103/4.06 |
| stroke, mm/in. | 90/3.54 |
| displacement, cc/ci | 2999/183.0 |
| valve operation | dohc |
| ignition | 2 Marelli distributors |
| spark plugs per cylinder | 2 |
| compression ratio | 8.6:1 |
| carburetion | 2 Weber 58 DCOA/3 |
| bhp | 260 at 6000 rpm |
| **drivetrain** | |
| clutch | double dry plate |
| transmission | 5-speed w/reverse; non-synchromesh, in unit with differential |
| **chassis** | |
| wheelbase, mm/in. | 2250/88.6 |
| track, front, mm/in. | 1278/50.3 |
| track, rear, mm/in. | 1284/50.6 |
| suspension, front | independent; double wishbone, transverse leaf spring |
| suspension, rear | De Dion; transverse leaf springs, trailing arms |
| brakes | hydraulic; aluminum drums, iron liners |
| wheels | Borrani wire, center lock, knockoff |
| **performance (approx.)** | |
| top speed, mph | 164 |
| 0-100 mph | 17 seconds |

---

<table>
<tr><td align="right">years</td><td>1955</td><td></td></tr>
<tr><td align="right">number built</td><td>4</td><td></td></tr>
</table>

# 121 LM

| | |
|---|---|
| **engine** | |
| configuration/placement | inline 6/front |
| bore, mm/in. | 102/4.02 |
| stroke, mm/in. | 90/3.54 |
| displacement, cc/ci | 4412/269.2 |
| valve operation | dohc |
| ignition | coil |
| spark plugs per cylinder | 2 |
| compression ratio | 8.6:1 |
| carburetion | 3 Weber 50 DCOA/3 |
| bhp | 330 at 6000 rpm |
| **drivetrain** | |
| clutch | multiple disc |
| transmission | 5-speed w/reverse; non-synchromesh, in unit with differential |
| **chassis** | |
| wheelbase, mm/in. | 2400/94.5 |
| track, front, mm/in. | 1278/50.3 |
| track, rear, mm/in. | 1284/50.6 |
| suspension, front | independent; double wishbone, coil springs |
| suspension, rear | De Dion; transverse leaf springs, trailing arms |
| brakes | hydraulic; aluminum drums, iron liners |
| wheels | Borrani wire, center lock, knockoff |
| **performance (approx.)** | |
| top speed, mph | 170 |
| 0-100 mph | 16 seconds |

# 250 Testa Rossa

| | |
|---|---|
| years | 1958-61 |
| number built | 33 |

**engine**

| | |
|---|---|
| configuration/placement | V-12 (60 degree)/front |
| bore, mm/in. | 73/2.87 |
| stroke, mm/in. | 58.8/2.31 |
| displacement, cc/ci | 2953/180.2 |
| valve operation | sohc |
| ignition | 2 Marelli distributors |
| spark plugs per cylinder | 1 |
| compression ratio | 9.8:1 |
| carburetion | 6 Weber 38 DCN |
| bhp | 300 at 7200 rpm |

**drivetrain**

| | |
|---|---|
| clutch | single dry plate |
| transmission | 4-speed; all synchromesh, in unit with engine |

**chassis**

| | |
|---|---|
| wheelbase, mm/in. | 2350/92.5 |
| track, front, mm/in. | 1308/51.5 |
| track, rear, mm/in. | 1300/51.2 |
| suspension, front | independent; double wishbone, coil springs |
| suspension, rear | live axle; semi-elliptic leaf springs, trailing arms |
| brakes | hydraulic; aluminum drums, iron liners |
| wheels | Borrani wire, center lock, knockoff |

**performance (approx.)**

| | |
|---|---|
| top speed, mph | 167 |
| 0-100 mph | 16 seconds |

---

# 250 GT SWB

| | |
|---|---|
| years | 1959-62 |
| number built | 175 |

**engine**

| | |
|---|---|
| configuration/placement | V-12 (60 degree)/front |
| bore, mm/in. | 73/2.87 |
| stroke, mm/in. | 58.8/2.31 |
| displacement, cc/ci | 2953/180.2 |
| valve operation | sohc |
| ignition | 2 Marelli distributors |
| spark plugs per cylinder | 1 |
| compression ratio | 9.2:1 |
| carburetion | 3 Weber 40 DCL/6 or 3 Weber 36 DCL/3 (road cars) |
| | 3 Weber 40 DCL/6 or 3 Weber 46 DCL/3 or 3 Weber 46 DCF/3 (competition) |
| bhp | 280 at 7000 rpm (competition) |
| | 240 at 7000 (road car) |

**drivetrain**

| | |
|---|---|
| clutch | single dry plate |
| transmission | 4-speed w/reverse in unit with engine, all synchromesh |

**chassis**

| | |
|---|---|
| wheelbase, mm/in. | 2400/94.5 |
| track, front, mm/in. | 1354/53.3 |
| track, rear, mm/in. | 1349/53.1 |
| suspension, front | independent; double wishbone, coil springs |
| suspension, rear | live axle; semi-elliptic leaf springs, trailing arms |
| brakes | disc |
| wheels | Borrani wire, center lock, knockoff |

**performance (approx.)**

| | |
|---|---|
| top speed, mph | 156 |
| 0-100 mph | 23 seconds |

# 400 Superamerica

| | |
|---|---|
| years | 1961-64 |
| number built | 45 |

**engine**

| | |
|---|---|
| configuration/placement | V-12 (60 degree)/front |
| bore, mm/in. | 77/3.03 |
| stroke, mm/in. | 71/2.80 |
| displacement, cc/ci | 3967/242.1 |
| valve operation | sohc |
| ignition | coil |
| spark plugs per cylinder | 1 |
| compression ratio | 8.8:1 |
| carburetion | 3 Weber 46 DCF |
| bhp | 340 at 7000 rpm |

**drivetrain**

| | |
|---|---|
| clutch | single dry plate |
| transmission | 4-speed w/reverse, all synchromesh |

**chassis**

| | |
|---|---|
| wheelbase, mm/in. | 2420/95.3, 2600/102.4 |
| track, front, mm/in. | 1359/53.5, 1395/54.9 |
| track, rear, mm/in. | 1350/53.1, 1387/54.6 |
| suspension, front | independent; double wishbone, coil springs |
| suspension, rear | live axle; semi-elliptic leaf springs, trailing arms |
| brakes | disc |
| wheels | Borrani wire; center lock, knockoff |

**performance (approx.)**

| | |
|---|---|
| top speed, mph | 160 |
| 0-100 mph | 18 seconds |

# 250 GTO

| | |
|---|---|
| years | 1962-64 |
| number built | 39 |

**engine**

| | |
|---|---|
| configuration/placement | V-12 (60 degree)/front |
| bore, mm/in. | 73/2.87 |
| stroke, mm/in. | 58.8/2.31 |
| displacement, cc/ci | 2953/180.2 |
| valve operation | sohc |
| ignition | single distributor |
| spark plugs per cylinder | 1 |
| compression ratio | 9.8:1 |
| carburetion | 6 Weber 36 DCN |
| bhp | 280 at 7500 rpm |

**drivetrain**

| | |
|---|---|
| clutch | single dry plate |
| transmission | 5-speed w/reverse; synchromesh, in unit with engine |

**chassis**

| | |
|---|---|
| wheelbase, mm/in. | 2600/102.4 |
| track, front, mm/in. | 1354/53.3 |
| track, rear, mm/in. | 1349/53.1 |
| suspension, front | independent; double wishbone, coil springs |
| suspension, rear | live axle; semi-elliptic leaf springs, trailing arms |
| brakes | disc |
| wheels | Borrani wire, center lock, knockoff |

**performance (approx.)**

| | |
|---|---|
| top speed, mph | 176 |
| 0-100 mph | 14.1 seconds |

# 250 LM

| | |
|---|---|
| years | 1963-66 |
| number built | 35 |
| **engine** | |
| configuration/placement | V-12 (60 degree)/mid |
| bore, mm/in. | 77/3.03 |
| stroke, mm/in. | 58.8/2.31 |
| displacement, cc/ci | 3286/200.5 |
| valve operation | sohc |
| ignition | coil |
| spark plugs per cylinder | 1 |
| compression ratio | 9.8:1 |
| carburetion | 6 Weber 38 DCN |
| bhp | 305 at 7500 rpm |
| **drivetrain** | |
| clutch | single dry plate |
| transmission | 5-speed w/reverse; non-synchromesh, in unit with differential |
| **chassis** | |
| wheelbase, mm/in. | 2400/94.5 |
| track, front, mm/in. | 1350/53.1 |
| track, rear, mm/in. | 1340/52.7 |
| suspension, front | independent; double wishbone, coil springs |
| suspension, rear | as for front |
| brakes | disc |
| wheels | Borrani wire; center lock, knockoff |
| **performance (approx.)** | |
| top speed, mph | 160 |
| 0-100 mph | 12 seconds |

# 330 GT

| | |
|---|---|
| years | 1965-66 |
| number built | 455 |
| **engine** | |
| configuration/placement | V-12 (60 degree)/front |
| bore, mm/in. | 77/3.03 |
| stroke, mm/in. | 71/2.80 |
| displacement, cc/ci | 3967/242.1 |
| valve operation | sohc |
| ignition | coil |
| spark plugs per cylinder | 1 |
| compression ratio | 8.8:1 |
| carburetion | 3 Weber 40 DCZ 6 |
| bhp | 300 at 6600 rpm |
| **drivetrain** | |
| clutch | single dry plate |
| transmission | 5-speed w/reverse; all synchromesh, rear mounted |
| **chassis** | |
| wheelbase, mm/in. | 2650/104.3 |
| track, front, mm/in. | 1397/55.0 |
| track, rear, mm/in. | 1389/54.7 |
| suspension, front | independent; double wishbone, coil springs |
| suspension, rear | live axle; semi-elliptic leaf springs, trailing arms |
| brakes | disc |
| wheels | Borrani wire, center lock, knockoff |
| **performance (approx.)** | |
| top speed, mph | 150 |
| 0-100 mph | 17 seconds |

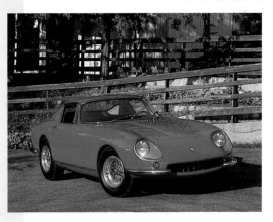

## 275 GTB/4

| | |
|---|---|
| years | 1966-68 |
| number built | 350 |

**engine**

| | |
|---|---|
| configuration/placement | V-12 (60 degree)/front |
| bore, mm/in. | 77/3.03 |
| stroke, mm/in. | 58.8/2.31 |
| displacement, cc/ci | 3286/200.5 |
| valve operation | dohc |
| ignition | coil |
| spark plugs per cylinder | 1 |
| compression ratio | 9.2:1 |
| carburetion | 6 Weber 40 DCN 17 |
| bhp | 300 at 8000 rpm |

**drivetrain**

| | |
|---|---|
| clutch | single dry plate |
| transmission | 5-speed w/reverse; all synchromesh, in unit with differential |

**chassis**

| | |
|---|---|
| wheelbase, mm/in. | 2400/94.5 |
| track, front, mm/in. | 1401/55.2 |
| track, rear, mm/in. | 1417/55.8 |
| suspension, front | independent; double wishbone, coil springs |
| suspension, rear | as for front |
| brakes | disc |
| wheels | Campagnolo light alloy |

**performance (approx.)**

| | |
|---|---|
| top speed, mph | 155 |
| 0-100 mph | 15 seconds |

---

## 365 GTB/4 Daytona

| | |
|---|---|
| years | 1968-73 |
| number built | 1300 |

**engine**

| | |
|---|---|
| configuration/placement | V-12 (60 degree)/front |
| bore, mm/in. | 81/3.19 |
| stroke, mm/in. | 71/2.80 |
| displacement, cc/ci | 4390/267.9 |
| valve operation | dohc |
| ignition | twin distributor |
| spark plugs per cylinder | 1 |
| compression ratio | 8.8:1 |
| carburetion | 6 Weber 40 DCN 20 |
| bhp | 352 at 7500 rpm |

**drivetrain**

| | |
|---|---|
| clutch | single dry plate |
| transmission | 5-speed w/reverse, in unit with differential |

**chassis**

| | |
|---|---|
| wheelbase, mm/in. | 2400/94.5 |
| track, front, mm/in. | 1440/56.7 |
| track, rear, mm/in. | 1425/56.1 |
| suspension, front | independent; double wishbone, coil springs |
| suspension, rear | as for front |
| brakes | disc |
| wheels | Cromodora 5-spoke light alloy |

**performance (approx.)**

| | |
|---|---|
| top speed, mph | 174 |
| 0-100 mph | 18.3 seconds |

## Dino 246 GT/GTS

| | |
|---|---|
| years | 1969-74 (Dino 246 GT), 1972-74 (Dino 246 GTS) |
| number built | 4000 plus |

**engine**

| | |
|---|---|
| configuration/placement | V-6 (65 degree)/transverse mid-engine |
| bore, mm/in. | 92.5/3.64 |
| stroke, mm/in. | 60/2.36 |
| displacement, cc/ci | 2418/147.6 |
| valve operation | dohc |
| ignition | coil |
| spark plugs per cylinder | 1 |
| compression ratio | 9.0:1 |
| carburetion | 3 Weber 40 DCN F/7 |
| bhp | 195 at 7600 rpm |

**drivetrain**

| | |
|---|---|
| clutch | single dry plate |
| transmission | 5-speed w/reverse; all synchromesh, in unit with differential |

**chassis**

| | |
|---|---|
| wheelbase, mm/in. | 2336/92.0 |
| track, front, mm/in. | 1427/56.2 |
| track, rear, mm/in. | 1430/56.3 |
| suspension, front | independent; double wishbone, coil springs, anti-roll bar |
| suspension, rear | as for front |
| brakes | disc |
| wheels | Cromodora light alloy |

**performance (approx.)**

| | |
|---|---|
| top speed, mph | 146 |
| 0-100 mph | 9 seconds |

---

## 365 GTC/4

| | |
|---|---|
| years | 1971-72 |
| number built | 500 |

**engine**

| | |
|---|---|
| configuration/placement | V-12 (60 degree)/front |
| bore, mm/in. | 81/3.19 |
| stroke, mm/in. | 71/2.80 |
| displacement, cc/ci | 4390/267.9 |
| valve operation | dohc |
| ignition | single distributor |
| spark plugs per cylinder | 1 |
| compression ratio | 8.8:1 |
| carburetion | 6 Weber DCOE sidedraft |
| bhp | 320 at 6200 rpm |

**drivetrain**

| | |
|---|---|
| clutch | single dry plate |
| transmission | 5-speed w/reverse, all synchromesh, in unit with engine |

**chassis**

| | |
|---|---|
| wheelbase, mm/in. | 2500/98.4 |
| track, front, mm/in. | 1470/57.9 |
| track, rear, mm/in. | 1470/57.9 |
| suspension, front | independent; double wishbone, coil springs |
| suspension, rear | as for front but with hydropneumatic self-leveling |
| brakes | disc |
| wheels | Cromodora light alloy |

**performance (approx.)**

| | |
|---|---|
| top speed, mph | 150 |
| 0-100 mph | 14 seconds |

## 308 GTBi/GTSi

| | |
|---|---|
| years | 1975-85 |
| number built | NA |
| **engine** | |
| configuration/placement | V-8 (90 degree)/transverse mid-engine |
| bore, mm/in. | 81/3.19 |
| stroke, mm/in. | 71/2.80 |
| displacement, cc/ci | 2927/178.6 |
| valve operation | dohc |
| ignition | coil |
| spark plugs per cylinder | 1 |
| compression ratio | 8.8:1 |
| carburetion | 4 Weber 40 DCNF (original); now Bosch fuel injection |
| bhp | quoted from 205 to 240 at 6600 rpm |
| **drivetrain** | |
| clutch | single dry plate |
| transmission | 5-speed w/reverse; all synchromesh, in unit with engine |
| **chassis** | |
| wheelbase, mm/in. | 2340/92.1 |
| track, front, mm/in. | 1460/57.5 |
| track, rear, mm/in. | 1460/57.5 |
| suspension, front | independent; double wishbone, coil springs |
| suspension, rear | as for front |
| brakes | disc |
| wheels | Cromodora light alloy |
| **performance (approx.)** | |
| top speed, mph | 150 |
| 0-100 mph | 11 seconds |

## 512 BBi

| | |
|---|---|
| years | 1976-84 |
| number built | NA |
| **engine** | |
| configuration/placement | flat 12/rear |
| bore, mm/in. | 82/3.23 |
| stroke, mm/in. | 78/3.07 |
| displacement, cc/ci | 4942/301.6 |
| valve operation | dohc |
| ignition | 1 distributor and electronic ignition |
| spark plugs per cylinder | 1 |
| compression ratio | 9.2:1 |
| carburetion | originally 4 Weber 40 LF/3C; now Bosch fuel injection |
| bhp | 360 at 6200 rpm |
| **drivetrain** | |
| clutch | multiple disc |
| transmission | 5-speed w/reverse; all synchromesh, in unit with engine |
| **chassis** | |
| wheelbase, mm/in. | 2500/98.4 |
| track, front, mm/in. | 1500/59.1 |
| track, rear, mm/in. | 1563/61.5 |
| suspension, front | independent; double wishbone, coil springs |
| suspension, rear | as for front |
| brakes | disc |
| wheels | Cromodora light alloy |
| **performance (approx.)** | |
| top speed, mph | 188 |
| 0-100 mph | 10 seconds |

# 400i Automatic

| | |
|---|---|
| years | 1979- |
| number built | NA |

### engine
| | |
|---|---|
| configuration/placement | V-12 (60 degree)/front |
| bore, mm/in. | 81/3.19 |
| stroke, mm/in. | 77/3.03 |
| displacement, cc/ci | 4823/294.3 |
| valve operation | dohc |
| ignition | single Marelli distributor |
| spark plugs per cylinder | 1 |
| compression ratio | 8.8:1 |
| carburetion | Bosch fuel injection |
| bhp | 310 at 6400 rpm |

### drivetrain
| | |
|---|---|
| clutch | not applicable |
| transmission | GM Turbo-Hydramatic; torque converter w/3-speed planetary gearbox |

### chassis
| | |
|---|---|
| wheelbase, mm/in. | 2700/106.3 |
| track, front, mm/in. | 1470/57.9 |
| track, rear, mm/in. | 1500/59.1 |
| suspension, front | independent; double wishbone, coil springs |
| suspension, rear | as for front with hydropneumatic self leveling |
| brakes | disc |
| wheels | Cromodora light alloy |

### performance (approx.)
| | |
|---|---|
| top speed, mph | 145 |
| 0-100 mph | 21 seconds |

---

# 328GTB

| | |
|---|---|
| years | 1986-89 |
| number built | approx. 1800 per year |

### engine
| | |
|---|---|
| configuration/placement | V-8 (90 degree)/transverse mid-engine |
| bore, mm/in. | 83/3.27 |
| stroke, mm/in. | 73.6/2.90 |
| displacement, cc/ci | 3186/194.4 |
| valve operation | dohc; 4-valves per cylinder |
| ignition | Twin Marelli Microplex (electronic/coil) |
| spark plugs per cylinder | 1 |
| compression ratio | 9.2:1 |
| carburetion | Bosch K-Jetronic with Lambda Control |
| bhp | 260 at 7000 rpm |

### drivetrain
| | |
|---|---|
| clutch | single dry plate |
| transmission | 5-speed w/reverse; all synchromesh, in unit with engine |

### chassis
| | |
|---|---|
| wheelbase, mm/in. | 2350/92.5 |
| track, front, mm/in. | 1473/58.0 |
| track, rear, mm/in. | 1468/57.8 |
| suspension, front | independent; double wishbone, coil springs |
| suspension, rear | as for front |
| brakes | ventilated disc; ABS |
| wheels | on-piece light alloy, various manufacturers |

### performance (approx.)
| | |
|---|---|
| top speed, mph | 156 |
| 0-100 mph | 15.9 seconds (328 GTS) |

## 3.2 Mondial

| | |
|---|---|
| years | 1986-89 |
| number built | approx. 500 per year |

**engine**

| | |
|---|---|
| configuration/placement | V-8 (90 degree)/transverse mid-engine |
| bore, mm/in. | 83/3.27 |
| stroke, mm/in. | 73.6/3.90 |
| displacement, cc/ci | 3186/194.4 |
| valve operation | dohc; 4 valves per cylinder |
| ignition | Twin Marelli Microplex (coil/electronic) |
| spark plugs per cylinder | 1 |
| compression ratio | 9.2:1 |
| carburetion | Bosch K-Jetronic fuel injection with Lambda Control |
| bhp | 260 at 7000 rpm |

**drivetrain**

| | |
|---|---|
| clutch | single dry plate |
| transmission | 5-speed w/reverse; all synchromesh, in unit with engine |

**chassis**

| | |
|---|---|
| wheelbase, mm/in. | 2650/104.3 |
| track, front, mm/in. | 1520/59.8 |
| track, rear, mm/in. | 1510/59.4 |
| suspension, front | independent; double wishbone, coil springs |
| suspension, rear | as for front |
| brakes | ventilated disc |
| wheels | one-piece light alloy, various manufacturers |

**performance (approx.)**

| | |
|---|---|
| top speed, mph | 150 |
| 0-100 mph | NA (quarter-mile in 15.3 seconds at 94 mph) |

---

## Testarossa

| | |
|---|---|
| years | 1985- |
| number built | 1074 (1988) |

**engine**

| | |
|---|---|
| configuration/placement | flat 12/transverse, mid-engine |
| bore, mm/in. | 82/3.22 |
| stroke, mm/in. | 78/3.07 |
| displacement, cc/ci | 4943/301.5 |
| valve operation | dohc; 4-valves per cylinder |
| ignition | Twin Marelli Microplex |
| spark plugs per cylinder | 1 |
| compression ratio | 8.8:1 |
| carburetion | Twin Bosch K-Jetronic fuel injection with Lambda Control |
| bhp | 390 at 6800 rpm |

**drivetrain**

| | |
|---|---|
| clutch | double dry plate, 9.5 inches |
| transmission | 5-speed w/reverse; all synchromesh, in unit with engine |

**chassis**

| | |
|---|---|
| wheelbase, mm/in. | 2550/100.4 |
| track, front, mm/in. | 1518/59.8 |
| track, rear, mm/in. | 1660/65.4 |
| suspension, front | independent; upper and lower transverse wishbone, coil springs |
| suspension, rear | as for front |
| brakes | disc |
| wheels | one-piece light alloy, various manufacturers |

**performance (approx.)**

| | |
|---|---|
| top speed, mph | 181 |
| 0-100 mph | 11.2 seconds |

315

# GTO

| | |
|---|---|
| years | 1984-85 |
| number built | approx. 260 |
| **engine** | |
| configuration/placement | V-8 (90 degree)/longitudinal, mid-engine |
| bore, mm/in. | 80/3.15 |
| stroke, mm/in. | 71/2.79 |
| displacement, cc/ci | 2855 |
| valve operation | dohc; 4-valves per cylinder |
| ignition | Weber Marelli IAW |
| spark plugs per cylinder | 1 |
| compression ratio | 7.6:1 |
| carburetion | fuel injection |
| bhp | 400 at 7000 rpm |
| **drivetrain** | |
| clutch | double dry plate, 8.5 inches |
| transmission | 5-speed; all synchromesh |
| **chassis** | |
| wheelbase, mm/in. | 2450/96.5 |
| track, front, mm/in. | 1589/62.5 |
| track, rear, mm/in. | 1562/61.5 |
| suspension, front | independent; double wishbone, coil springs |
| suspension, rear | as for front |
| brakes | ventilated disc |
| wheels | three-piece alloy, various manufacturers |
| **performance (approx.)** | |
| top speed, mph | 180 |
| 0-100 mph | 11.0 seconds |

# F40

| | |
|---|---|
| years | 1988-89 |
| number built | planned production, 800 |
| **engine** | |
| configuration/placement | V-8 (90 degree)/longitudinal, mid-engine |
| bore, mm/in. | 82/NA |
| stroke, mm/in. | 69.5/NA |
| displacement, cc/ci | 2936.24/NA |
| valve operation | dohc; 4-valves per cylinder |
| ignition | Weber Marelli (coil/electronic) |
| spark plugs per cylinder | 1 |
| compression ratio | 7.7:1 |
| carburetion | Weber Marelli fuel injection |
| bhp | 478 at 7000 rpm |
| **drivetrain** | |
| clutch | twin dry plate |
| transmission | 5-speed; all synchromesh |
| **chassis** | |
| wheelbase, mm/in. | 2450/NA |
| track, front, mm/in. | 1594/NA |
| track, rear, mm/in. | 1606/NA |
| suspension, front | independent; double wishbone, coil springs |
| suspension, rear | as for front |
| brakes | disc |
| wheels | three-piece alloy, various manufacturers |
| **performance (approx.)** | |
| top speed, mph | 201.3 |
| 0-100 mph | NA |

# Index